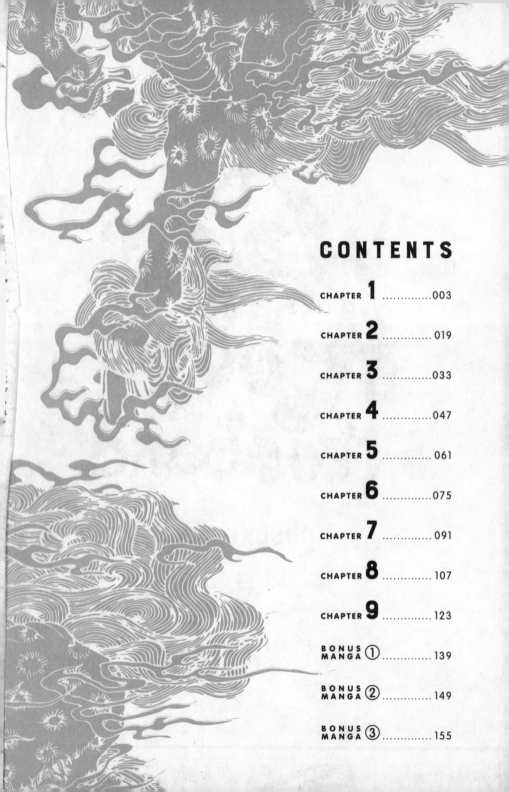

# CONTENTS

CHAPTER **1** .............003

CHAPTER **2** ............. 019

CHAPTER **3** .............033

CHAPTER **4** .............047

CHAPTER **5** ............. 061

CHAPTER **6** .............075

CHAPTER **7** ............. 091

CHAPTER **8** ............. 107

CHAPTER **9** .............123

BONUS MANGA ① .............139

BONUS MANGA ② ............. 149

BONUS MANGA ③ .............155

# The Way of the House Husband

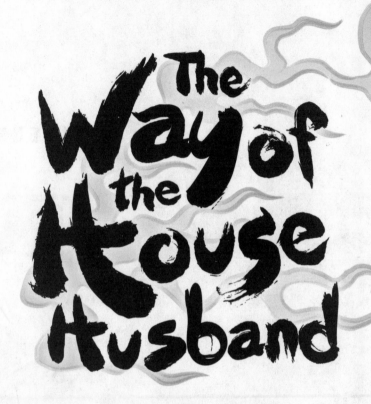

KOUSUKE OONO

1

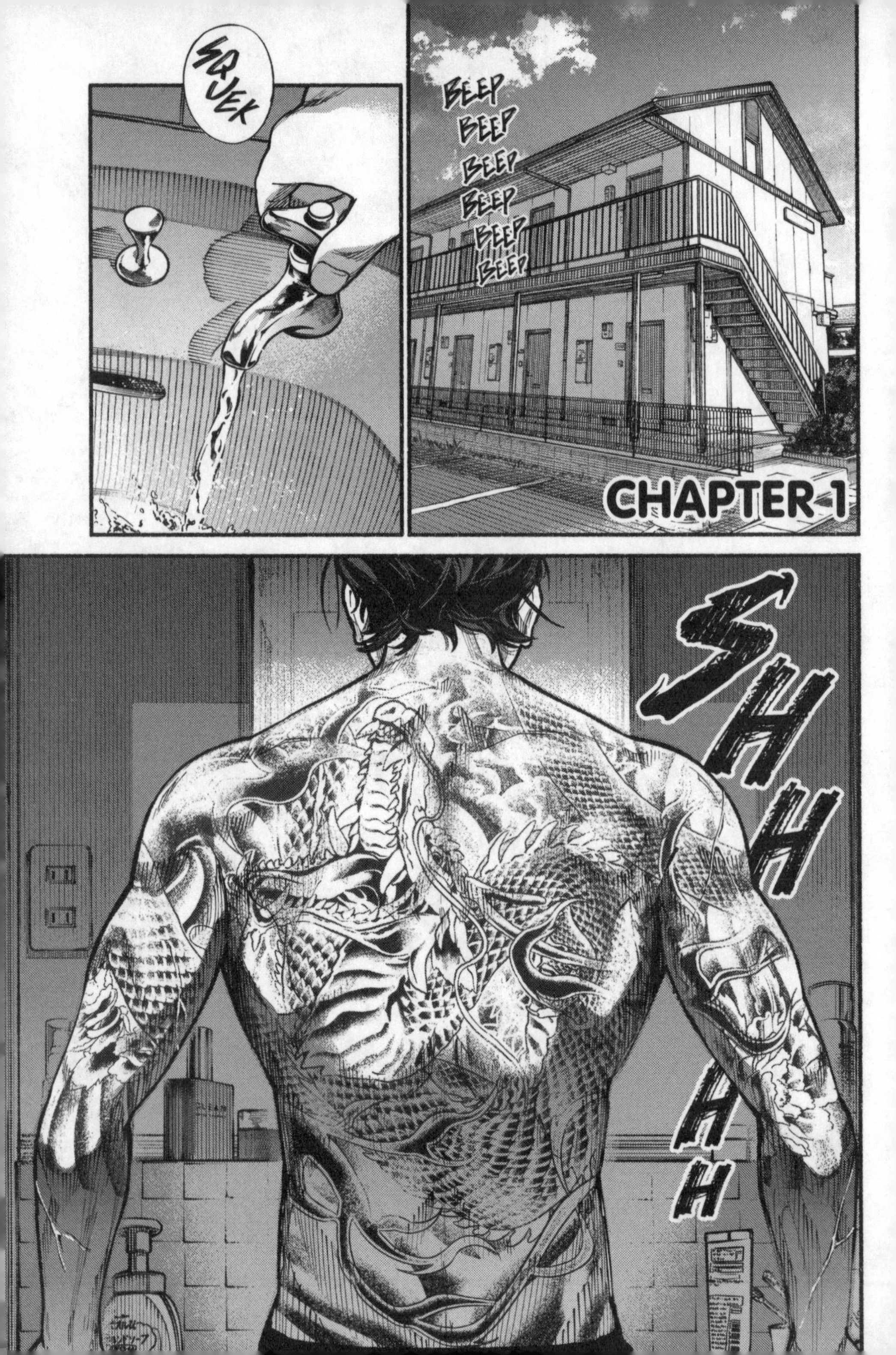
BEEP
BEEP
BEEP
BEEP
BEEP
BEEP
CHAPTER 1
SQUEK
SHHHHH

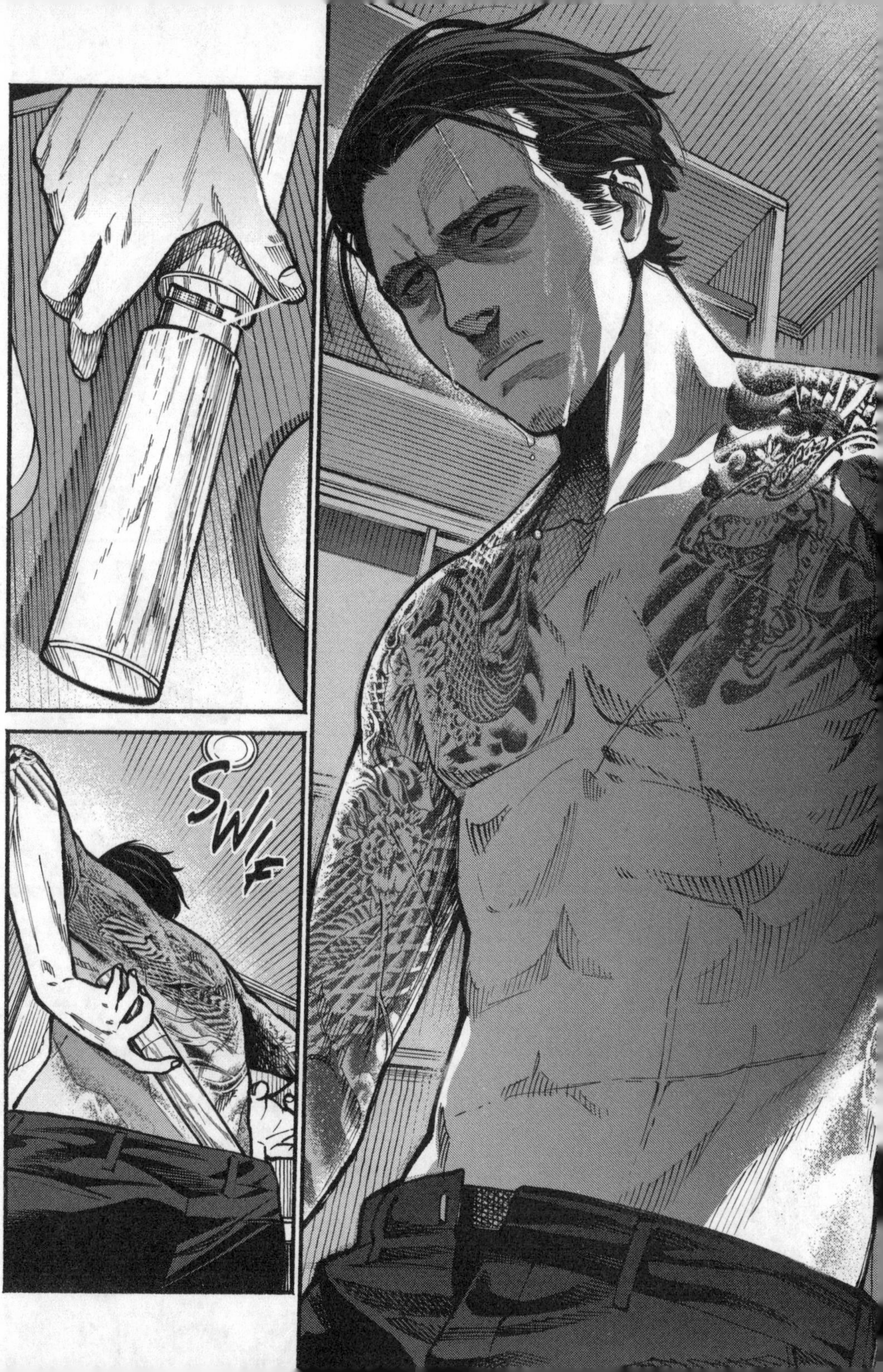
SWIF

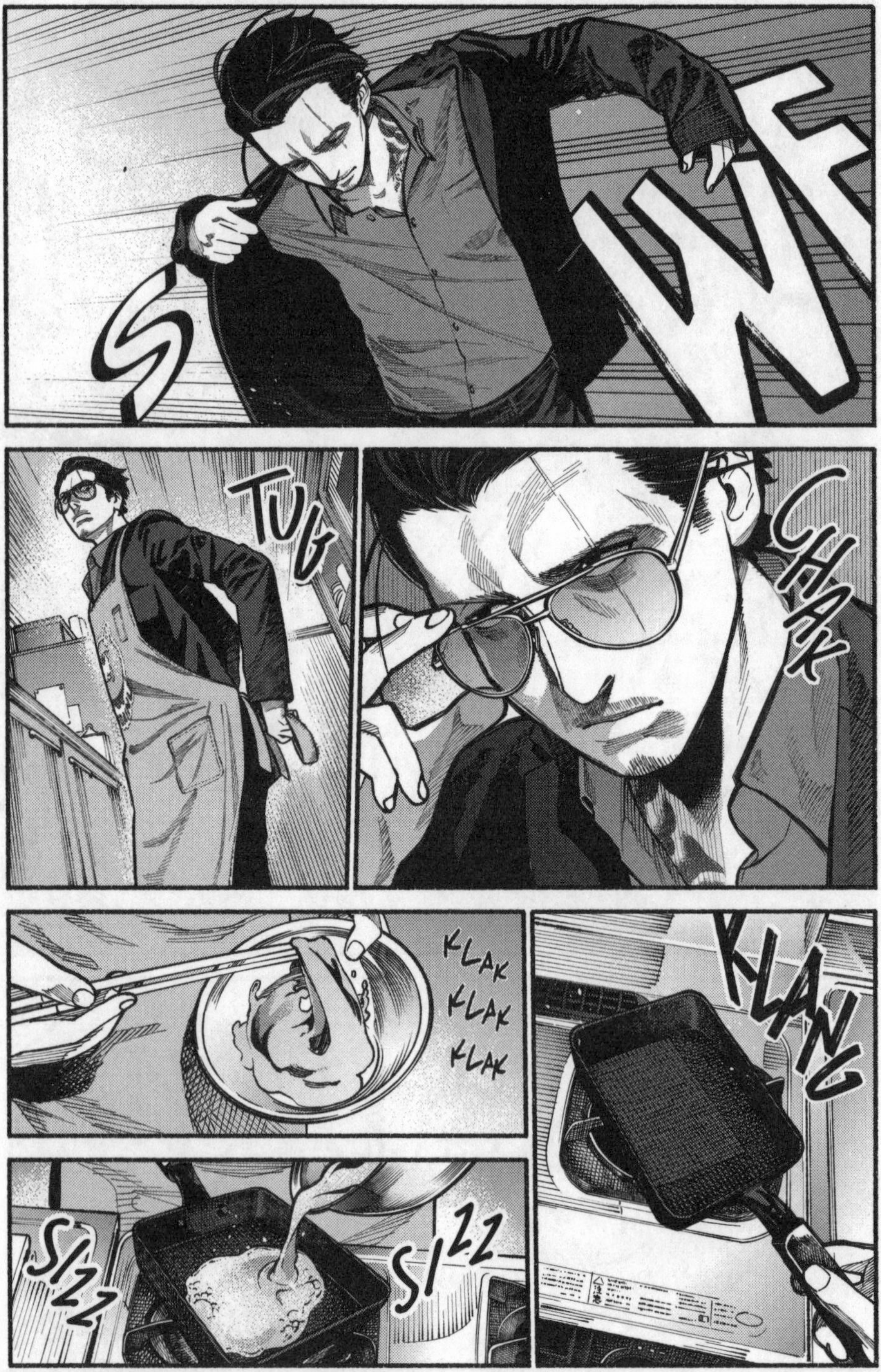
SWF
CHAK
TUG
KLANG
KLAK
KLAK
KLAK
SIZZ
SIZZ

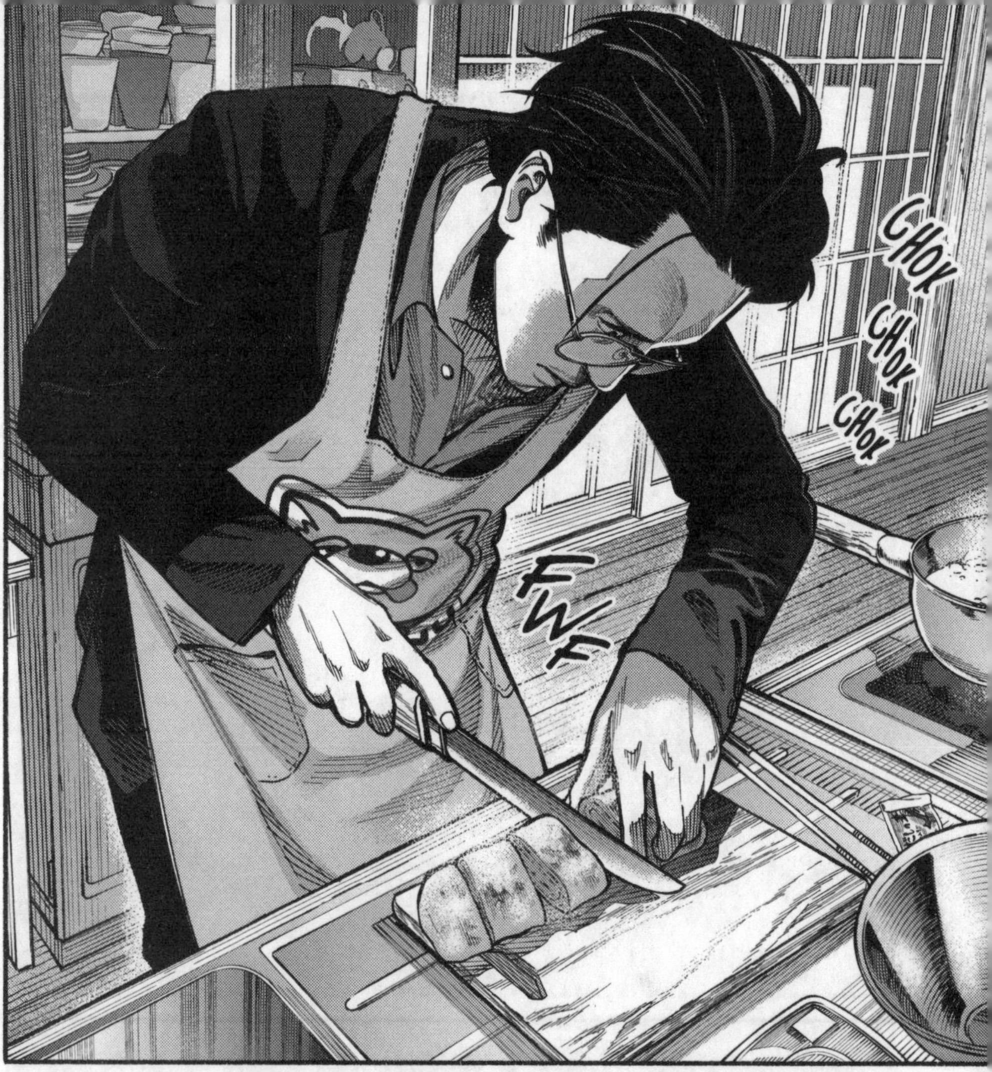
CHOK
CHOK
CHOK
FWF

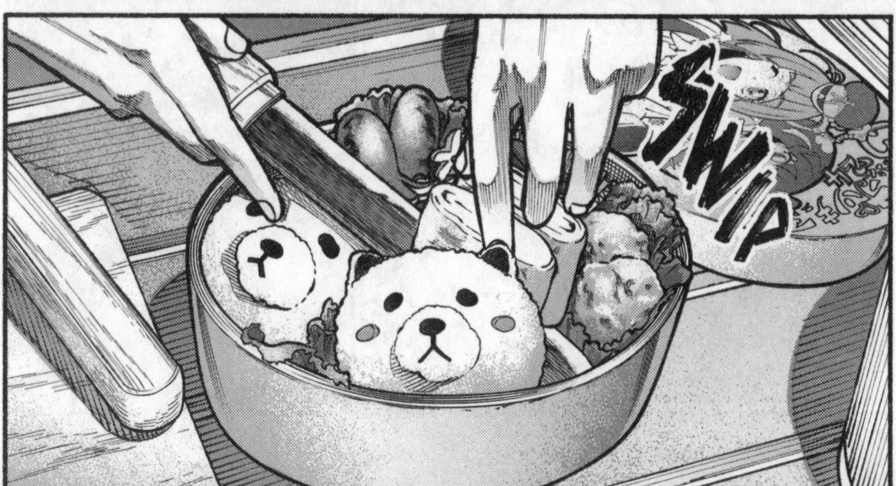
SWIP

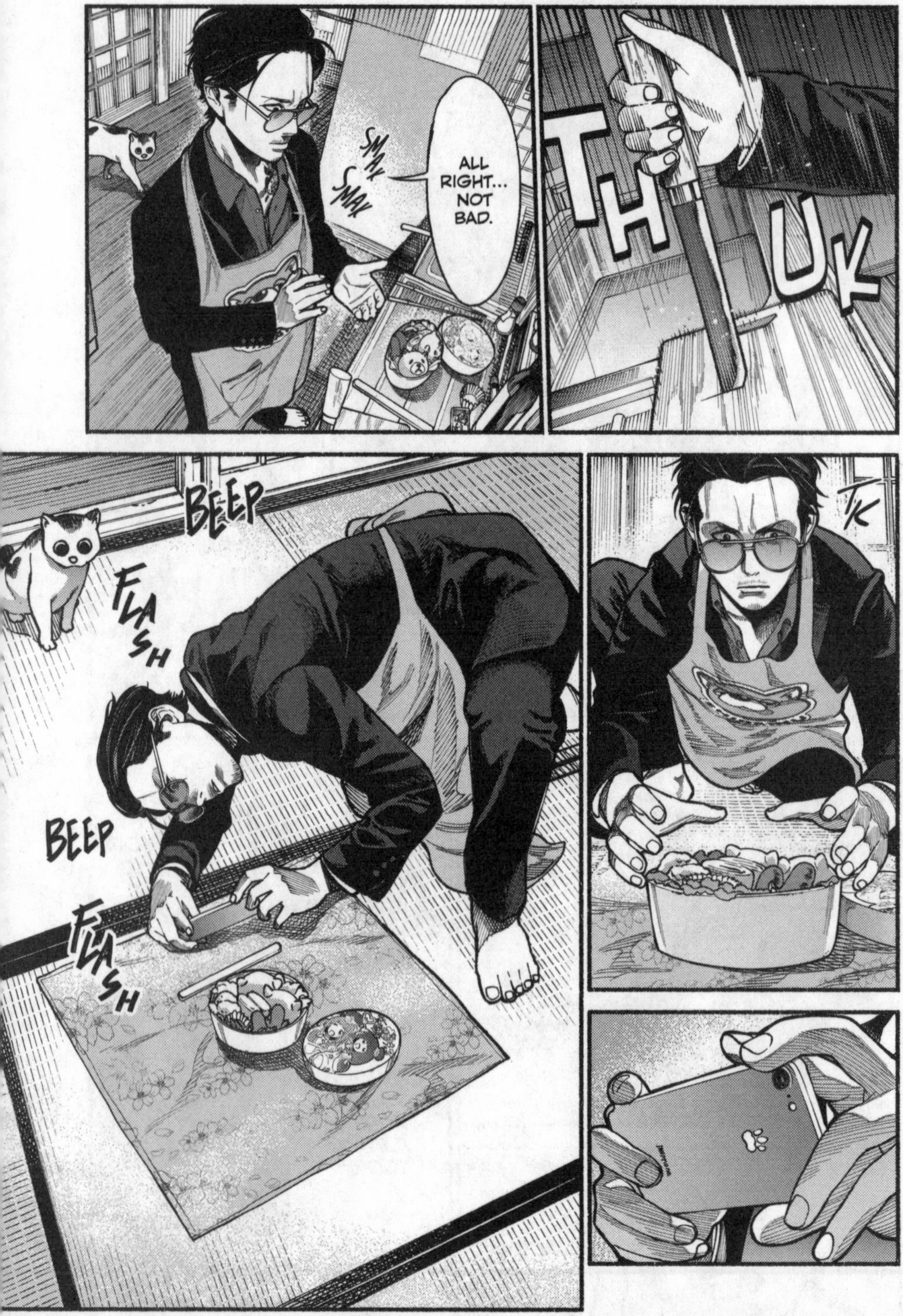
THUK
SMAK SMAK
ALL RIGHT... NOT BAD.
TK
BEEP
FLASH
BEEP
FLASH

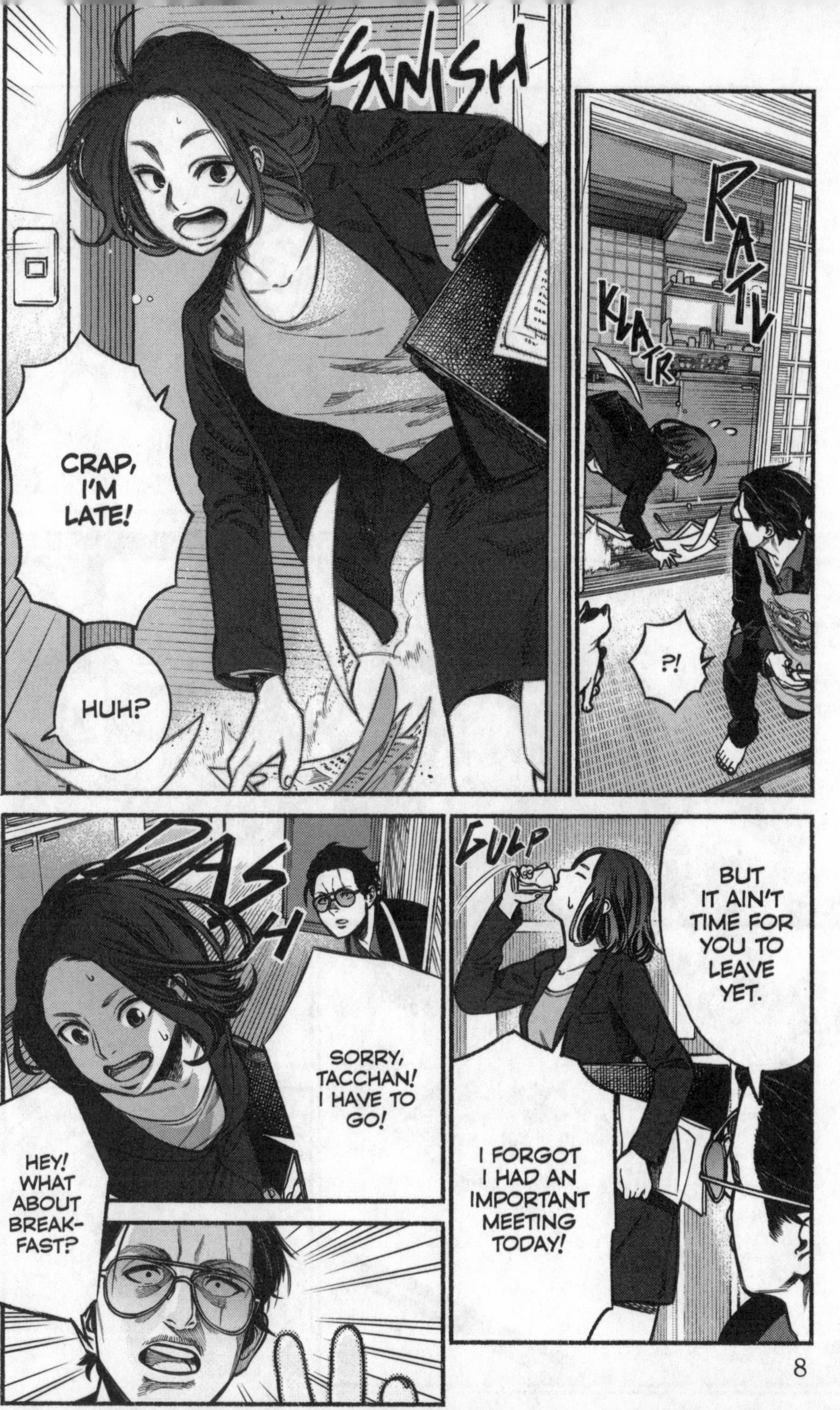
RATTL
KLATR
?!
SWISH
CRAP, I'M LATE!
HUH?
GULP
BUT IT AIN'T TIME FOR YOU TO LEAVE YET.
I FORGOT I HAD AN IMPORTANT MEETING TODAY!
DASH
SORRY, TACCHAN! I HAVE TO GO!
HEY! WHAT ABOUT BREAK-FAST?

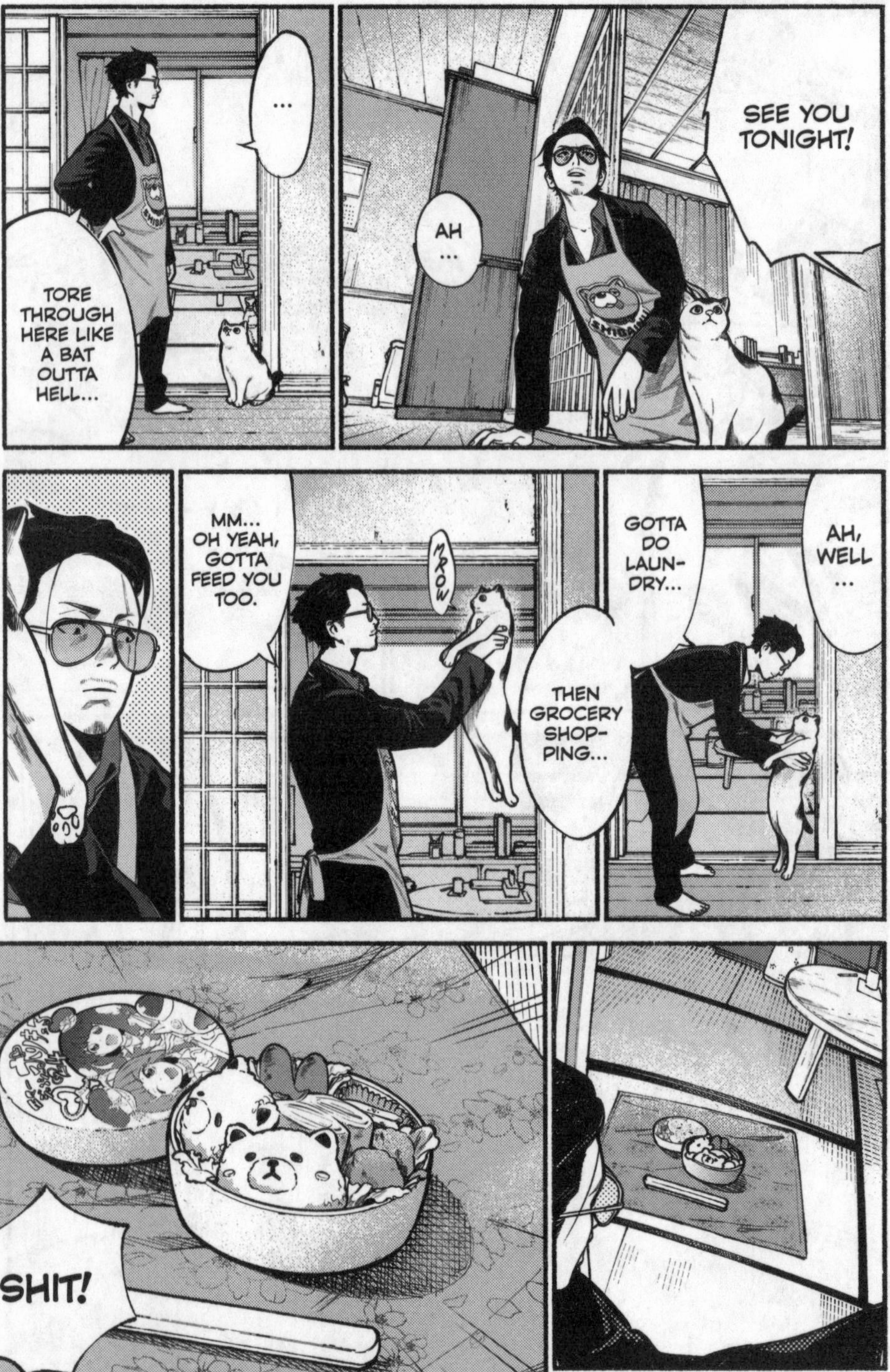
SEE YOU TONIGHT!
AH ...
...
TORE THROUGH HERE LIKE A BAT OUTTA HELL...
AH, WELL ...
GOTTA DO LAUN-DRY...
THEN GROCERY SHOP-PING...
MROW
MM... OH YEAH, GOTTA FEED YOU TOO.
SHIT!

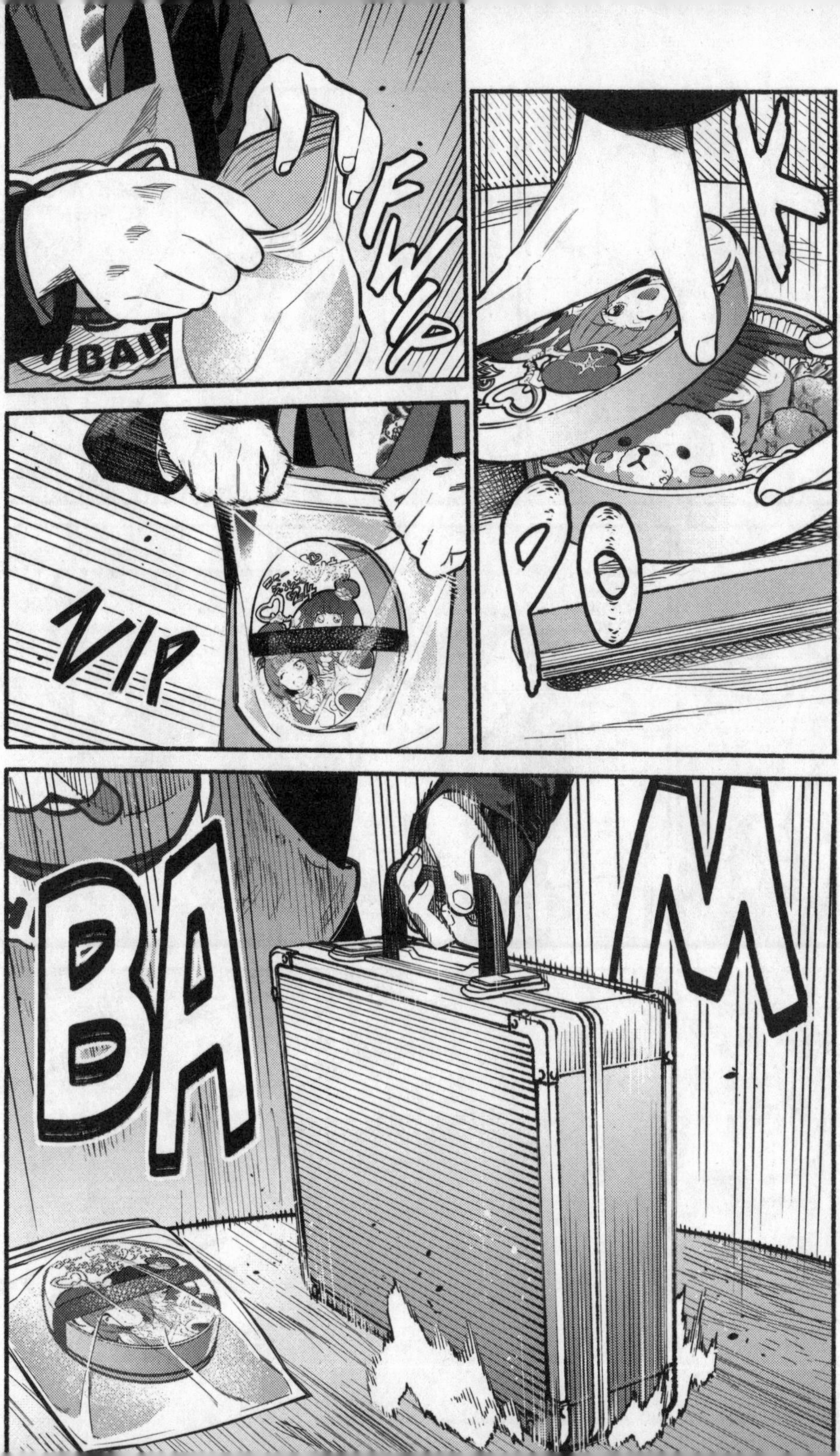
POK
FWIP
VIP
BAM

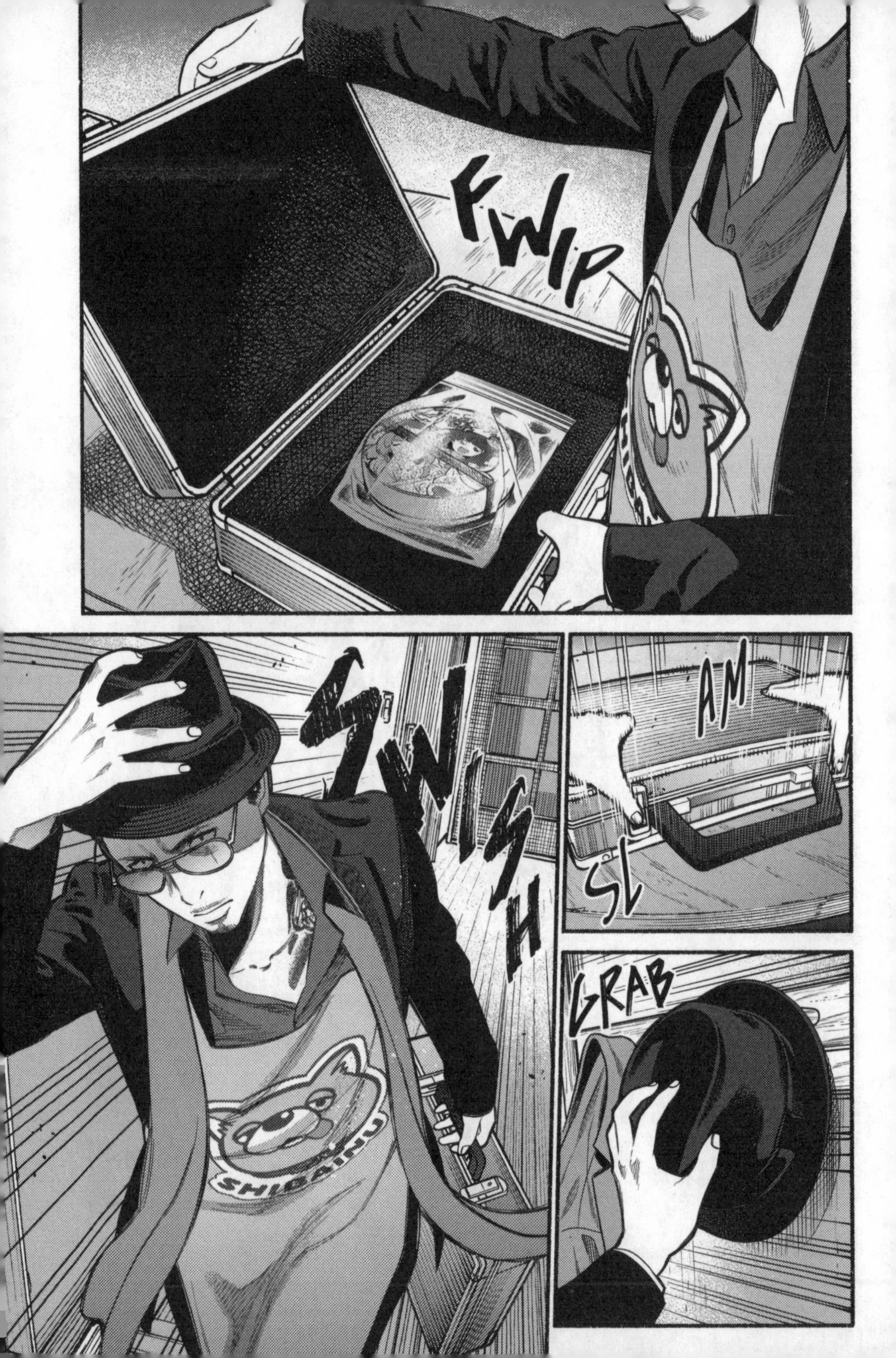
FWIP
SLAM
GRAB
SWISH

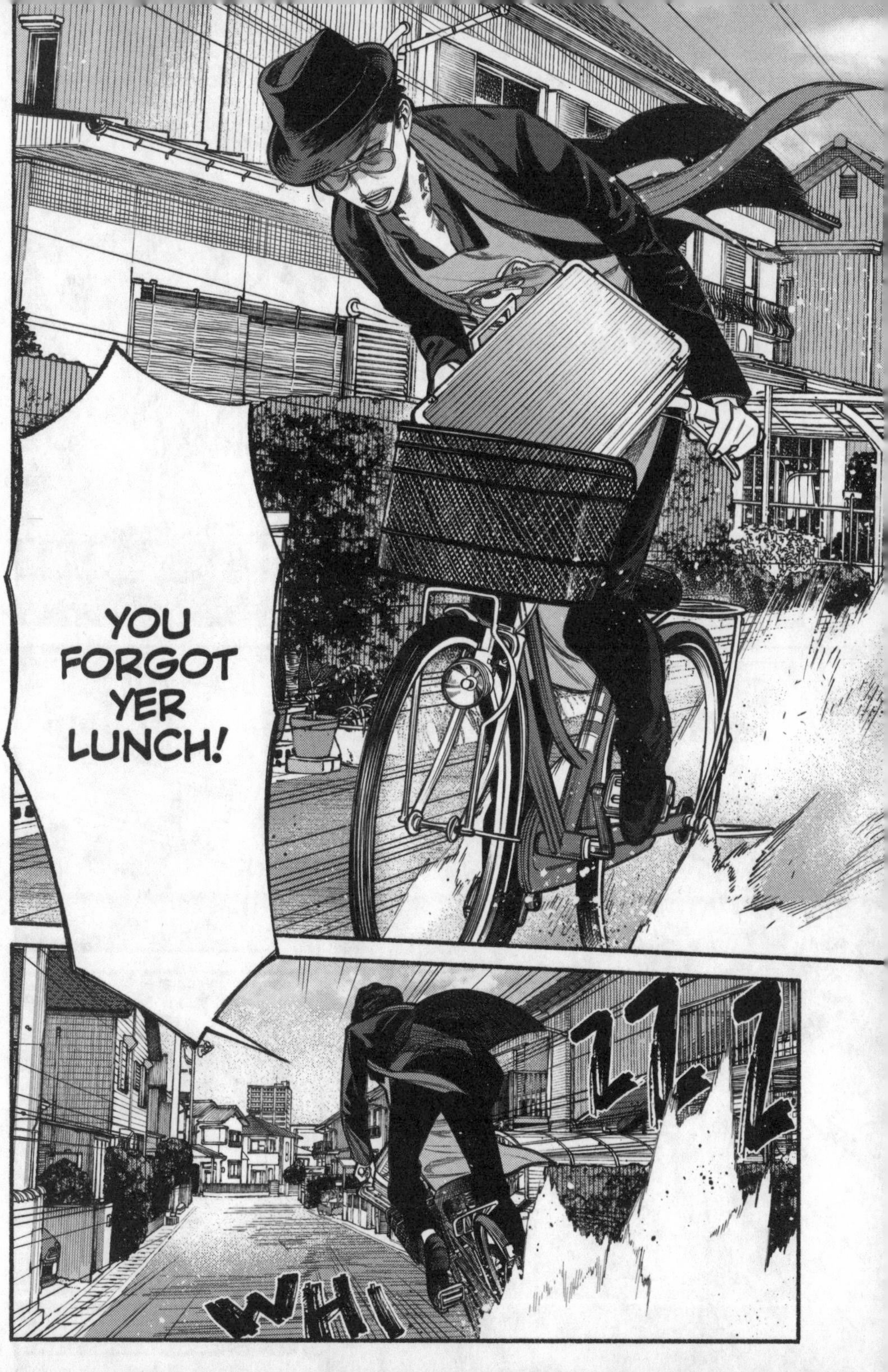
YOU FORGOT YER LUNCH!
WHIZZ

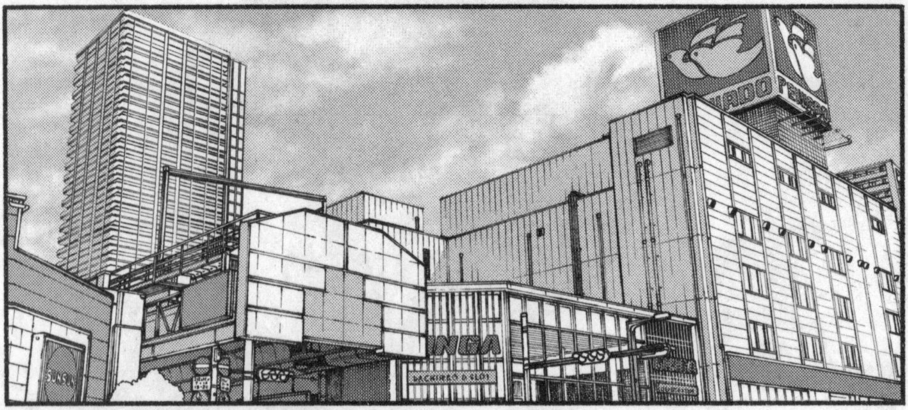

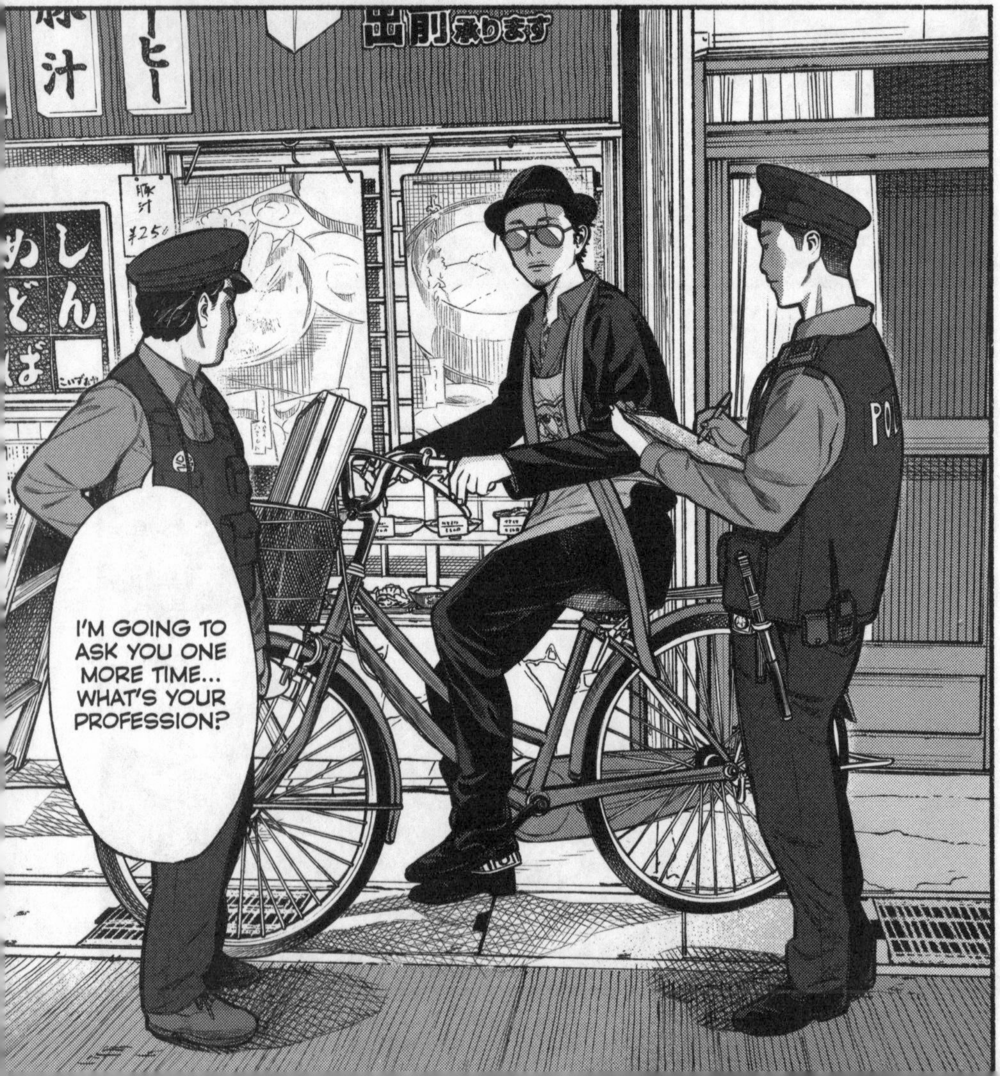
豚汁
豚汁 ¥250
I'M GOING TO ASK YOU ONE MORE TIME... WHAT'S YOUR PROFESSION?

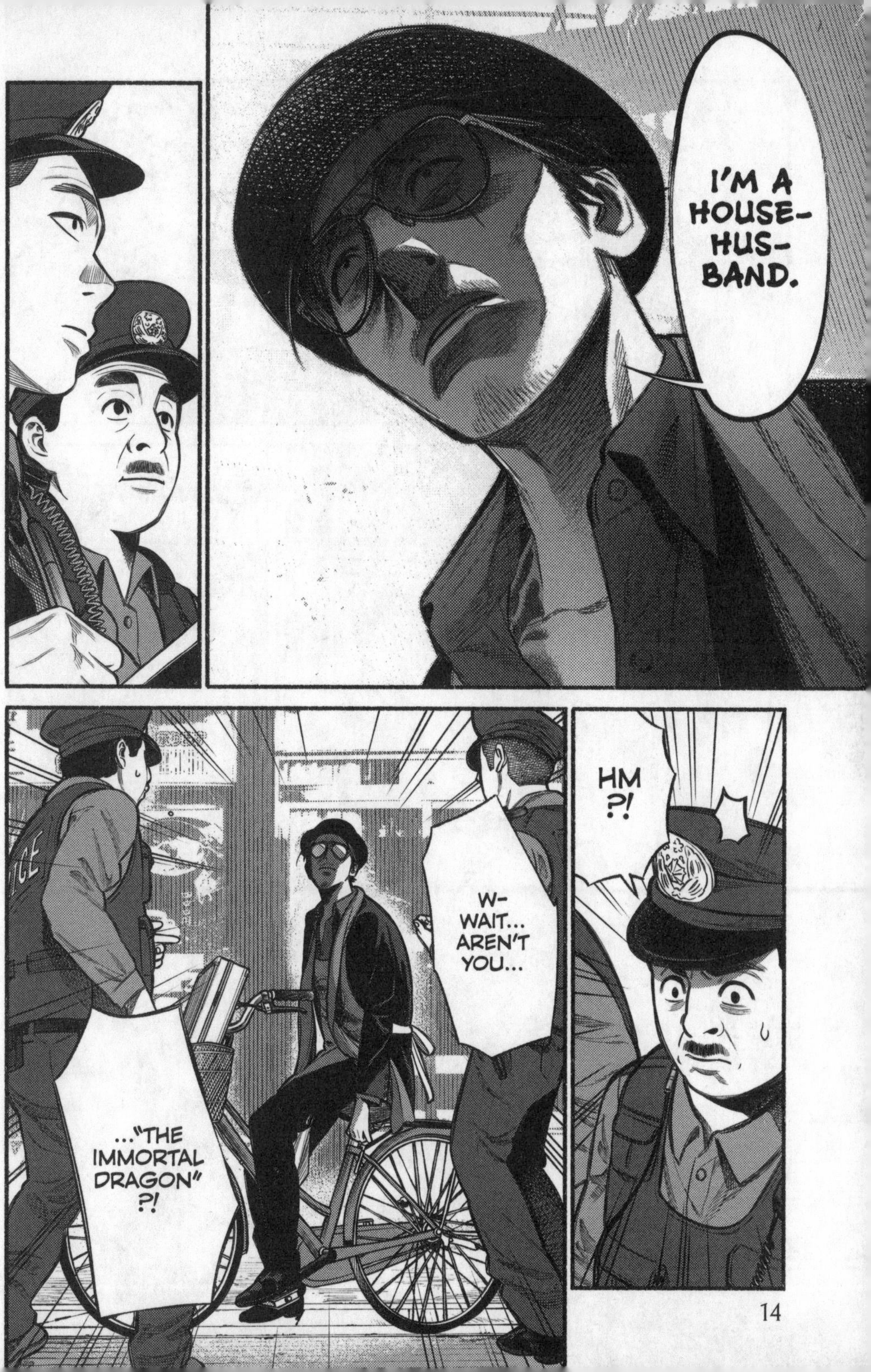
I'M A HOUSE-HUSBAND.
HM ?!
W-WAIT... AREN'T YOU...
..."THE IMMORTAL DRAGON" ?!

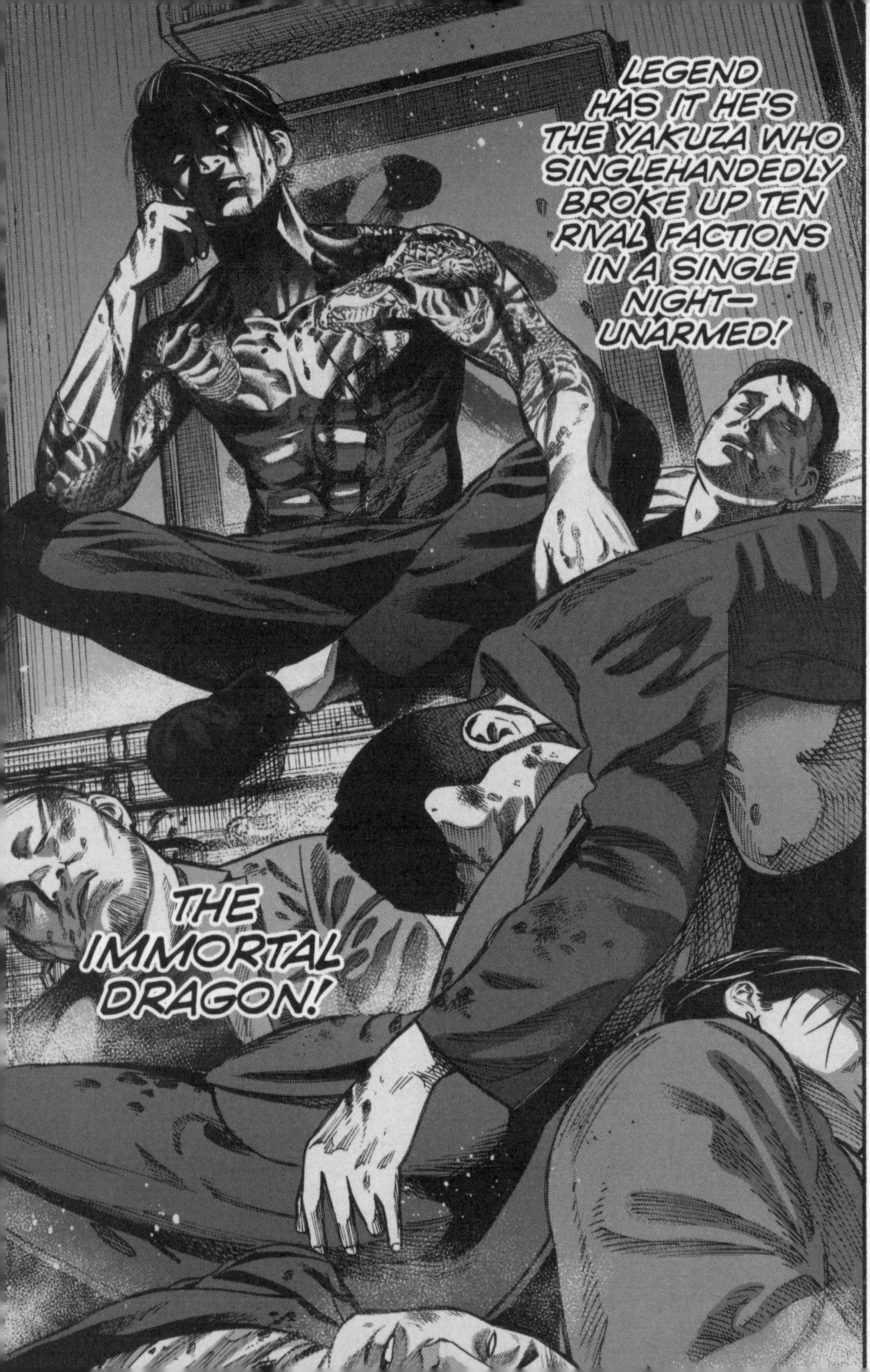
LEGEND HAS IT HE'S THE YAKUZA WHO SINGLEHANDEDLY BROKE UP TEN RIVAL FACTIONS IN A SINGLE NIGHT—UNARMED!
THE IMMORTAL DRAGON!

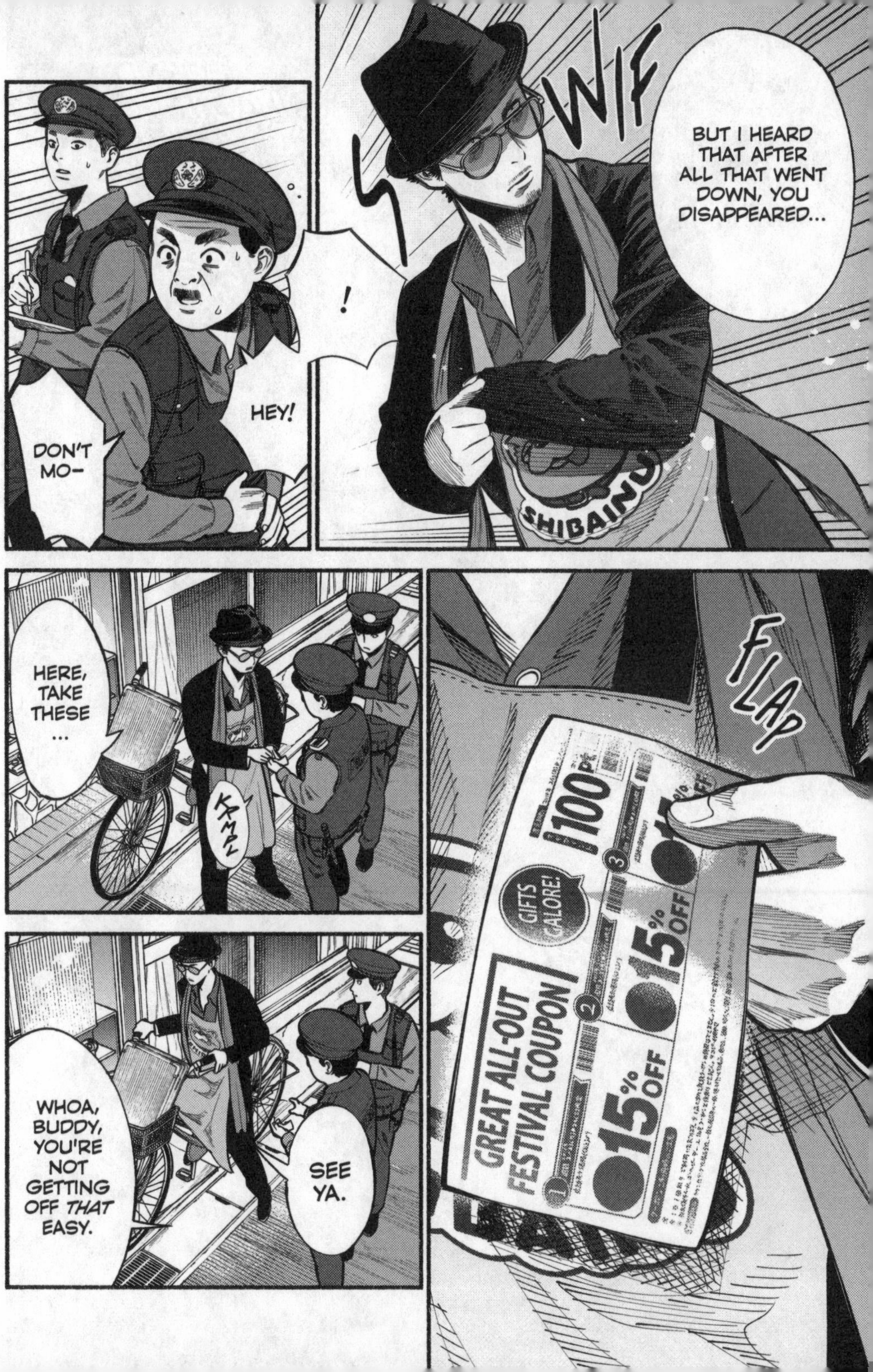
SWIF
BUT I HEARD THAT AFTER ALL THAT WENT DOWN, YOU DISAPPEARED...
SHIBAINU
!
HEY!
DON'T MO—
FLAP
GREAT ALL-OUT FESTIVAL COUPON
GIFTS GALORE!
100
15% OFF
15% OFF
15% OFF
HERE, TAKE THESE ...
KRMPL
SEE YA.
WHOA, BUDDY, YOU'RE NOT GETTING OFF *THAT* EASY.

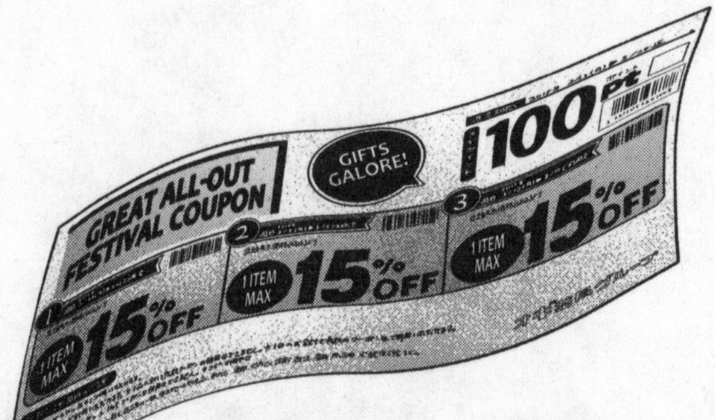
GREAT ALL-OUT FESTIVAL COUPON
GIFTS GALORE!
100pt
1 ITEM MAX
15% OFF
1 ITEM MAX
15% OFF
1 ITEM MAX
15% OFF

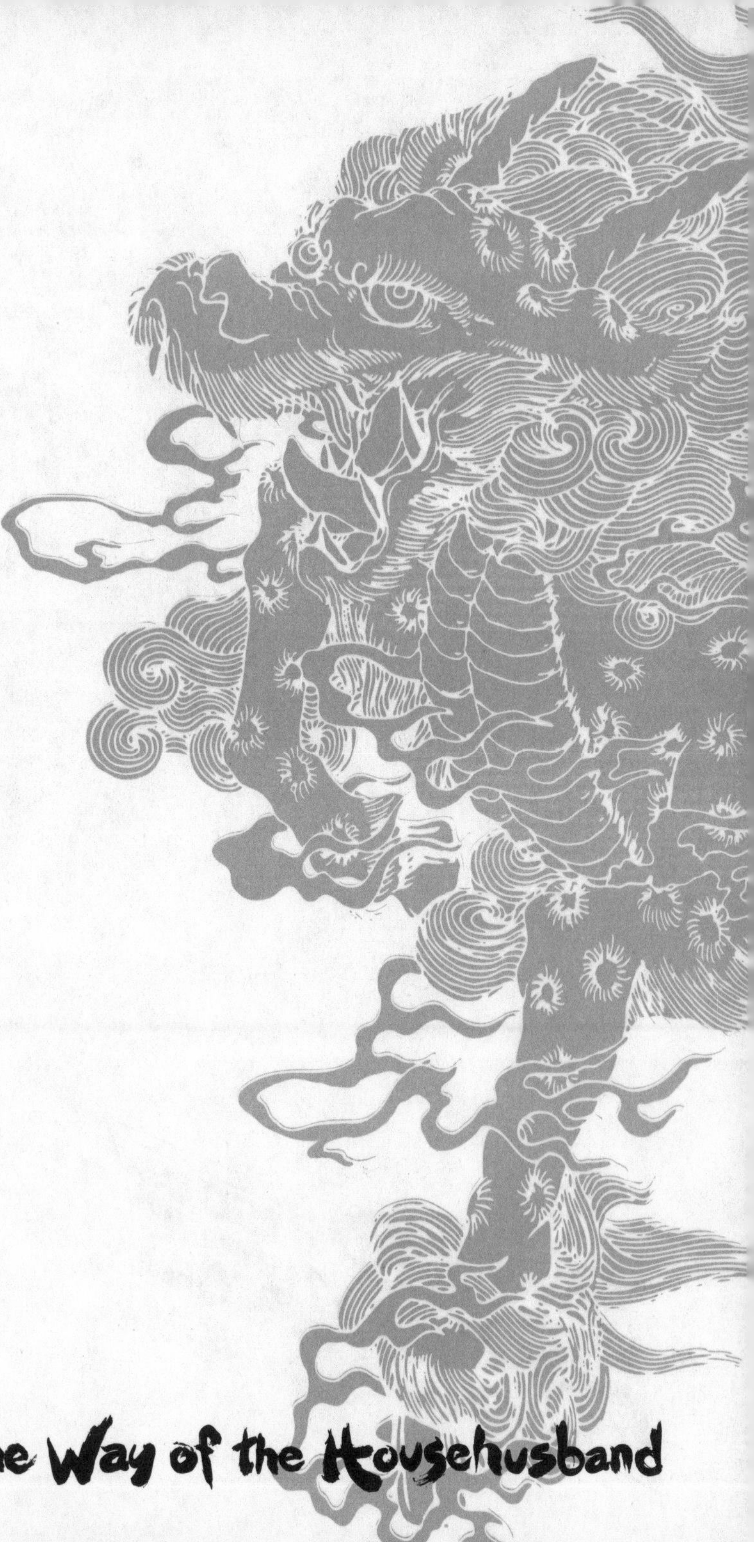

The Way of the Househusband

# CHAPTER 2

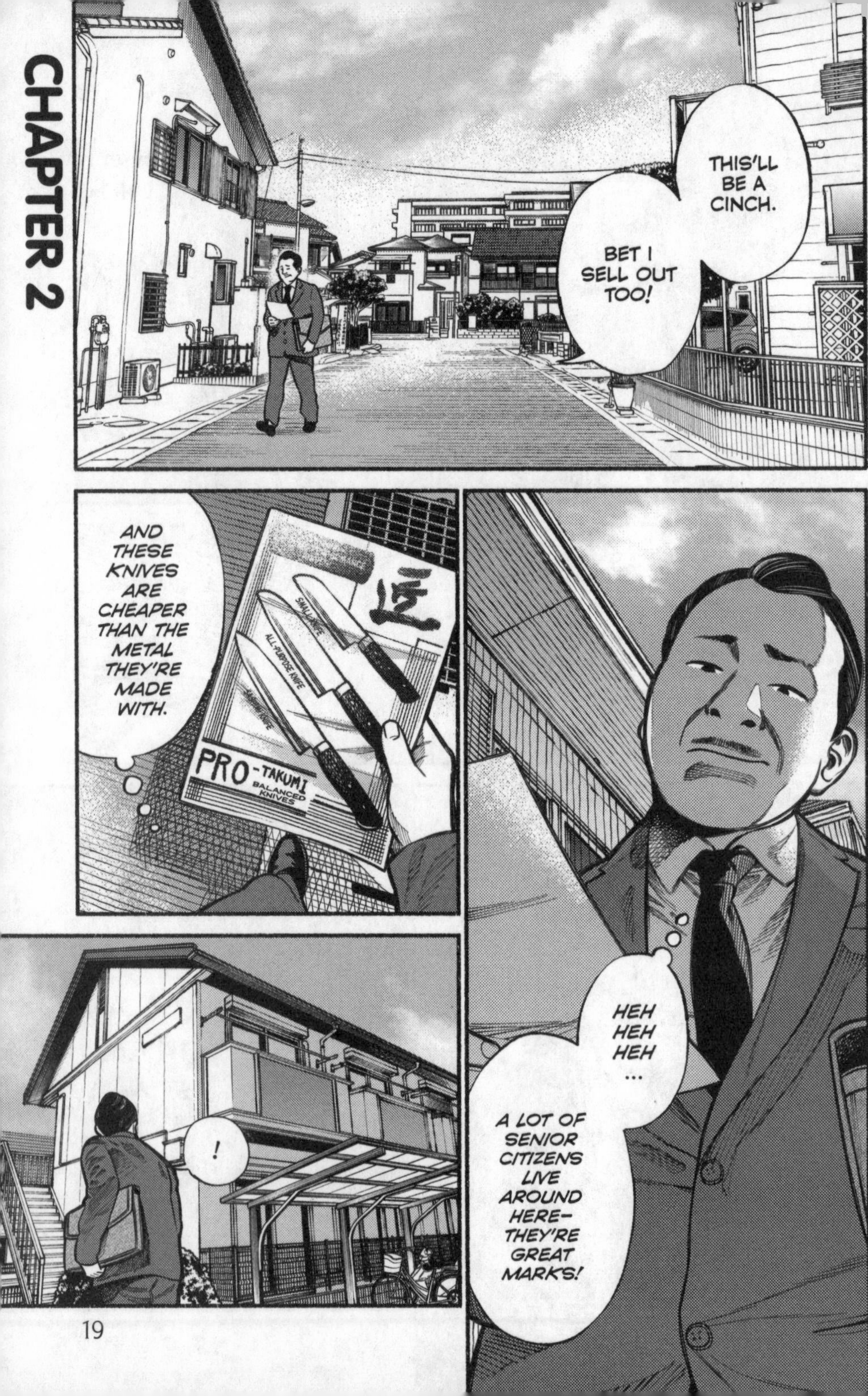
THIS'LL BE A CINCH.
BET I SELL OUT TOO!
HEH HEH HEH ...
A LOT OF SENIOR CITIZENS LIVE AROUND HERE— THEY'RE GREAT MARKS!
AND THESE KNIVES ARE CHEAPER THAN THE METAL THEY'RE MADE WITH.
匠
SMALL KNIFE
ALL-PURPOSE KNIFE
PRO-TAKUMI BALANCED KNIVES
!

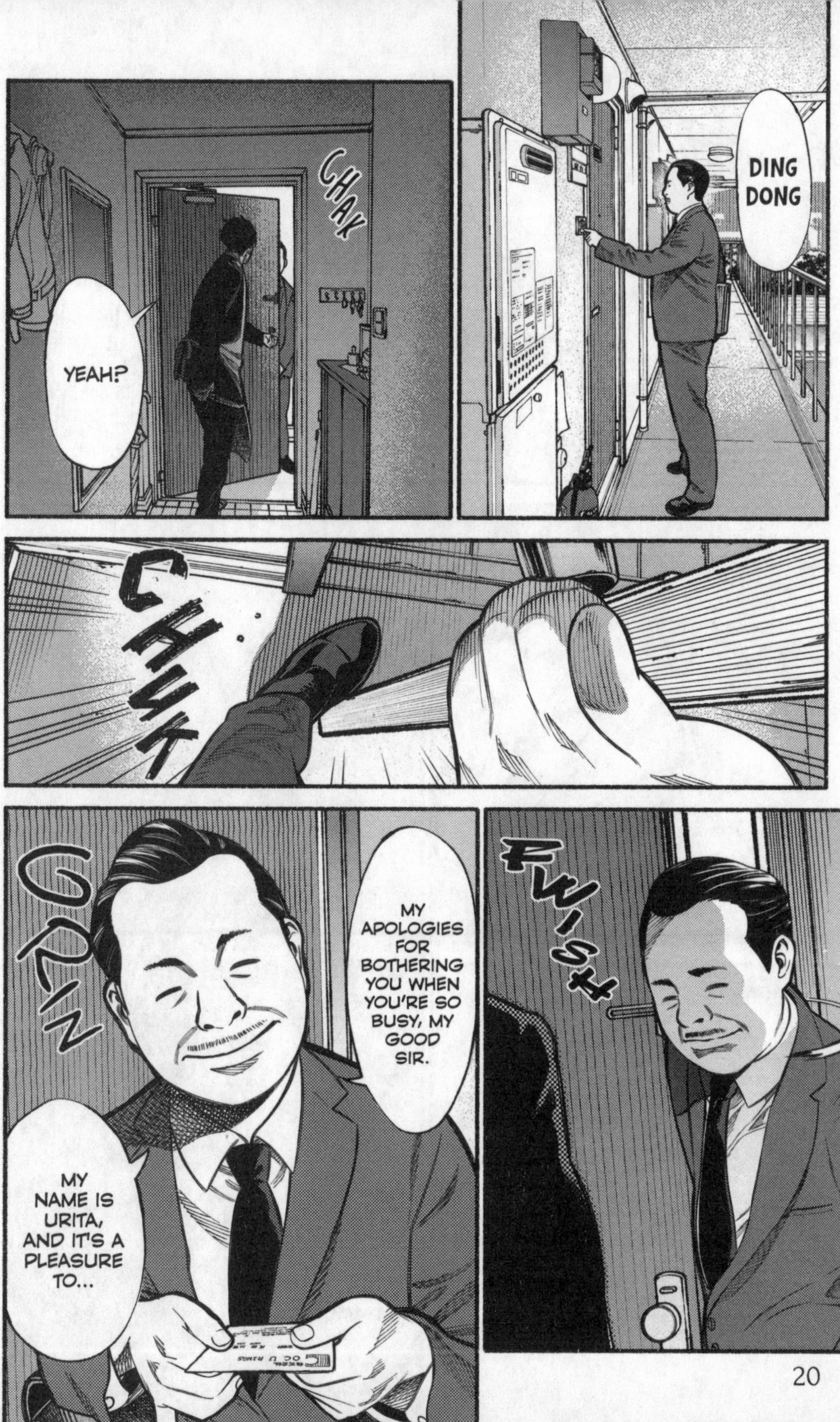
DING DONG
CHAK
YEAH?
CHUNK
FWISH
GRIN
MY APOLOGIES FOR BOTHERING YOU WHEN YOU'RE SO BUSY, MY GOOD SIR.
MY NAME IS URITA, AND IT'S A PLEASURE TO...

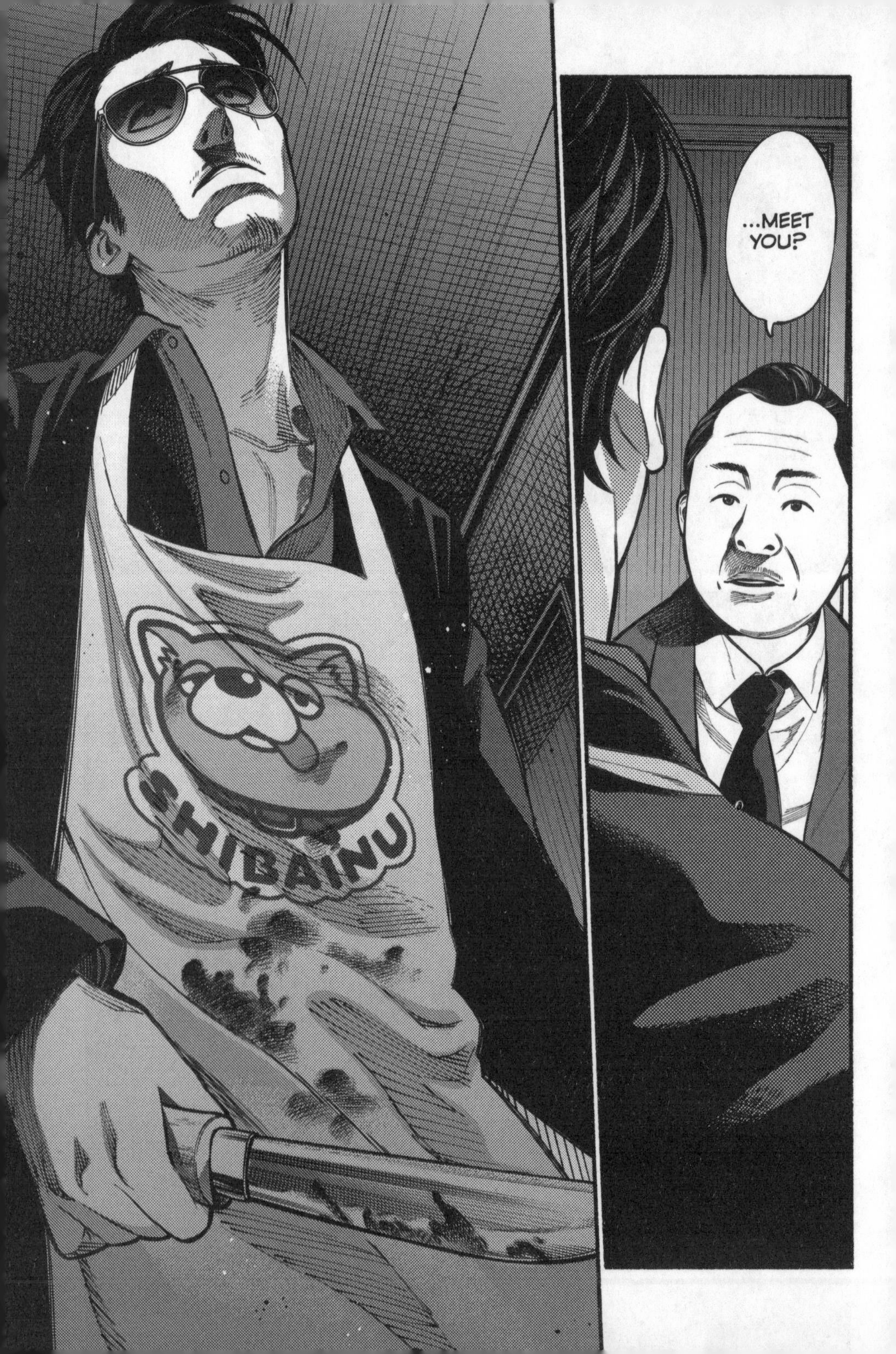
...MEET YOU?
SHIBAINU

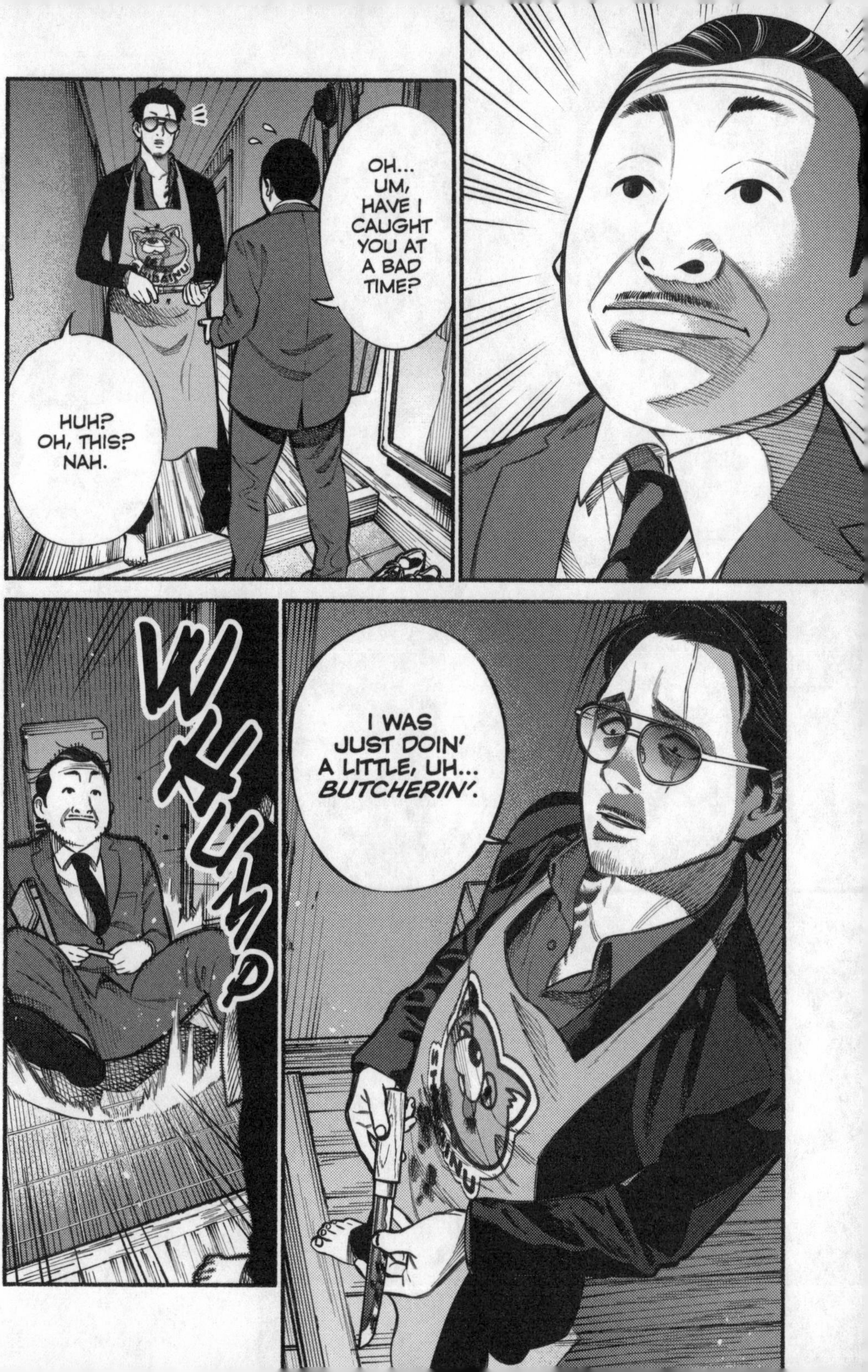
OH... UM, HAVE I CAUGHT YOU AT A BAD TIME?
HUH? OH, THIS? NAH.
I WAS JUST DOIN' A LITTLE, UH... *BUTCHERIN'*.
WHUMP

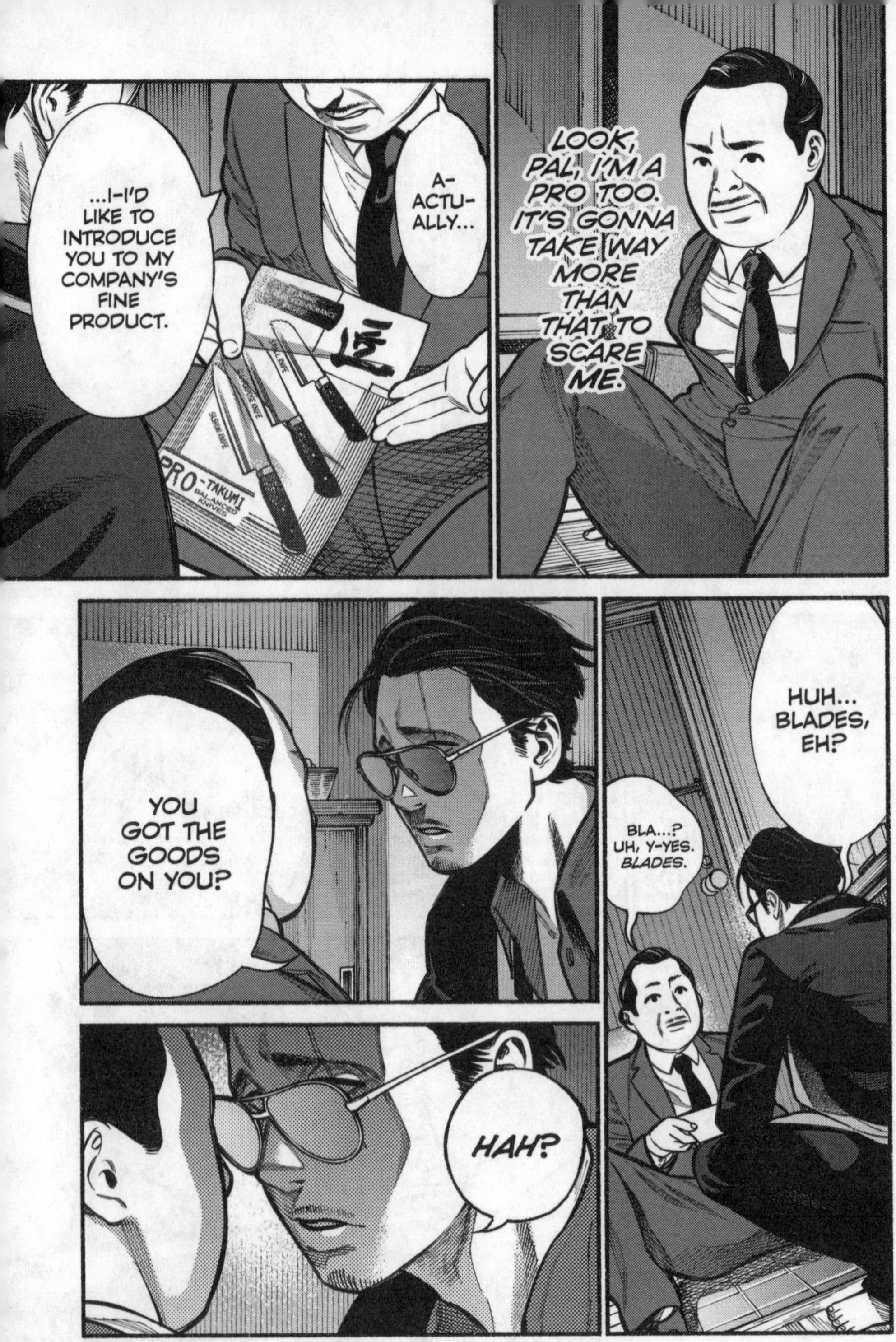
LOOK, PAL, I'M A PRO TOO. IT'S GONNA TAKE WAY MORE THAN THAT TO SCARE ME.
A-ACTU-ALLY...
...I-I'D LIKE TO INTRODUCE YOU TO MY COMPANY'S FINE PRODUCT.
PRO-TAKUMI BALANCED KNIVES
HUH... BLADES, EH?
BLA...? UH, Y-YES. BLADES.
YOU GOT THE GOODS ON YOU?
HAH?

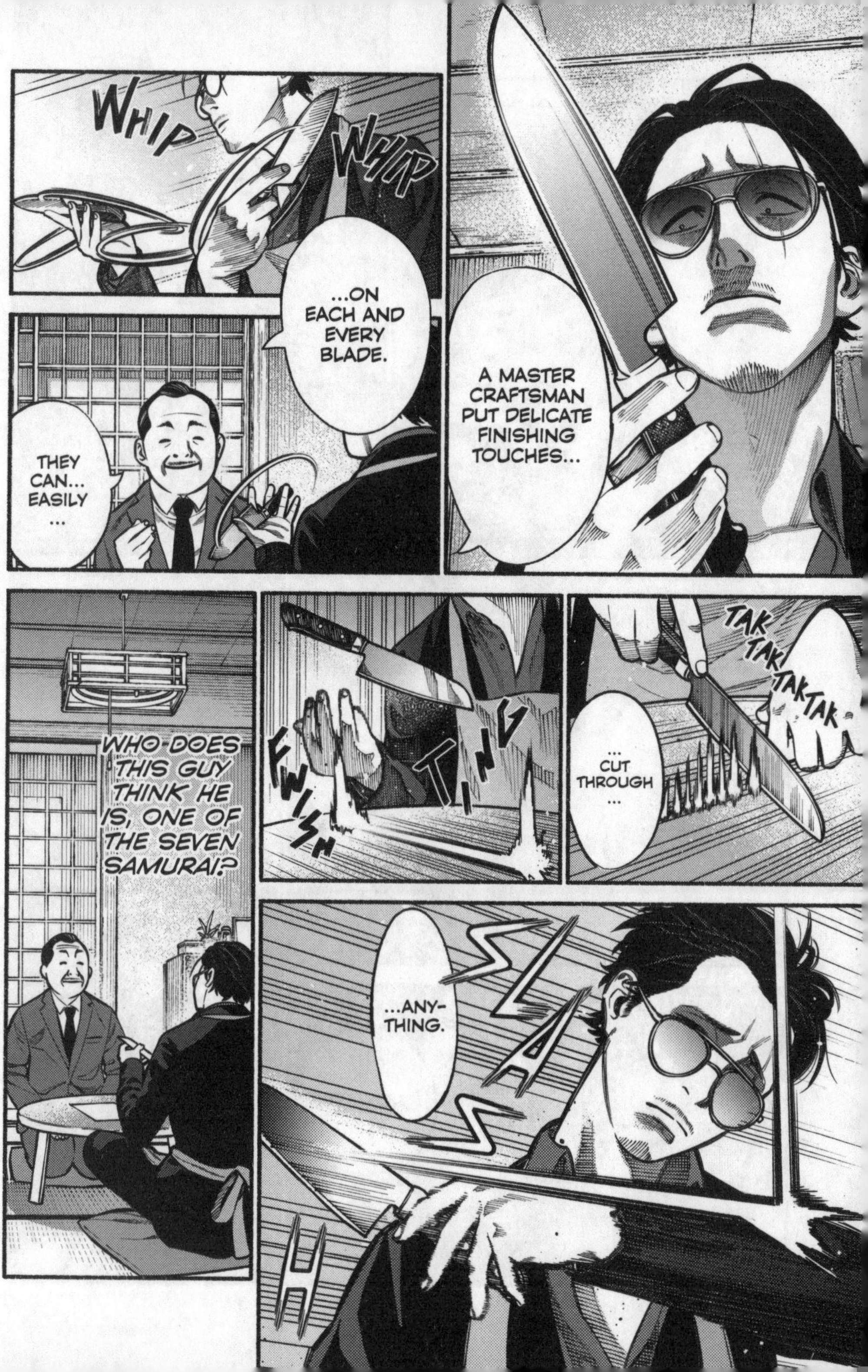
A MASTER CRAFTSMAN PUT DELICATE FINISHING TOUCHES...
WHIP
WHIP
...ON EACH AND EVERY BLADE.
THEY CAN... EASILY ...
TAK TAK TAK TAK
... CUT THROUGH ...
TING
FWISH
...ANY-THING.
WHO DOES THIS GUY THINK HE IS, ONE OF THE SEVEN SAMURAI?

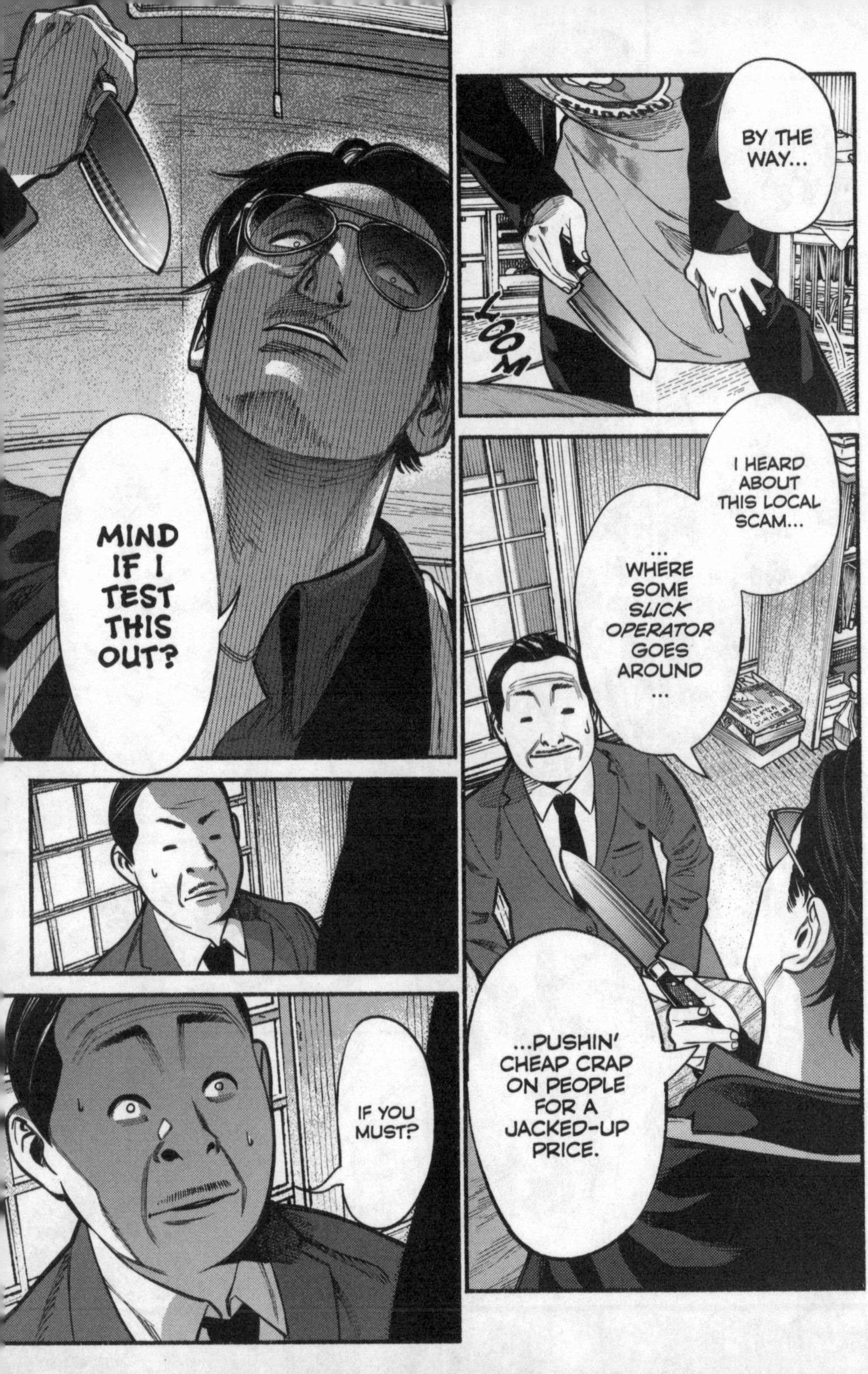

BY THE WAY...
LOOM
I HEARD ABOUT THIS LOCAL SCAM...
... WHERE SOME *SLICK OPERATOR* GOES AROUND ...
...PUSHIN' CHEAP CRAP ON PEOPLE FOR A JACKED-UP PRICE.
MIND IF I TEST THIS OUT?
IF YOU MUST?

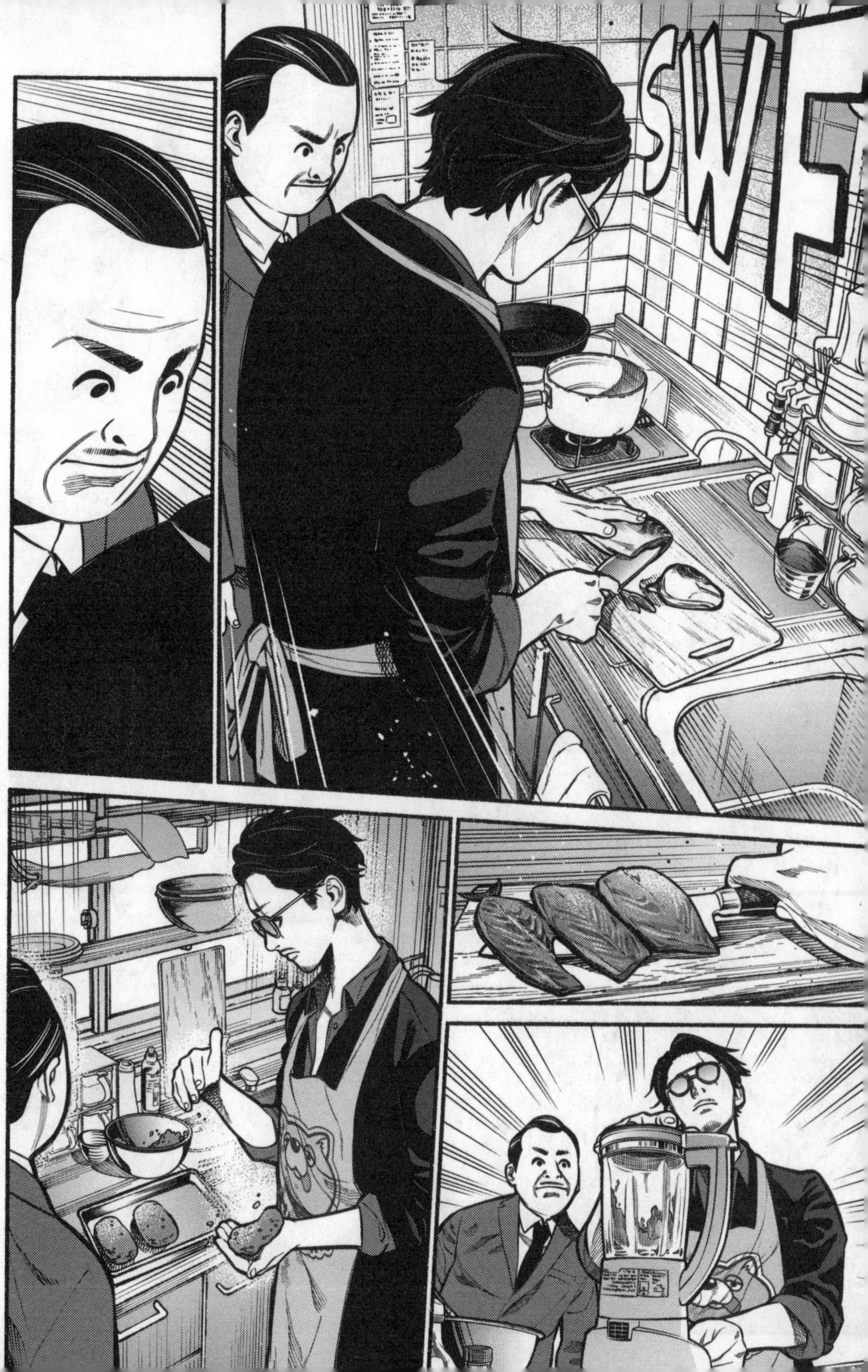
SWF

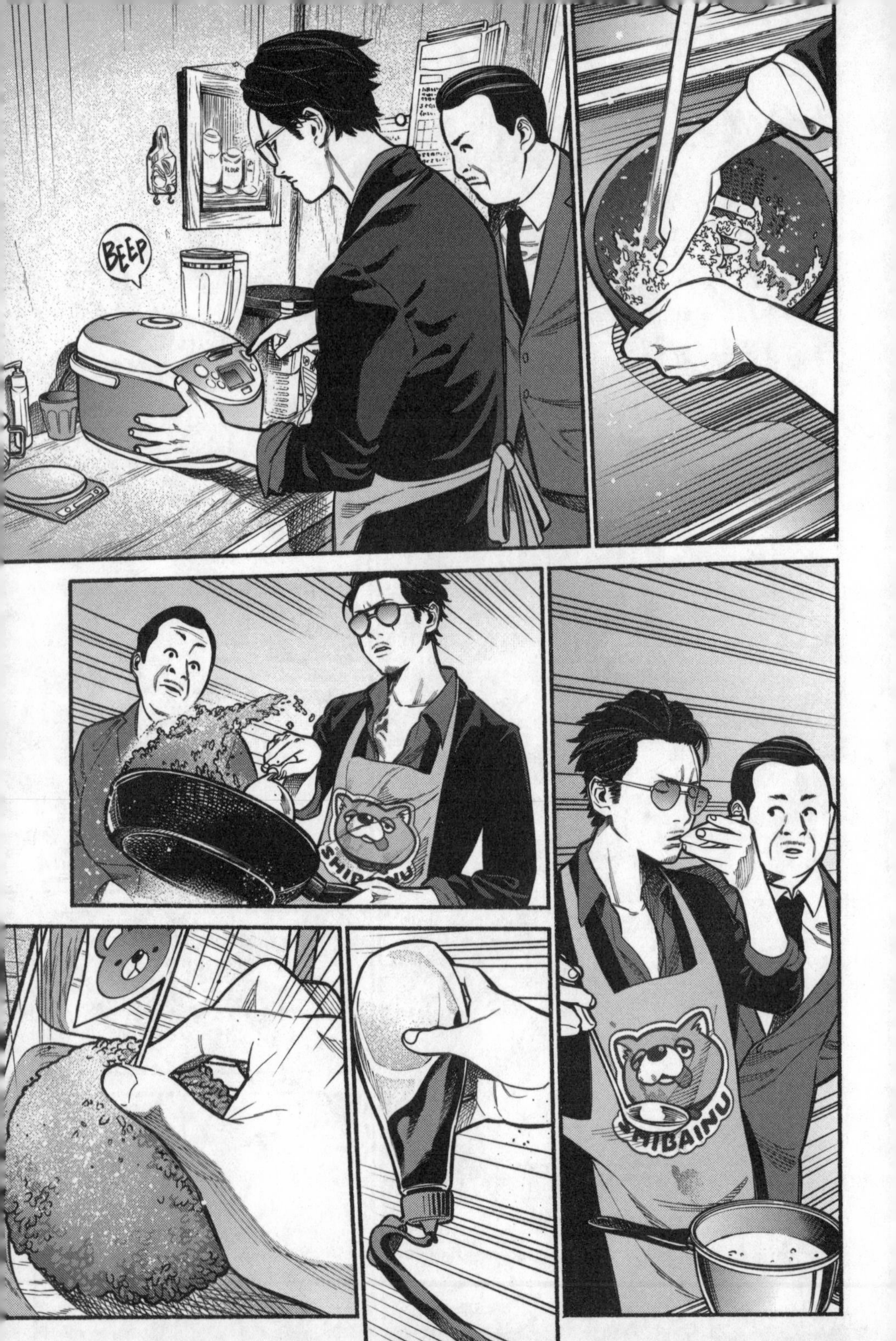
BEEP
FLOUR
SHIBAINU
SHIBAINU

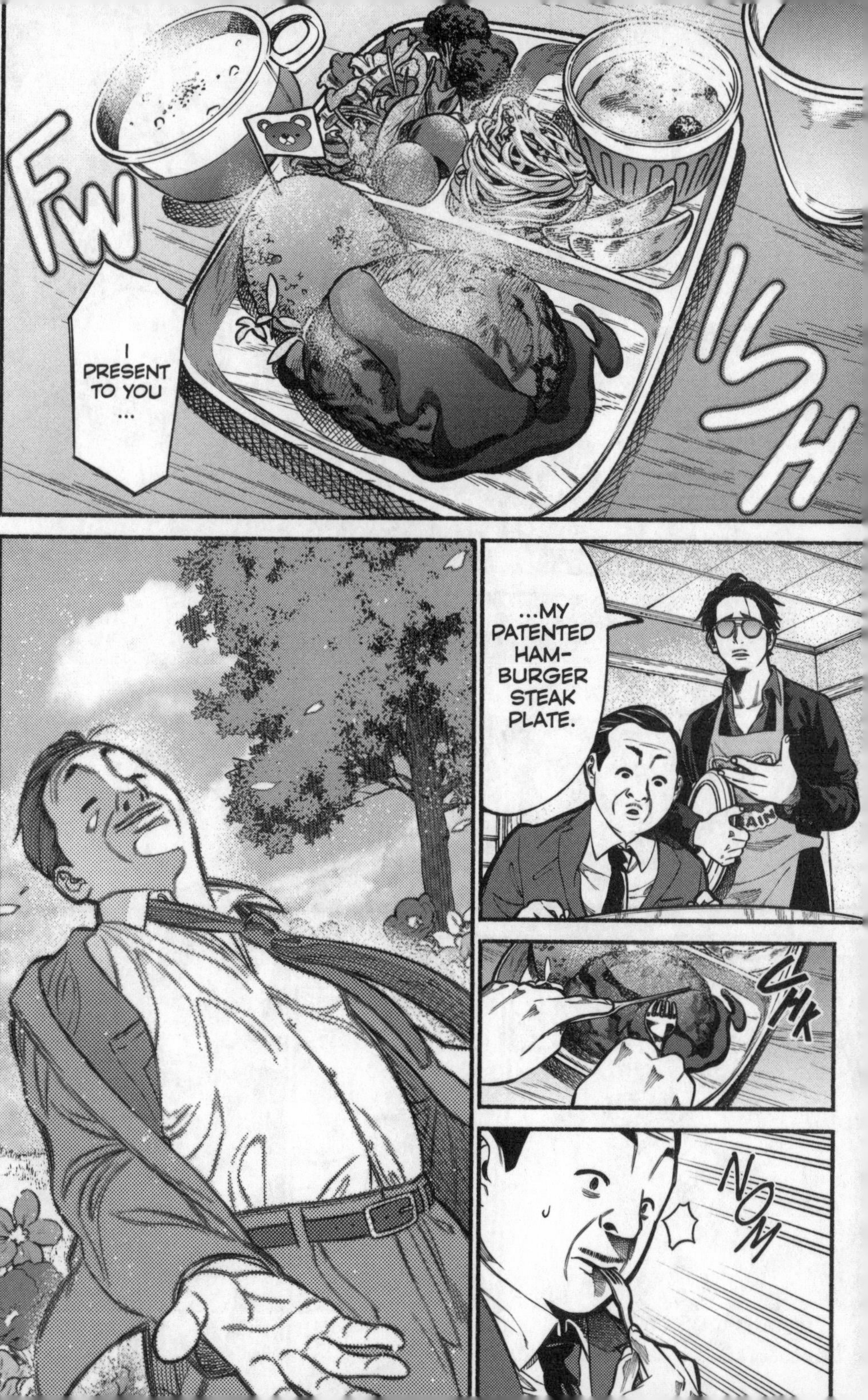
FWISH
I PRESENT TO YOU ...
...MY PATENTED HAMBURGER STEAK PLATE.
CHK
NOM

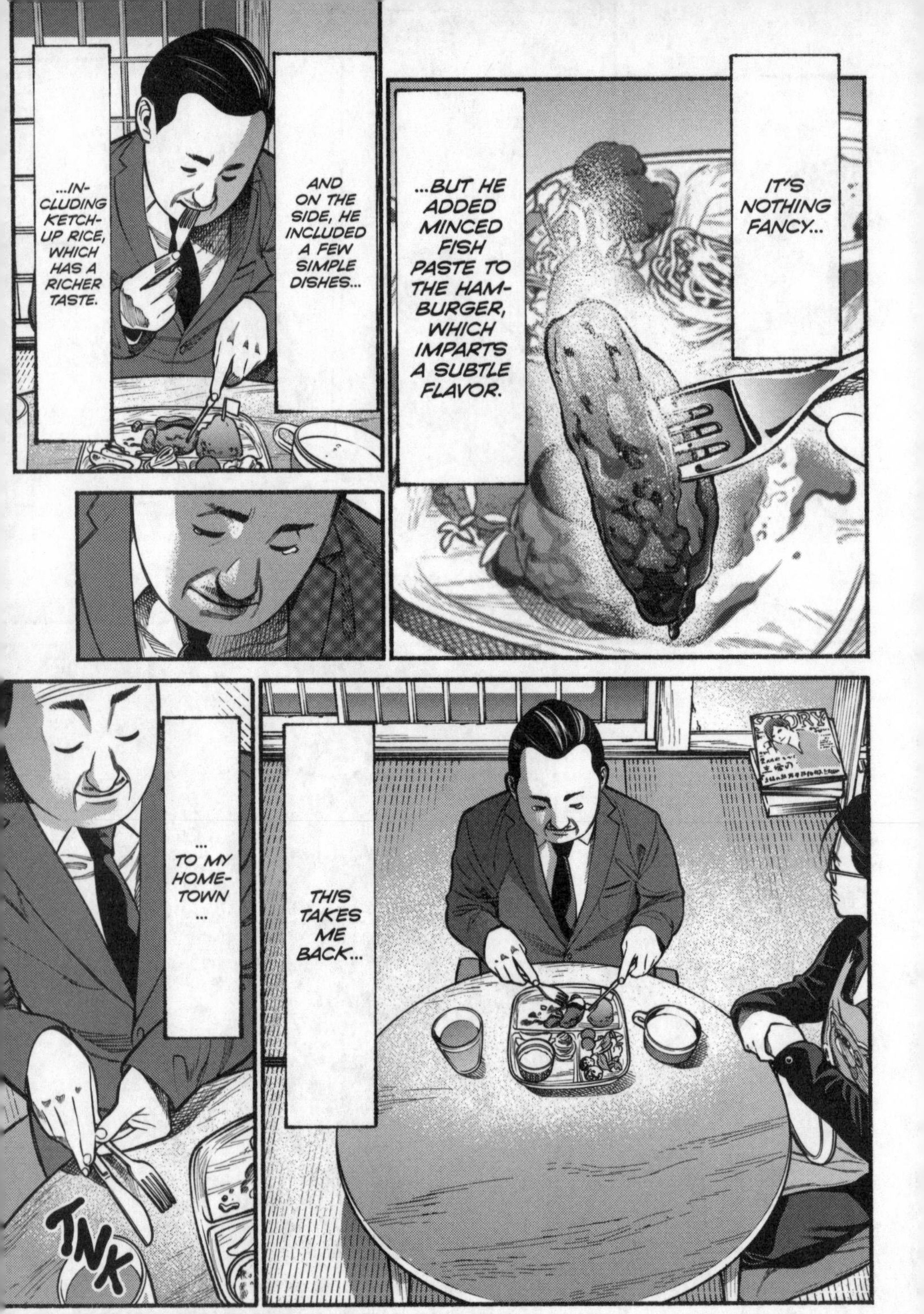
IT'S NOTHING FANCY...
...BUT HE ADDED MINCED FISH PASTE TO THE HAMBURGER, WHICH IMPARTS A SUBTLE FLAVOR.
AND ON THE SIDE, HE INCLUDED A FEW SIMPLE DISHES...
...INCLUDING KETCHUP RICE, WHICH HAS A RICHER TASTE.
THIS TAKES ME BACK...
...TO MY HOMETOWN...
TINK

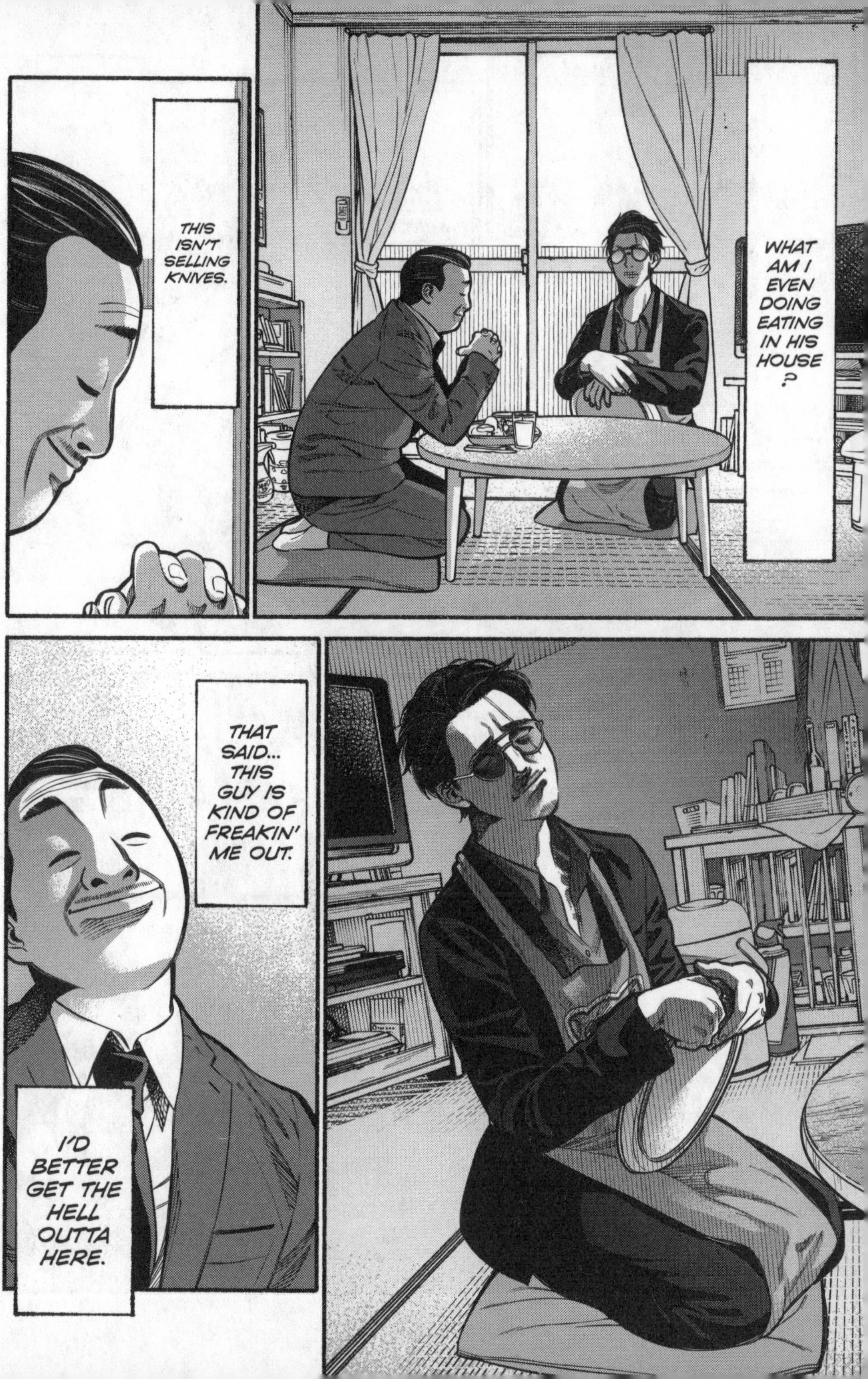
WHAT AM I EVEN DOING EATING IN HIS HOUSE?
THIS ISN'T SELLING KNIVES.
THAT SAID... THIS GUY IS KIND OF FREAKIN' ME OUT.
I'D BETTER GET THE HELL OUTTA HERE.

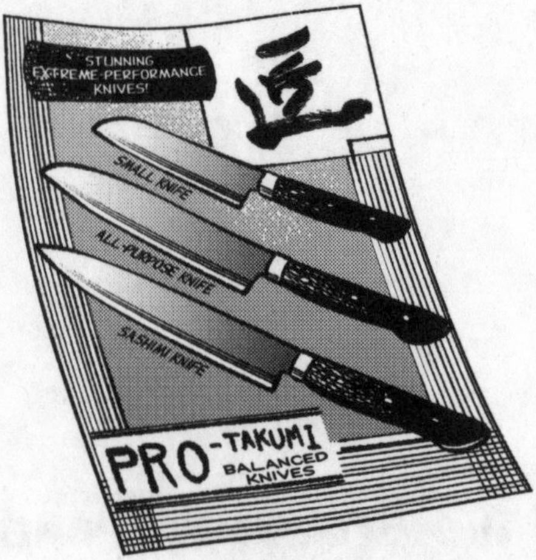
STUNNING
EXTREME-PERFORMANCE
KNIVES!
SMALL KNIFE
ALL-PURPOSE KNIFE
SASHIMI KNIFE
PRO-TAKUMI
BALANCED
KNIVES

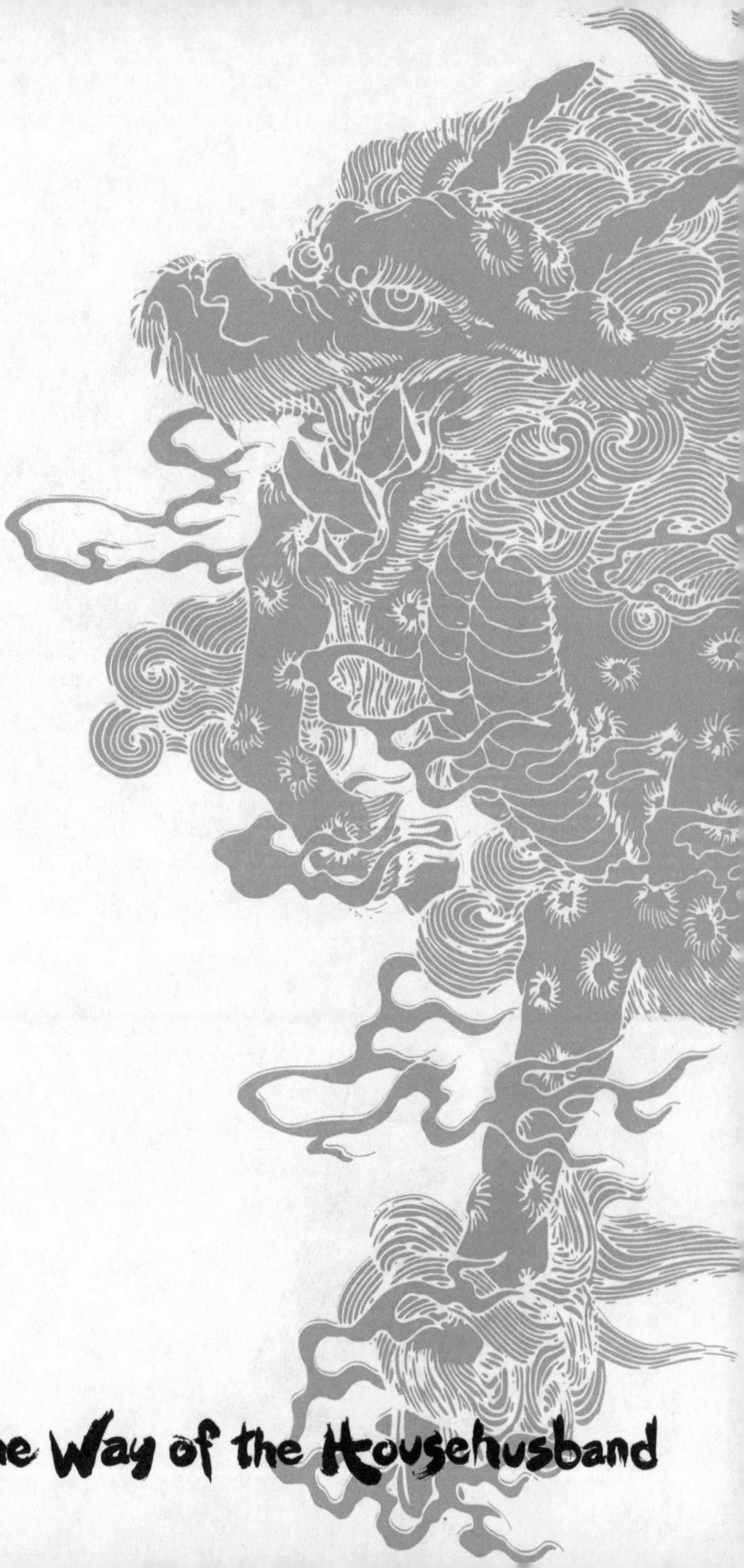

The Way of the Househusband

# CHAPTER 3

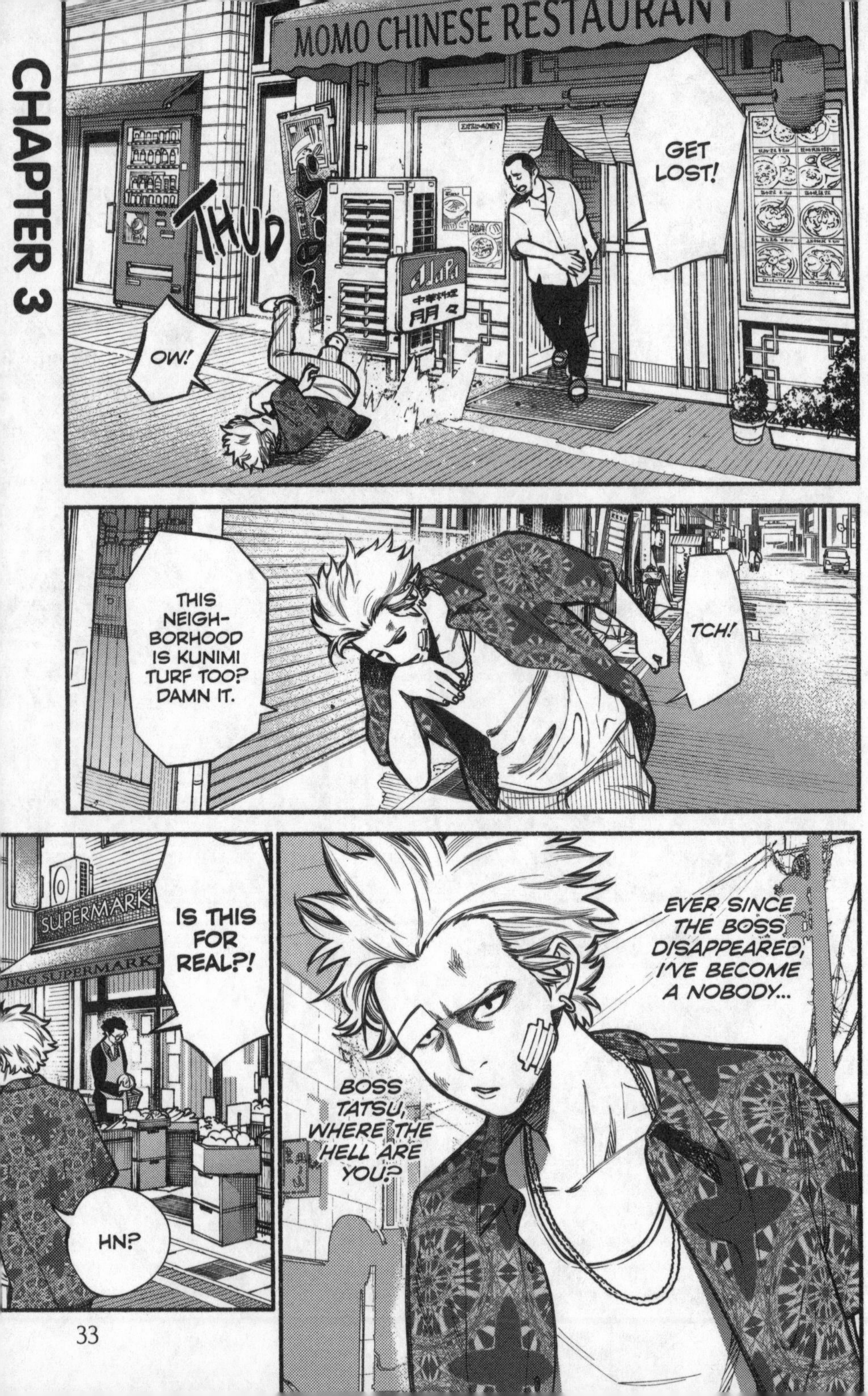

MOMO CHINESE RESTAURANT
GET LOST!
THUD
OW!
TCH!
THIS NEIGHBORHOOD IS KUNIMI TURF TOO? DAMN IT.
EVER SINCE THE BOSS DISAPPEARED, I'VE BECOME A NOBODY...
BOSS TATSU, WHERE THE HELL ARE YOU?
SUPERMARKET
IS THIS FOR REAL?!
HN?

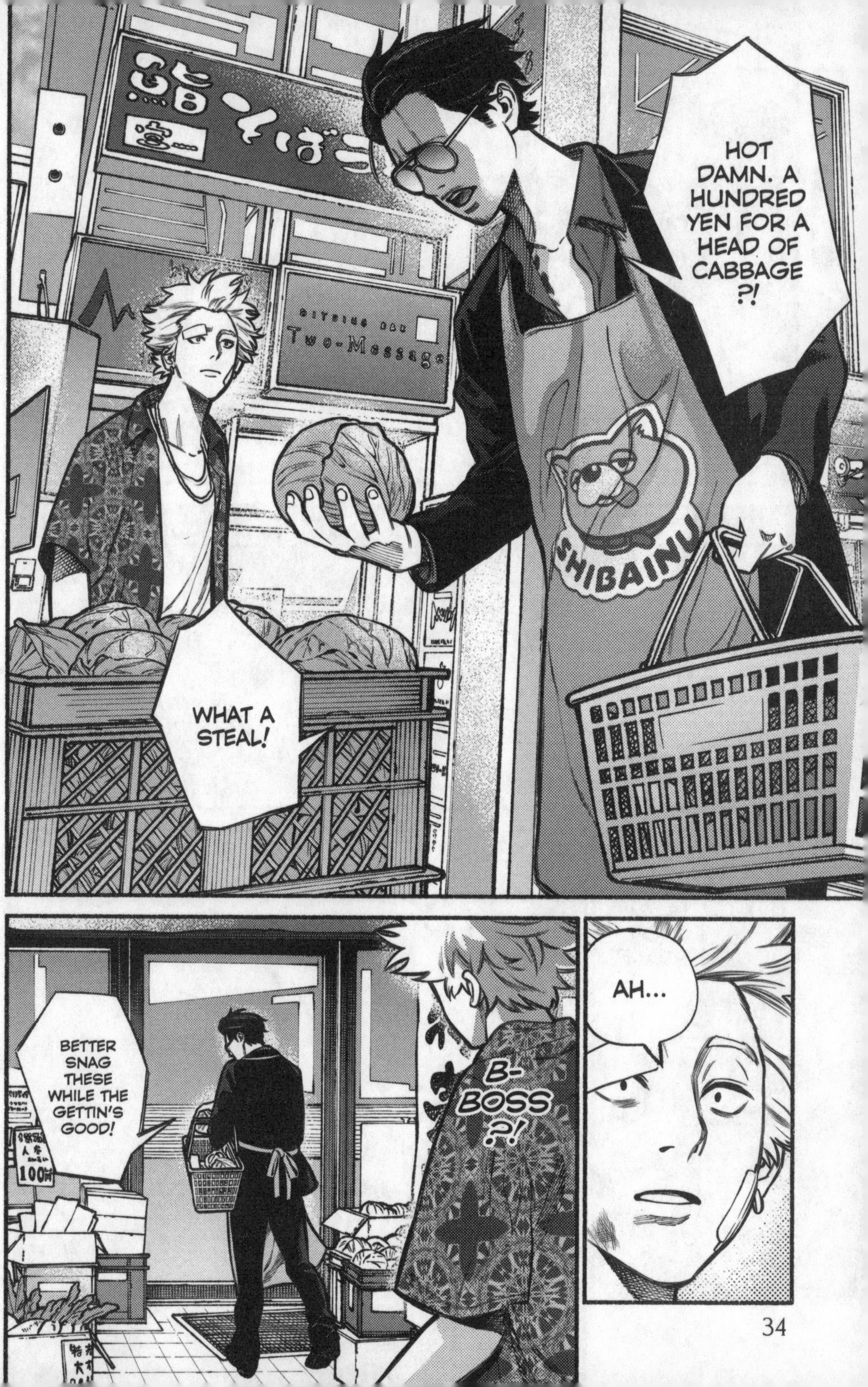
HOT DAMN. A HUNDRED YEN FOR A HEAD OF CABBAGE ?!
Two-Message
SHIBAINU
WHAT A STEAL!
AH...
B-BOSS ?!
BETTER SNAG THESE WHILE THE GETTIN'S GOOD!
100円

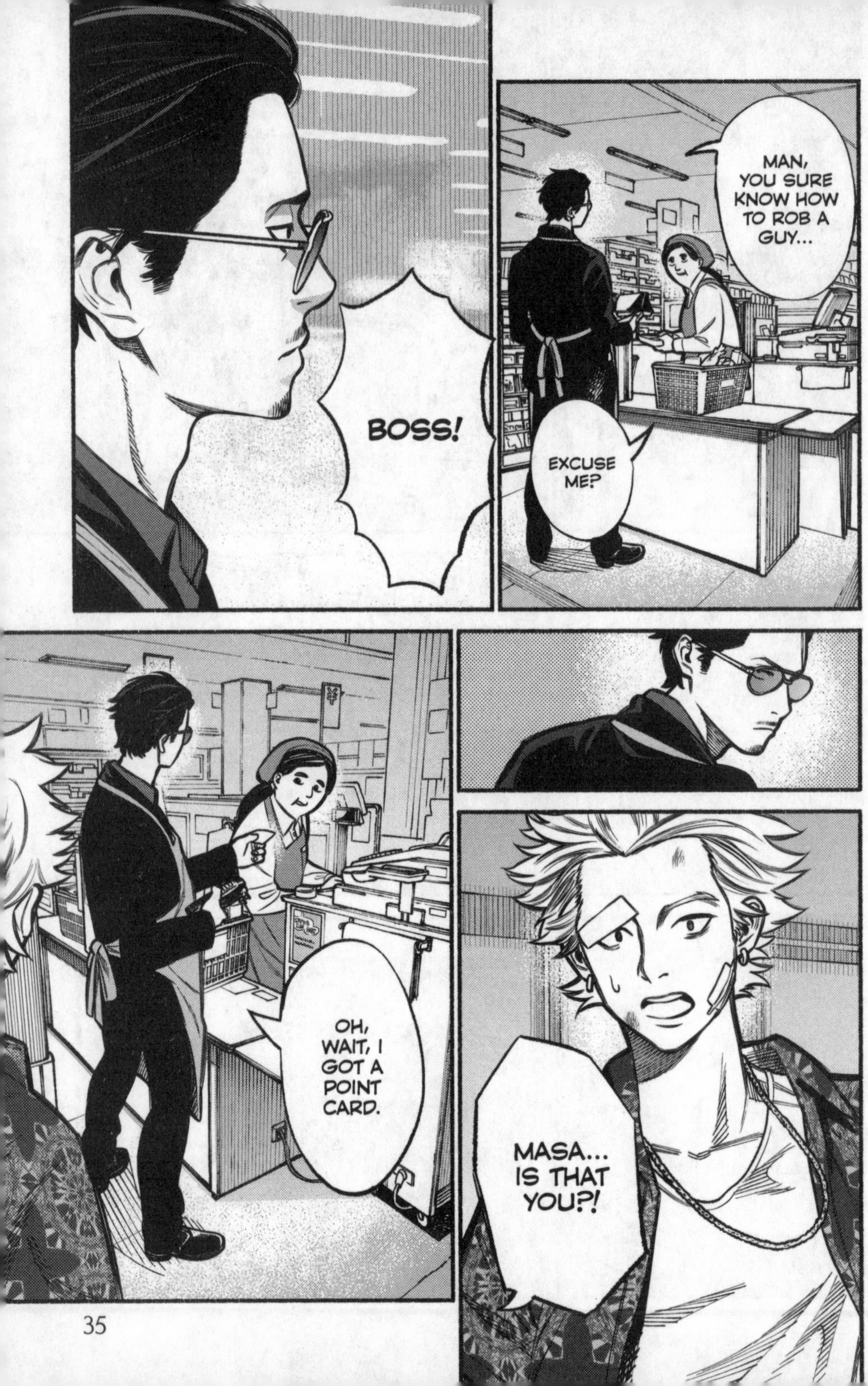
MAN, YOU SURE KNOW HOW TO ROB A GUY...
EXCUSE ME?
BOSS!
MASA... IS THAT YOU?!
OH, WAIT, I GOT A POINT CARD.

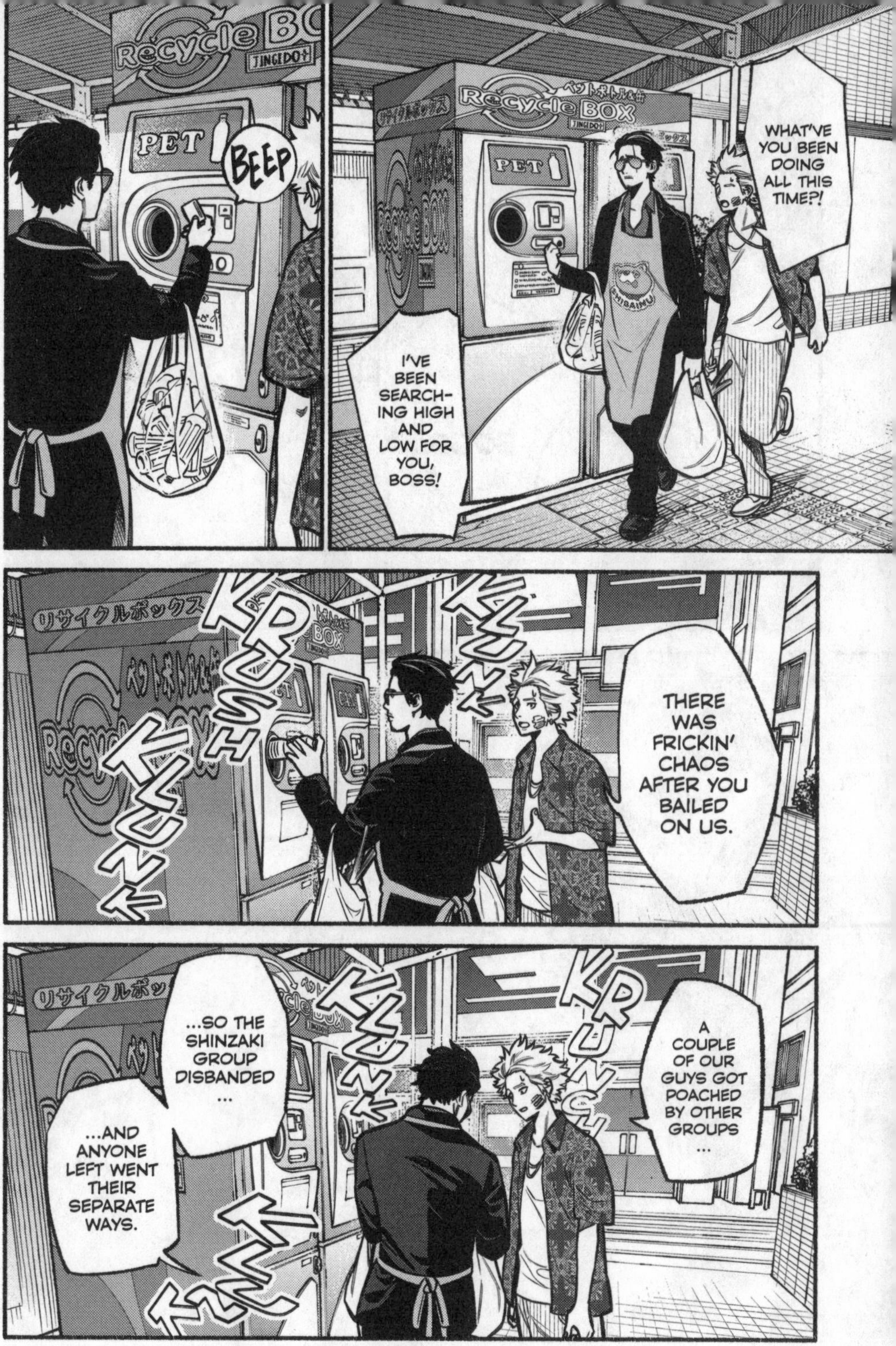
WHAT'VE YOU BEEN DOING ALL THIS TIME?!
I'VE BEEN SEARCHING-ING HIGH AND LOW FOR YOU, BOSS!
BEEP
KLUNK
THERE WAS FRICKIN' CHAOS AFTER YOU BAILED ON US.
KRUSH
KLUNK
KRUNCH
A COUPLE OF OUR GUYS GOT POACHED BY OTHER GROUPS ...
KLUNK
...SO THE SHINZAKI GROUP DISBANDED ...
...AND ANYONE LEFT WENT THEIR SEPARATE WAYS.
KLUNK

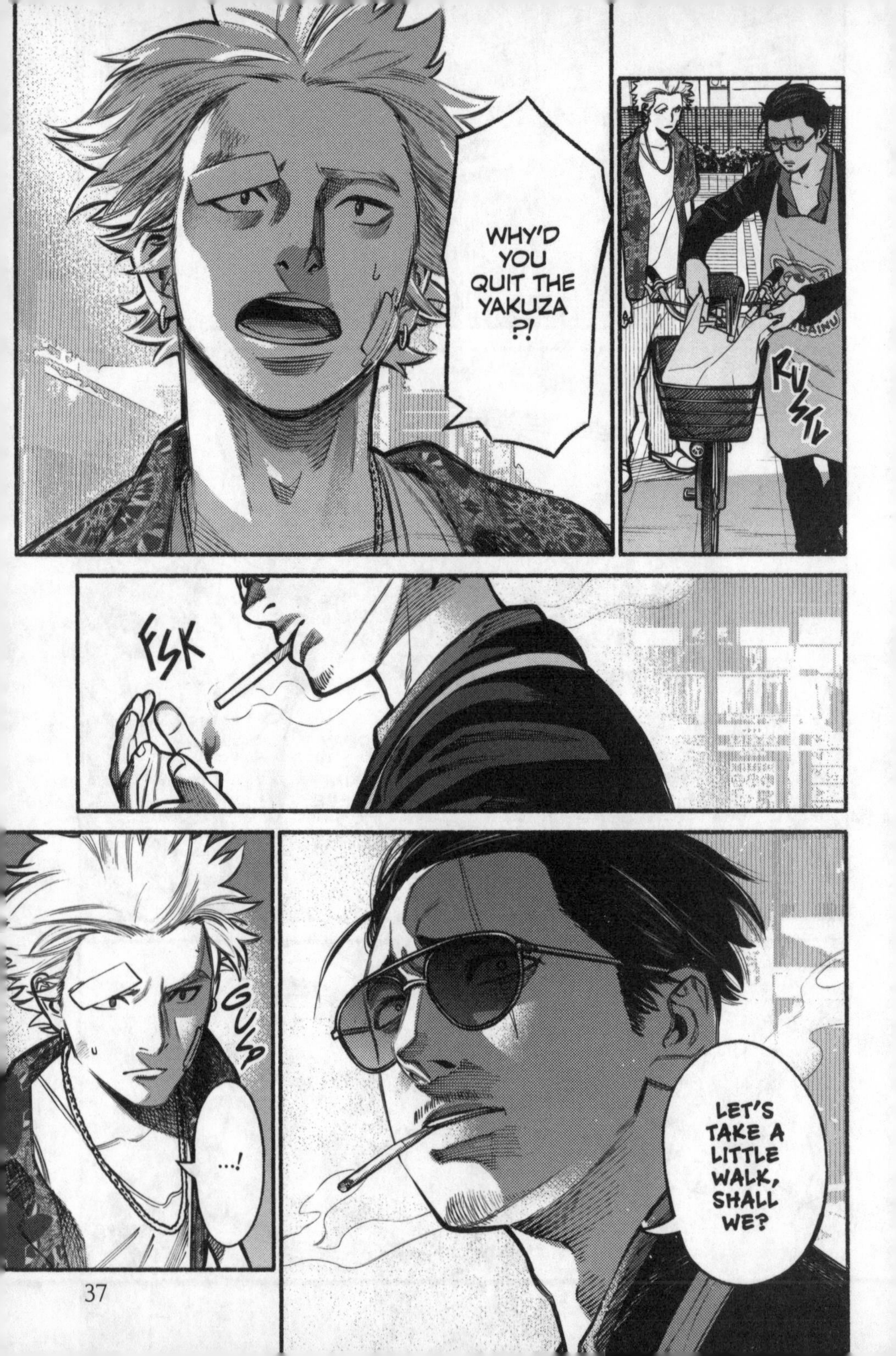
RUSTL
WHY'D YOU QUIT THE YAKUZA?!
FSK
LET'S TAKE A LITTLE WALK, SHALL WE?
GULP
...!

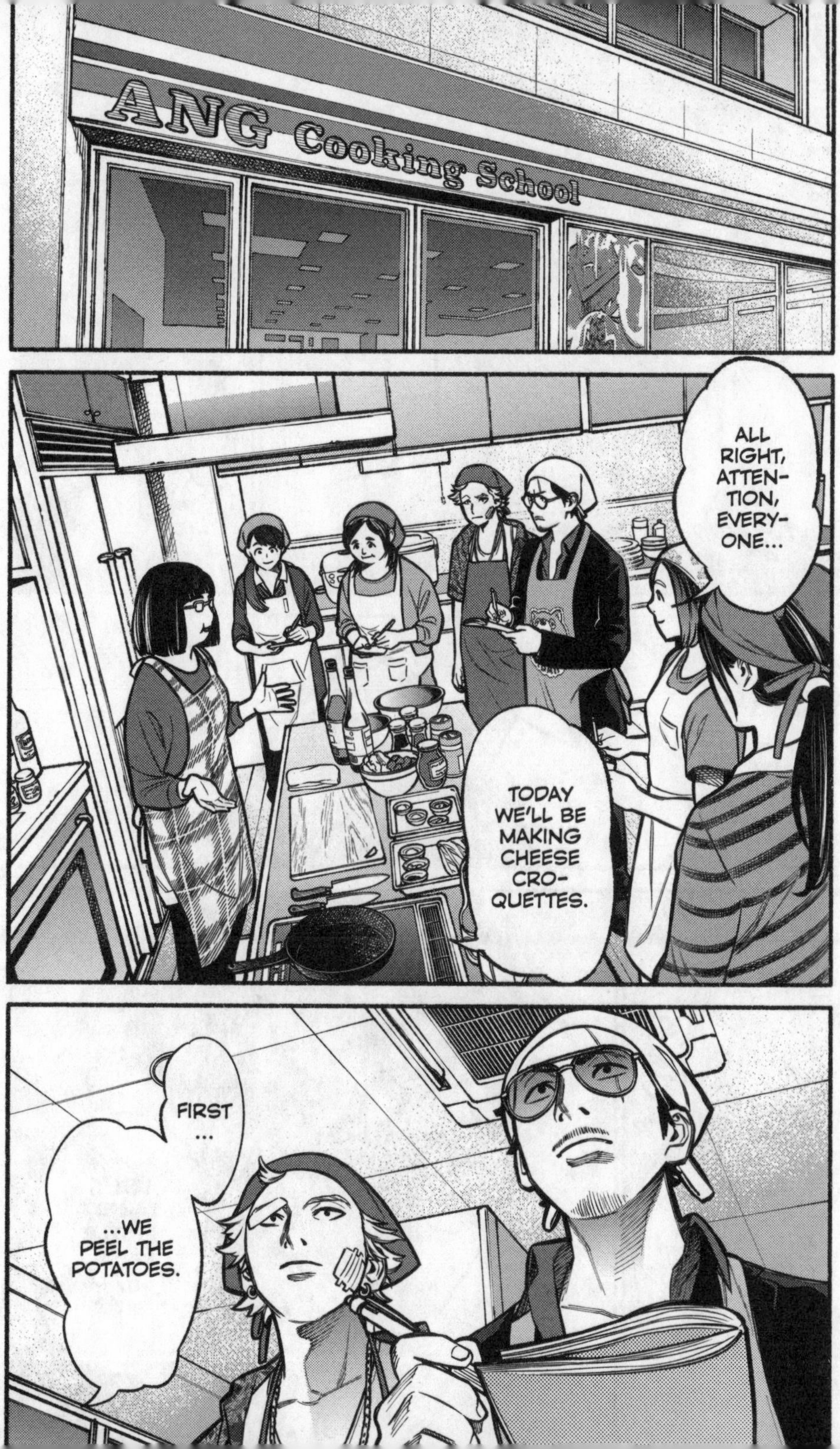
ANG Cooking School
ALL RIGHT, ATTENTION, EVERYONE...
TODAY WE'LL BE MAKING CHEESE CROQUETTES.
FIRST...
...WE PEEL THE POTATOES.

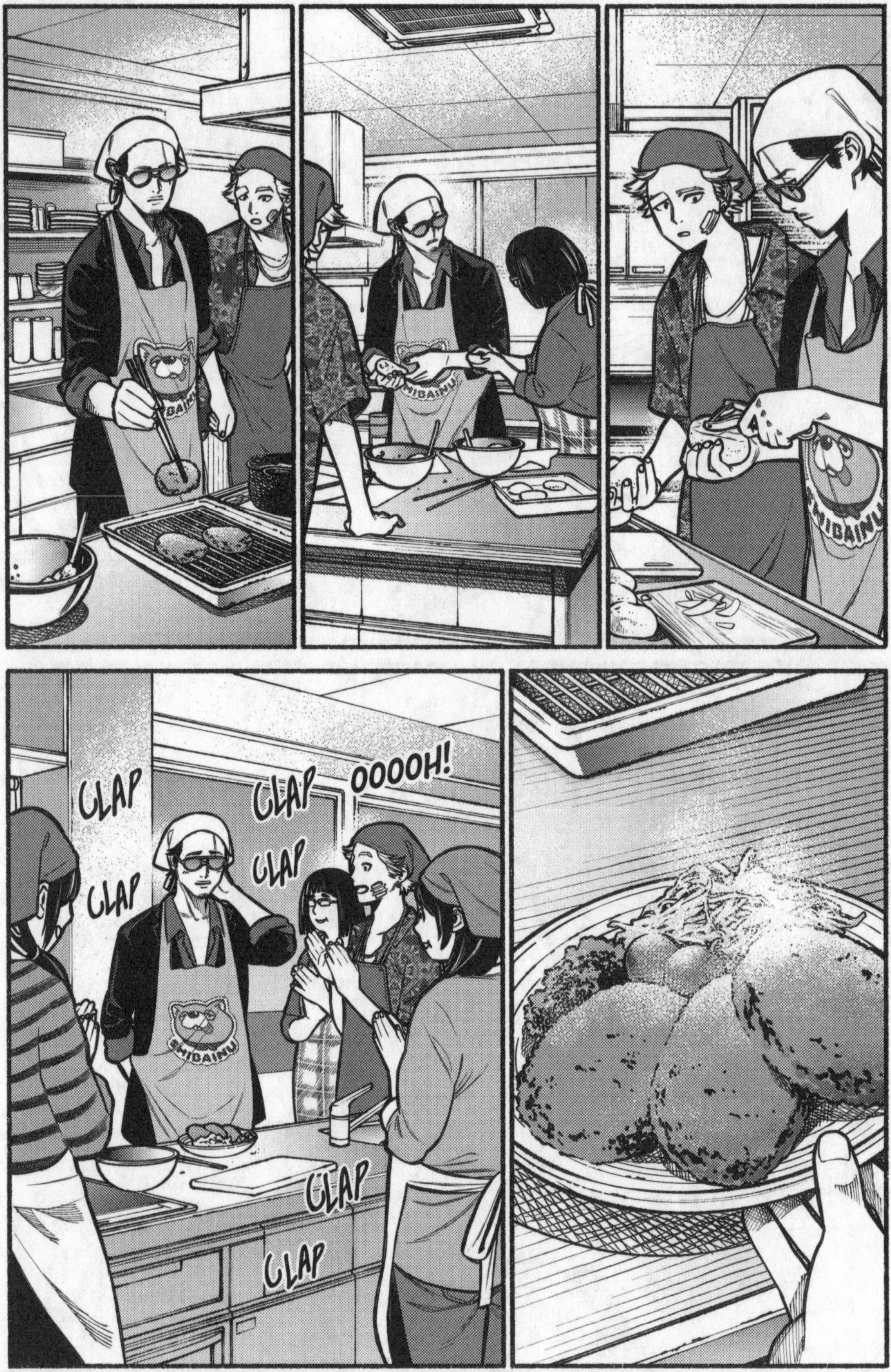
OOOOH!
CLAP
CLAP
CLAP
CLAP
CLAP
CLAP

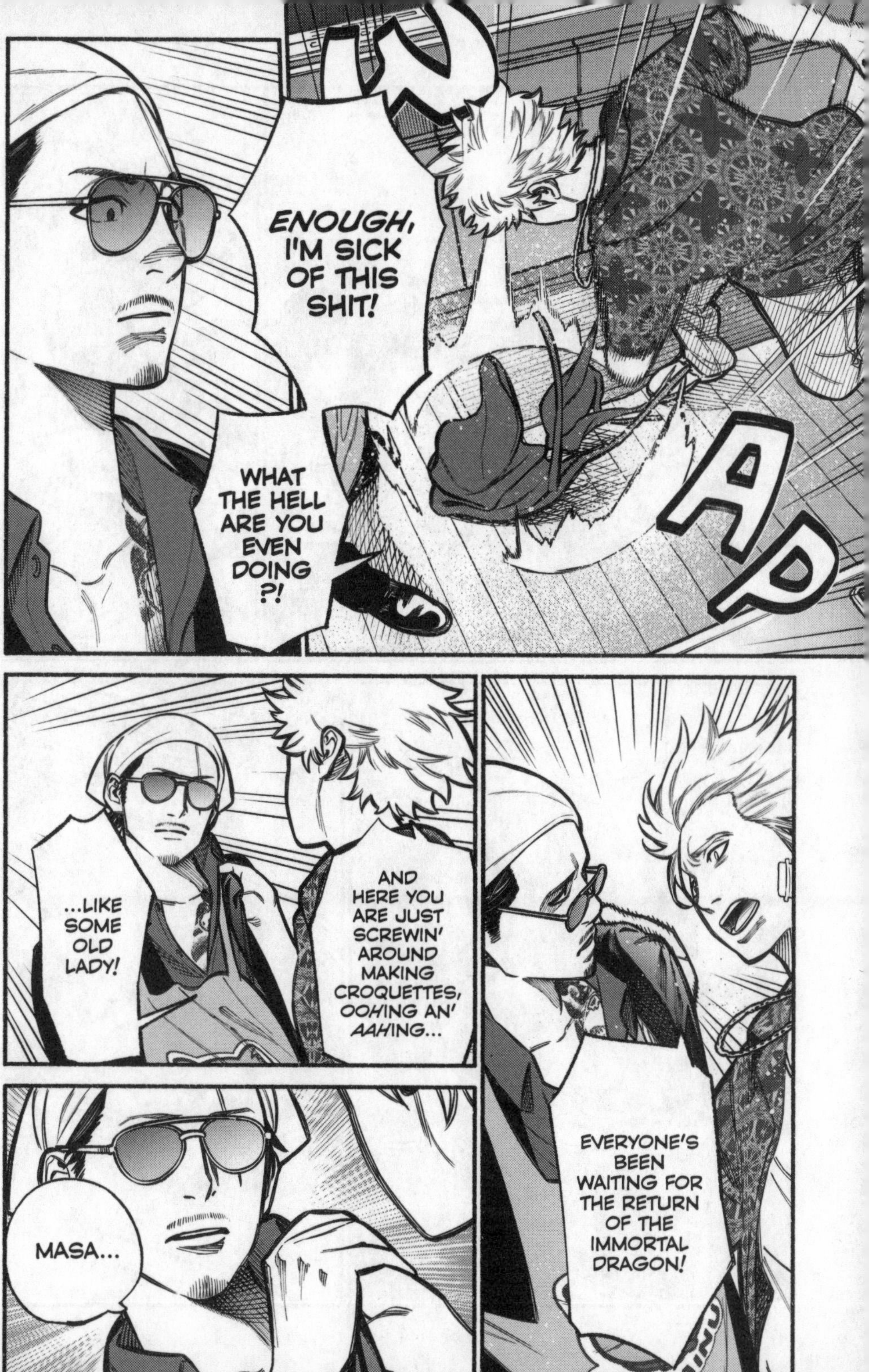
ENOUGH, I'M SICK OF THIS SHIT!
WHAT THE HELL ARE YOU EVEN DOING?!
AP
EVERYONE'S BEEN WAITING FOR THE RETURN OF THE IMMORTAL DRAGON!
AND HERE YOU ARE JUST SCREWIN' AROUND MAKING CROQUETTES, *OOH*ING AN' *AAH*ING...
...LIKE SOME OLD LADY!
MASA...

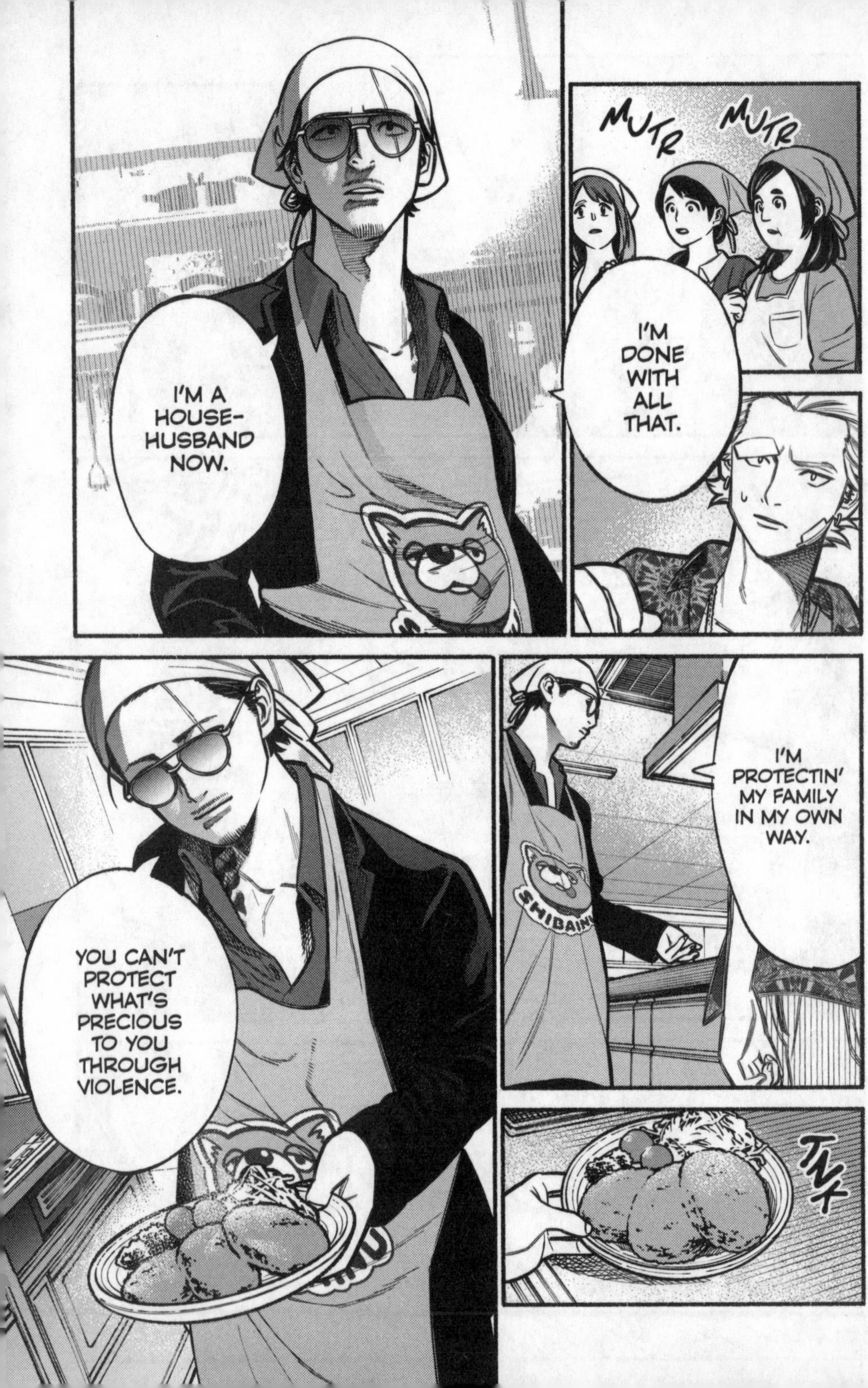
MUTR MUTR
I'M DONE WITH ALL THAT.
I'M A HOUSE-HUSBAND NOW.
I'M PROTECTIN' MY FAMILY IN MY OWN WAY.
SHIBAINU
TNK
YOU CAN'T PROTECT WHAT'S PRECIOUS TO YOU THROUGH VIOLENCE.

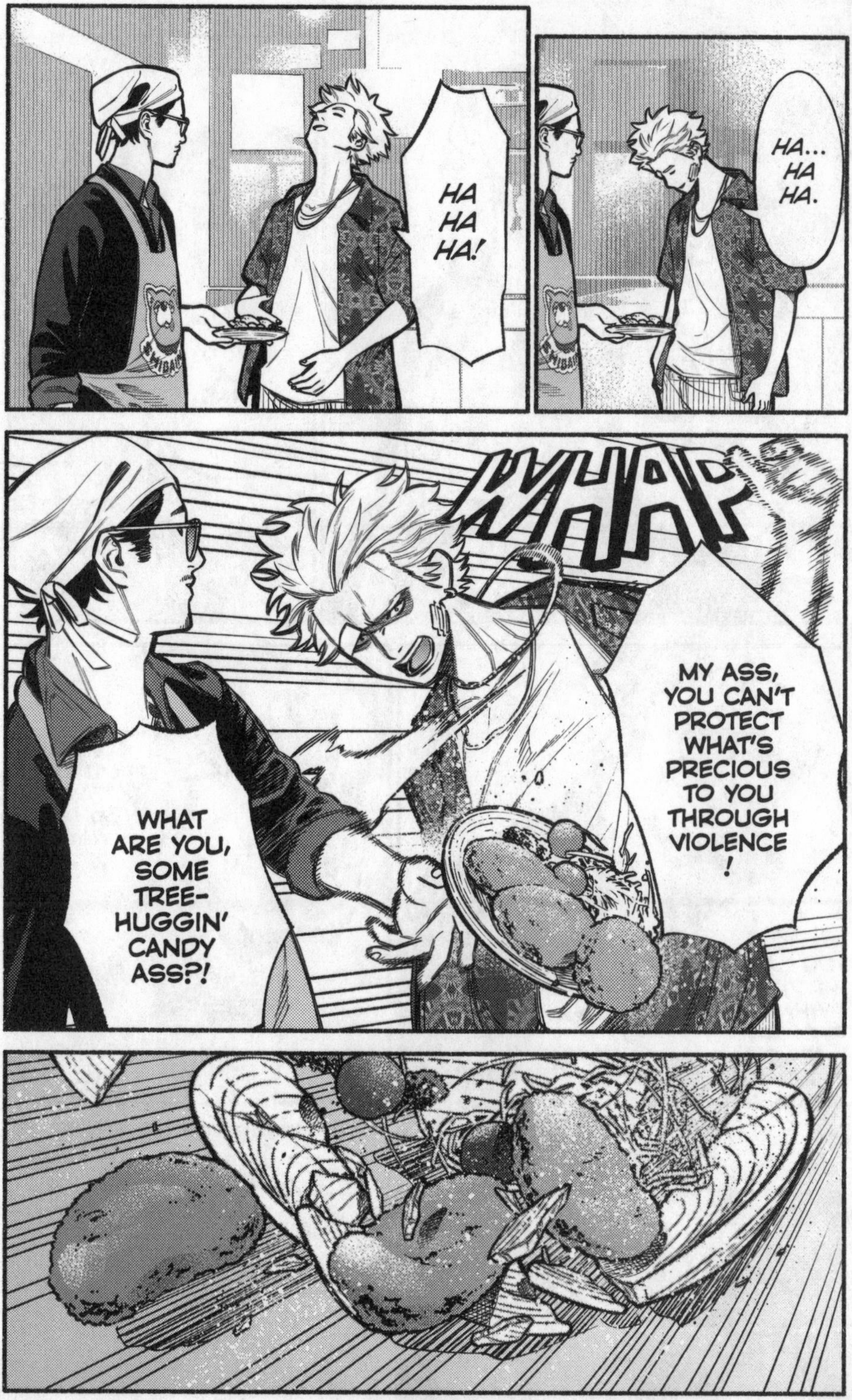
HA... HA HA.
HA HA HA!
WHAP
MY ASS, YOU CAN'T PROTECT WHAT'S PRECIOUS TO YOU THROUGH VIOLENCE!
WHAT ARE YOU, SOME TREE-HUGGIN' CANDY ASS?!

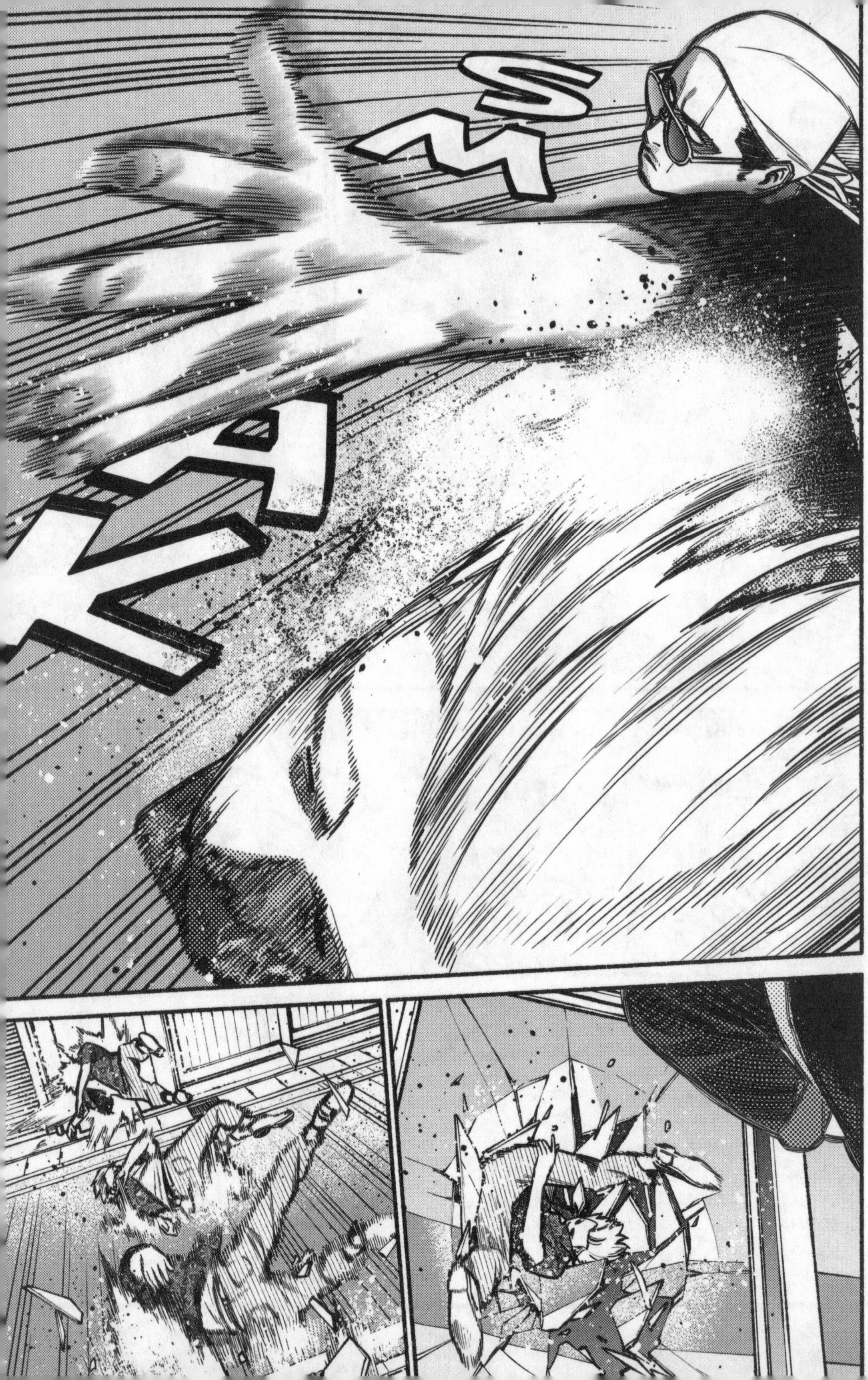
SMAS

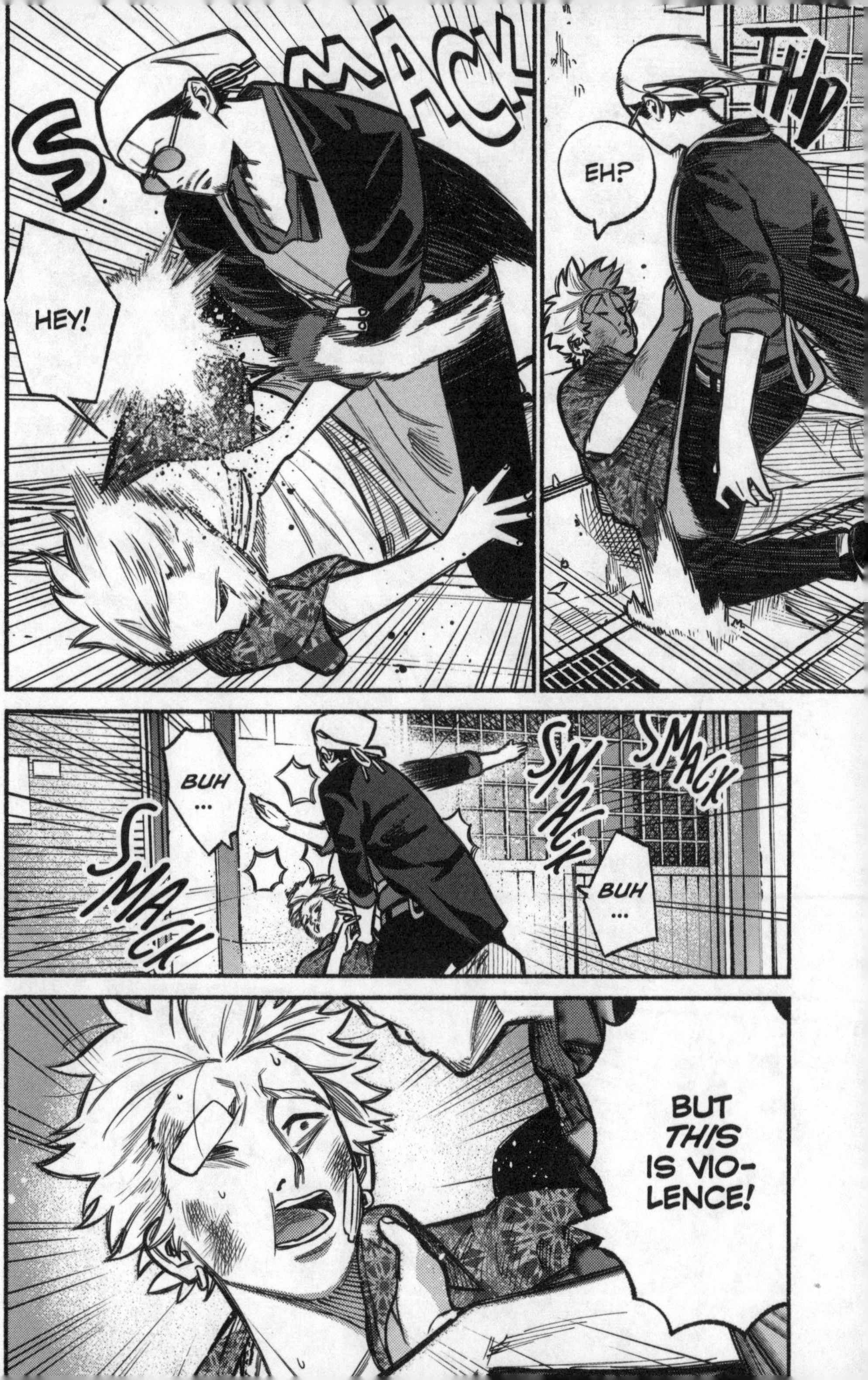
THD
EH?
SMACK
HEY!
SMACK
SMACK
BUH ...
BUH ...
SMACK
BUT THIS IS VIO-LENCE!

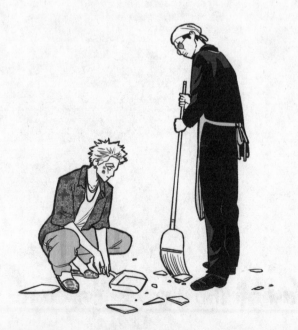

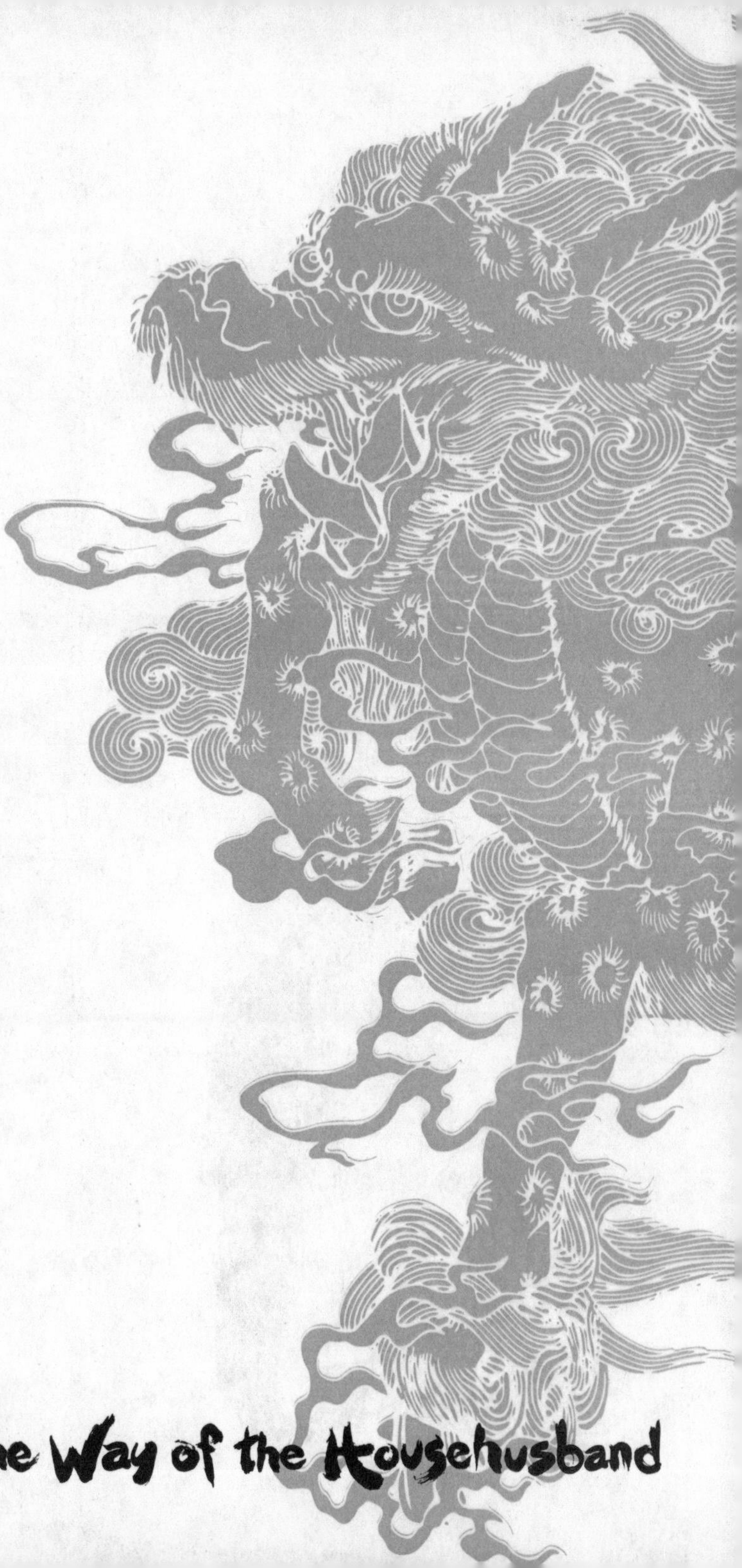

The Way of the Househusband

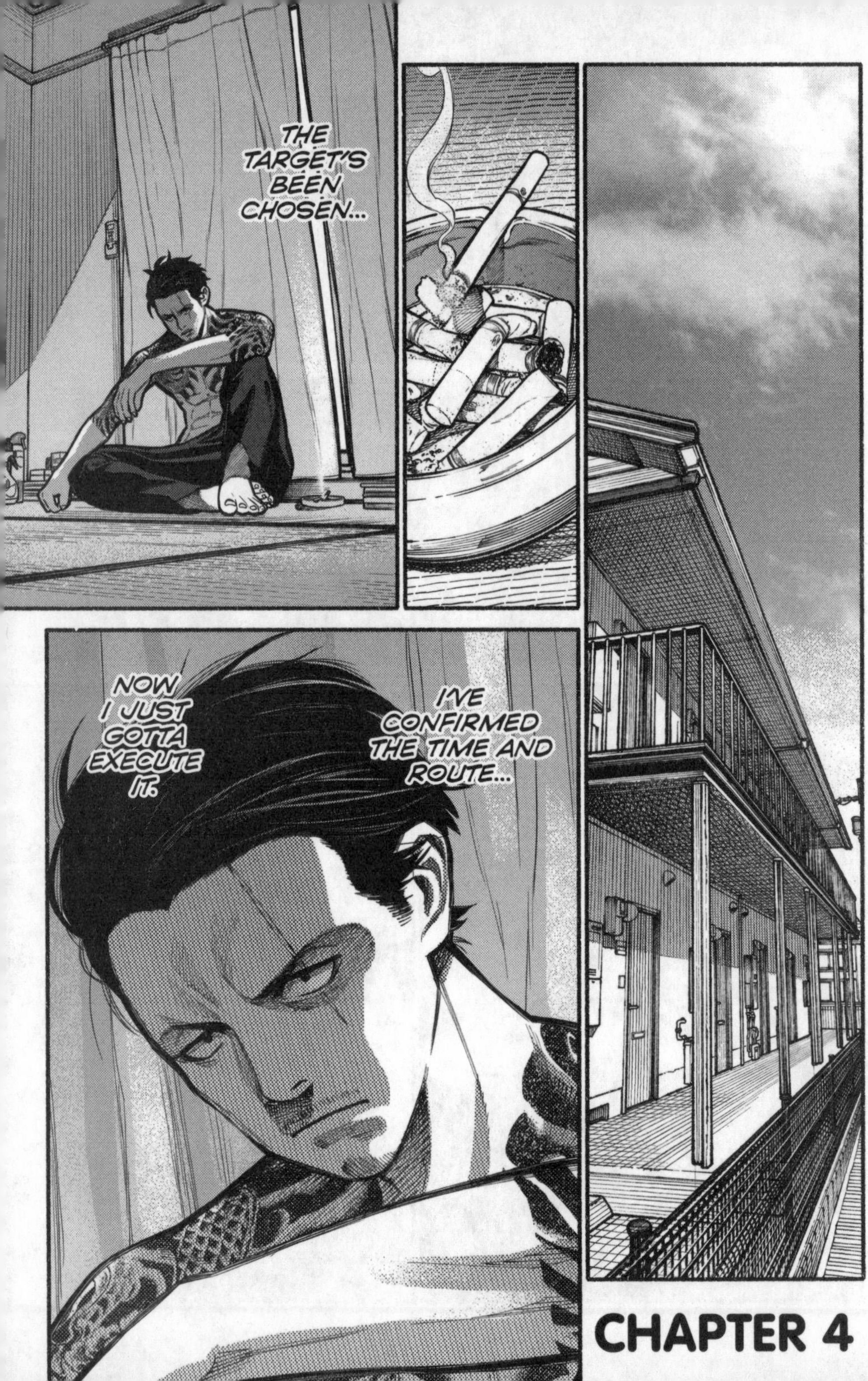
THE TARGET'S BEEN CHOSEN...
I'VE CONFIRMED THE TIME AND ROUTE...
NOW I JUST GOTTA EXECUTE IT.

# CHAPTER 4

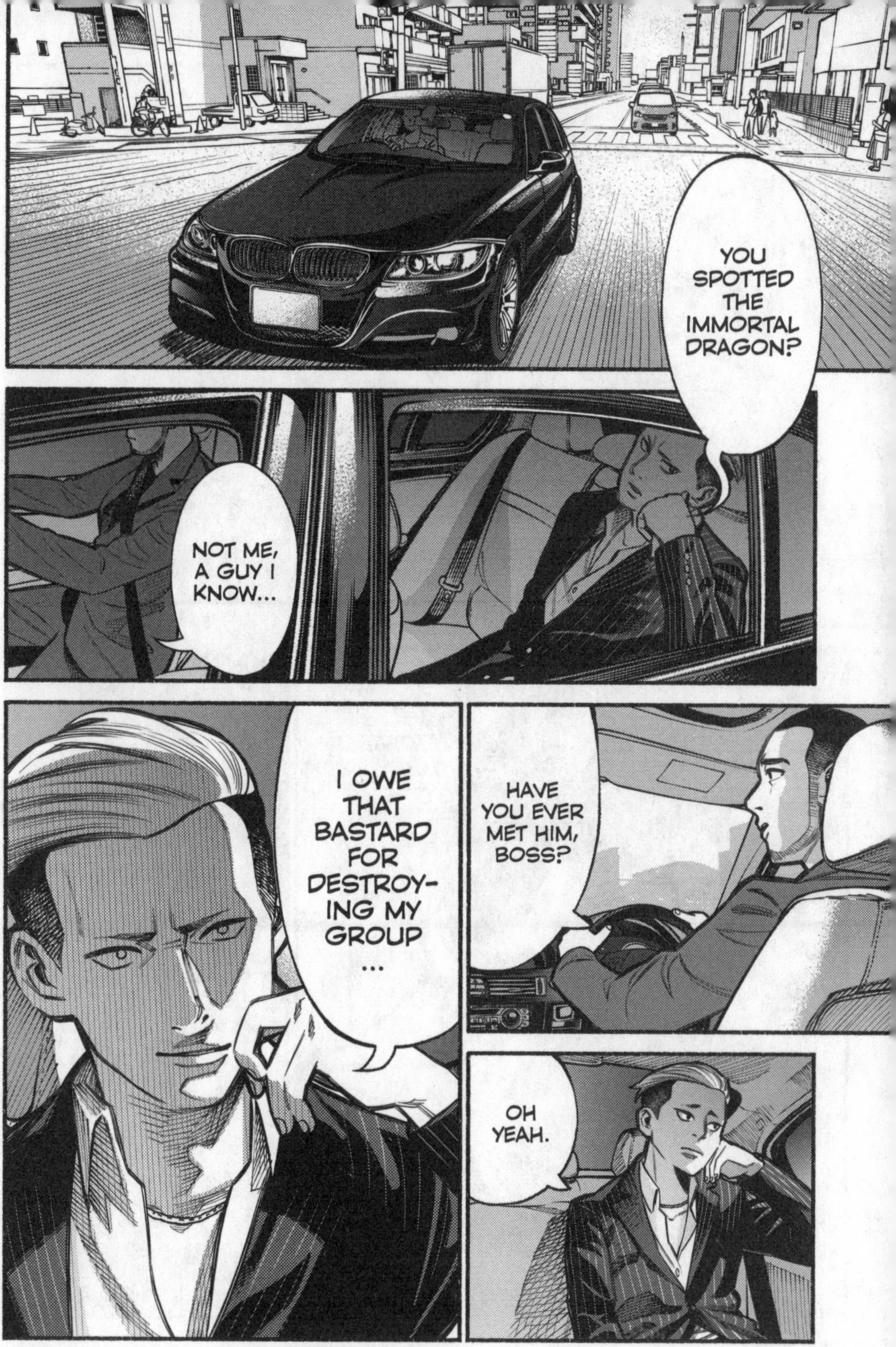
YOU SPOTTED THE IMMORTAL DRAGON?
NOT ME, A GUY I KNOW...
HAVE YOU EVER MET HIM, BOSS?
OH YEAH.
I OWE THAT BASTARD FOR DESTROYING MY GROUP...

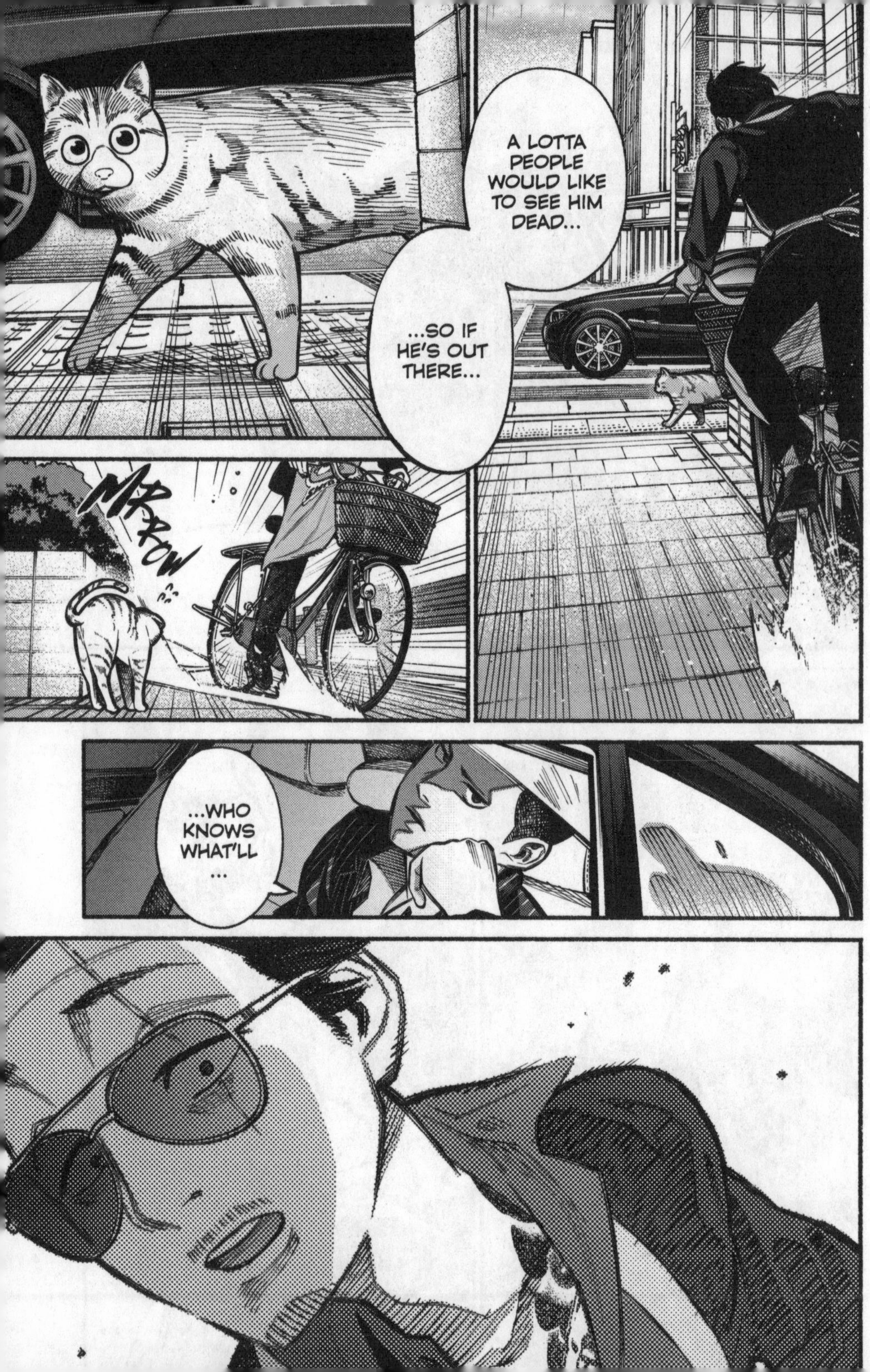
A LOTTA PEOPLE WOULD LIKE TO SEE HIM DEAD...
...SO IF HE'S OUT THERE...
MRROW
...WHO KNOWS WHAT'LL ...

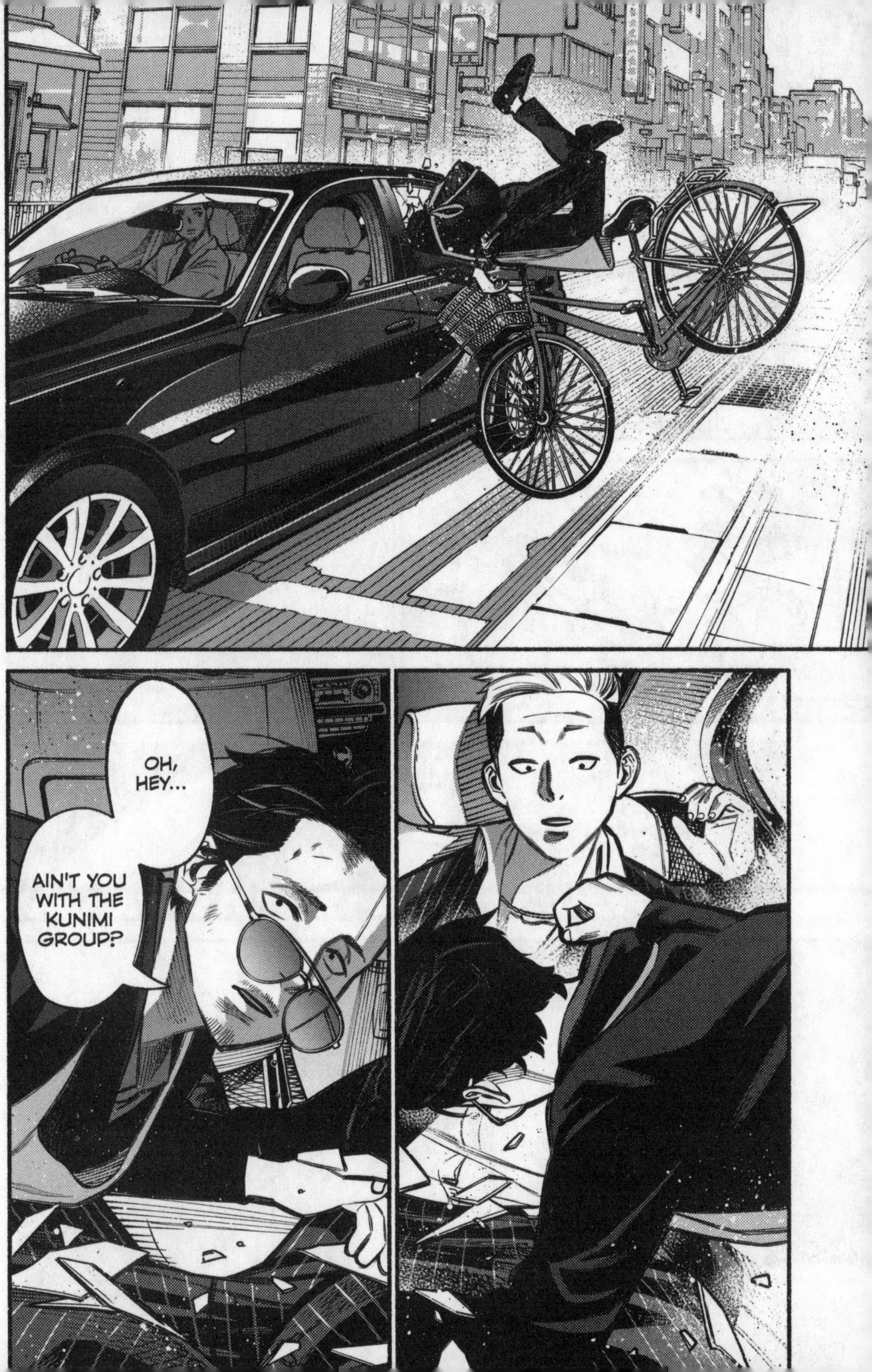
OH, HEY...
AIN'T YOU WITH THE KUNIMI GROUP?

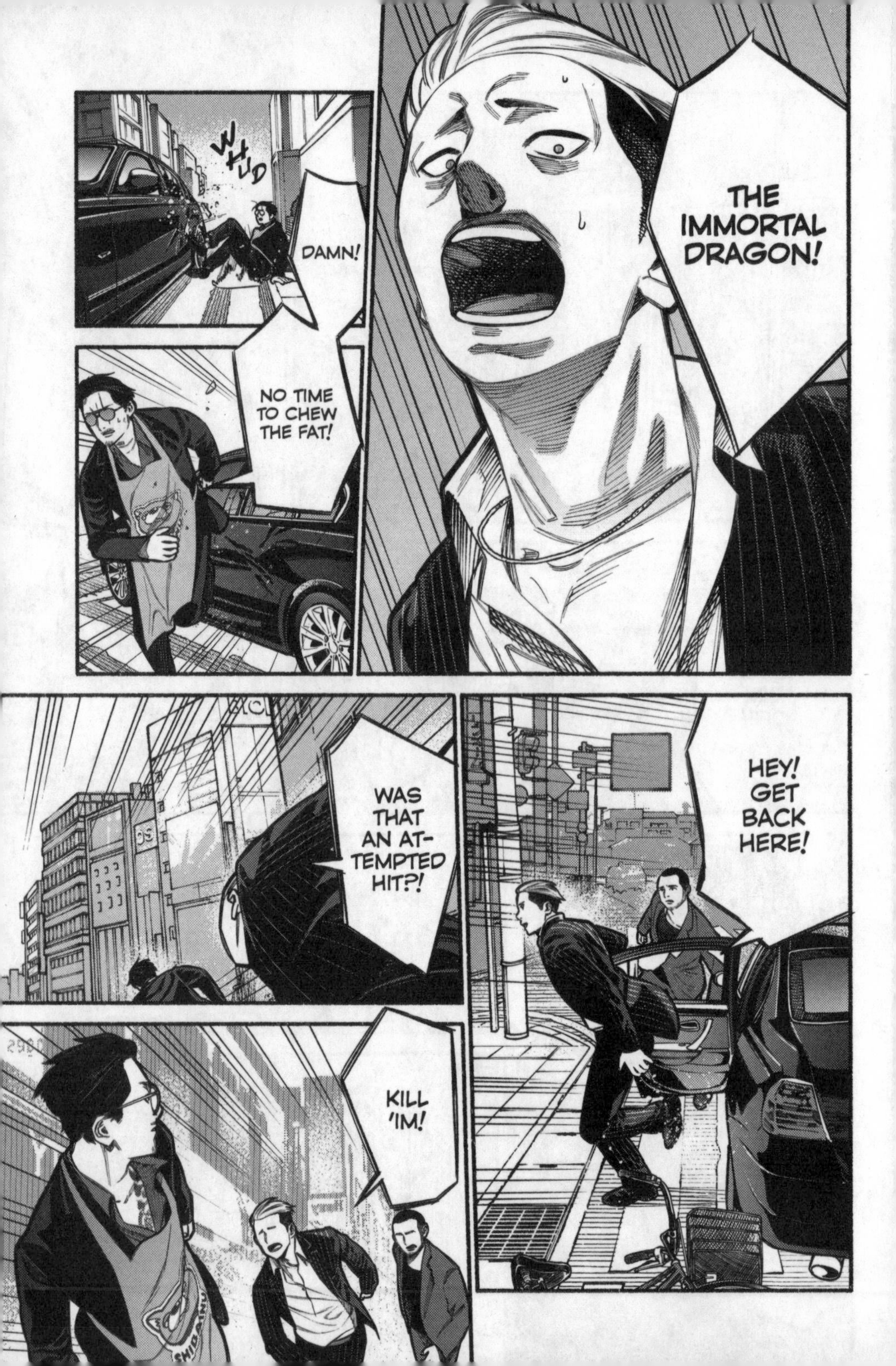
THE IMMORTAL DRAGON!
WHUD
DAMN!
NO TIME TO CHEW THE FAT!
HEY! GET BACK HERE!
WAS THAT AN ATTEMPTED HIT?!
KILL 'IM!

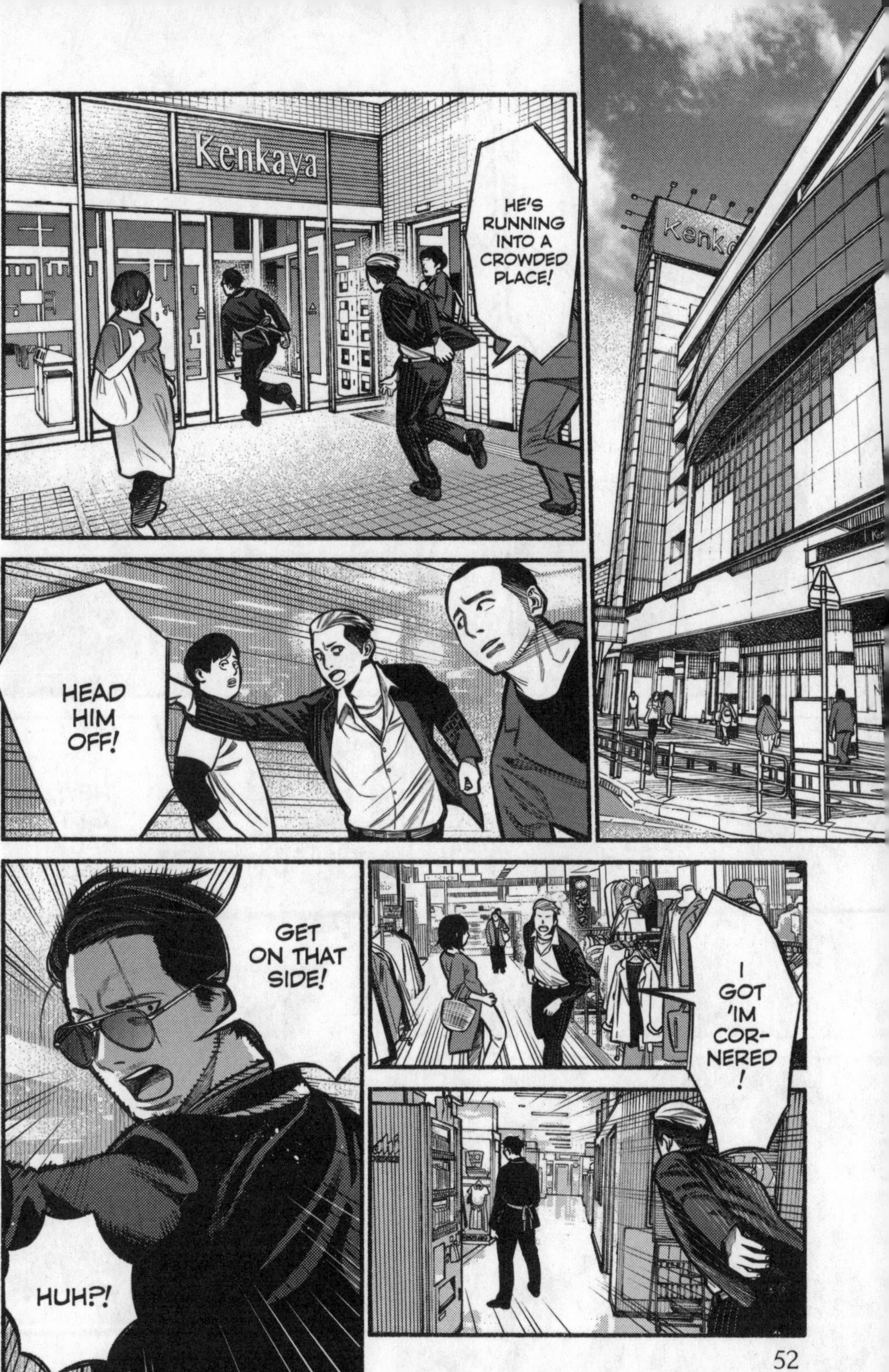
HE'S RUNNING INTO A CROWDED PLACE!
HEAD HIM OFF!
I GOT 'IM COR-NERED!
GET ON THAT SIDE!
HUH?!

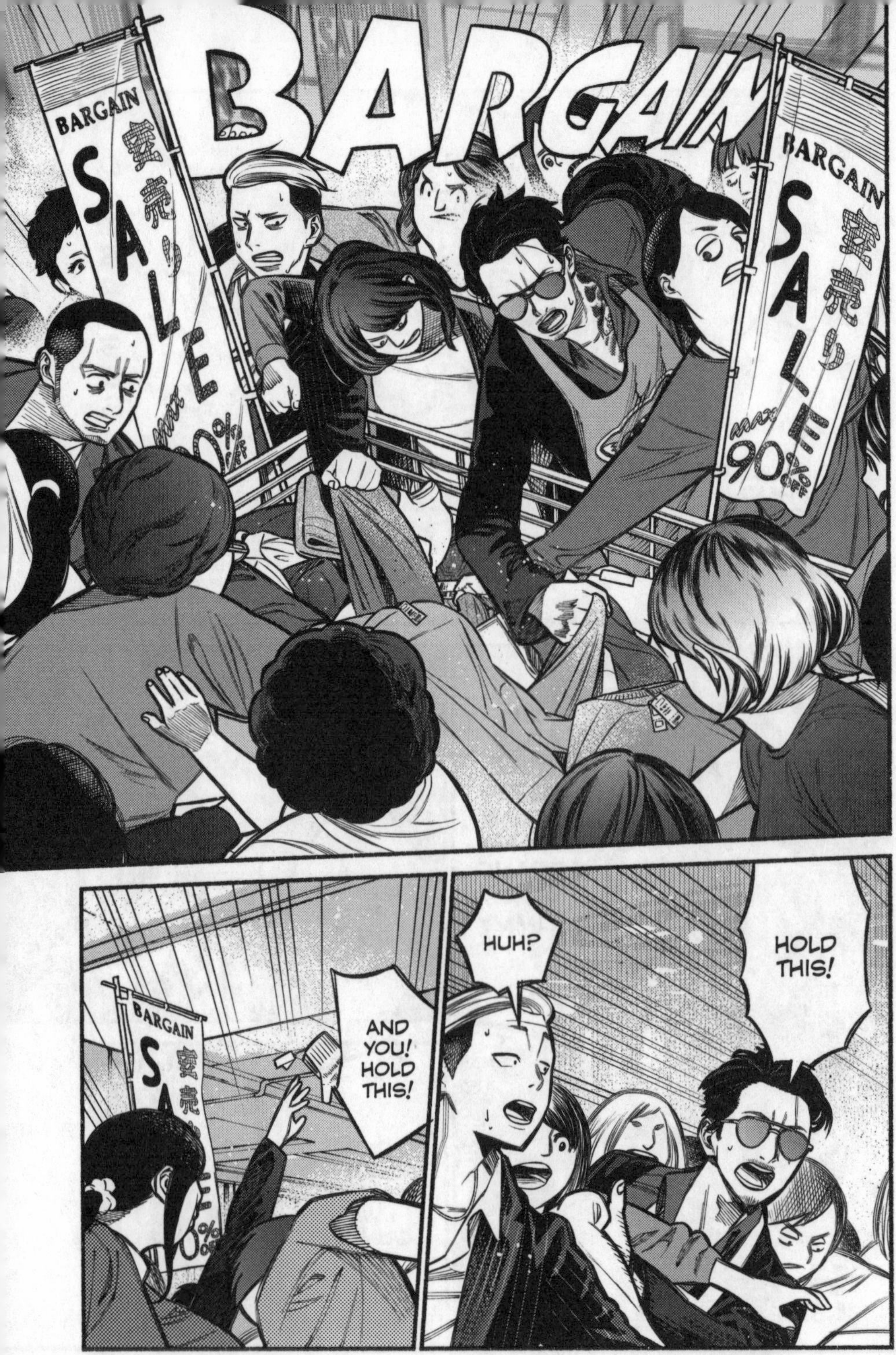
BARGAIN
BARGAIN
SALE
安売り
MAX 90% OFF
BARGAIN
SALE
安売り
BARGAIN
SALE
安売り
HOLD THIS!
HUH?
AND YOU! HOLD THIS!

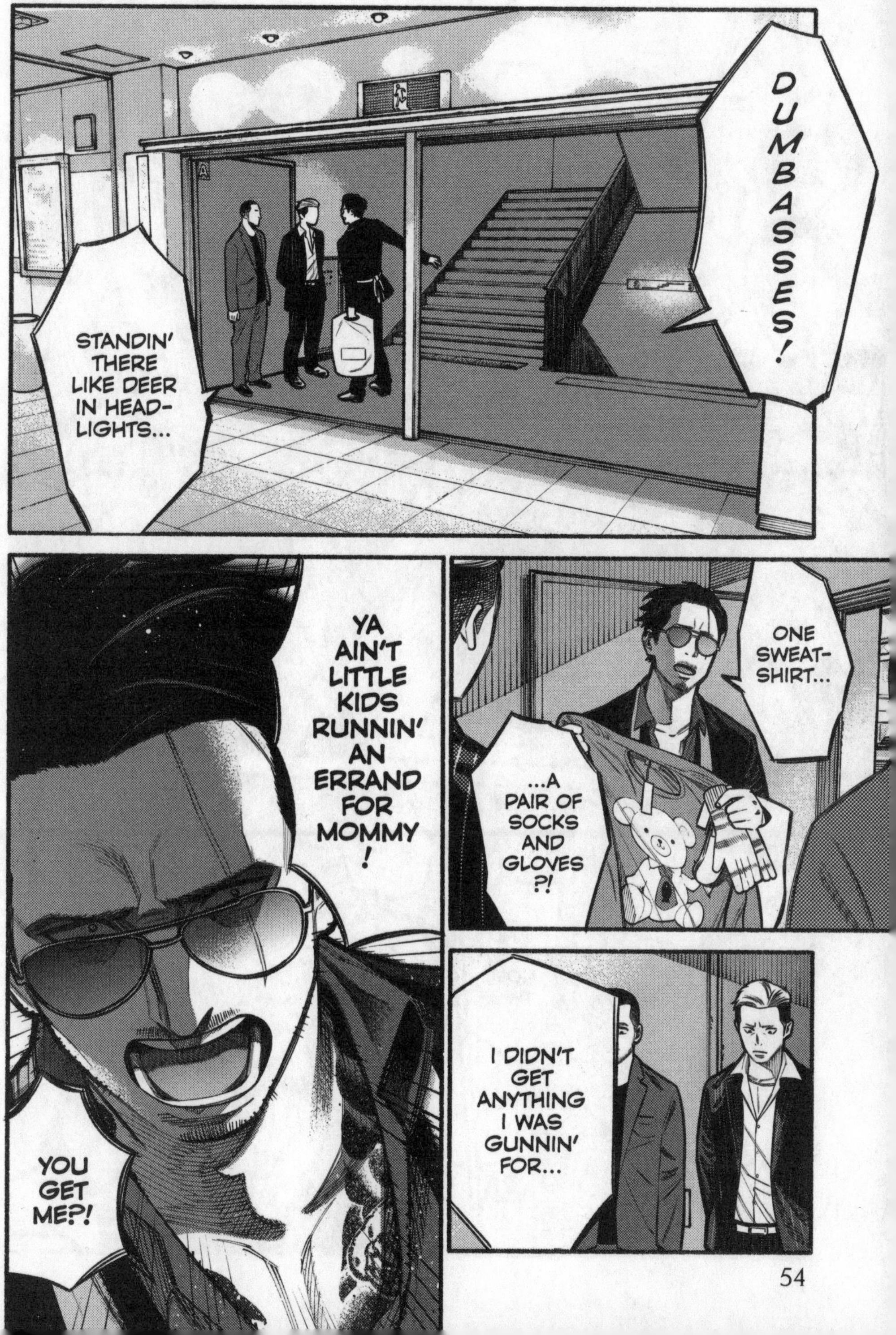
DUMBASSES!
STANDIN' THERE LIKE DEER IN HEAD-LIGHTS...
ONE SWEAT-SHIRT...
...A PAIR OF SOCKS AND GLOVES?!
I DIDN'T GET ANYTHING I WAS GUNNIN' FOR...
YA AIN'T LITTLE KIDS RUNNIN' AN ERRAND FOR MOMMY!
YOU GET ME?!

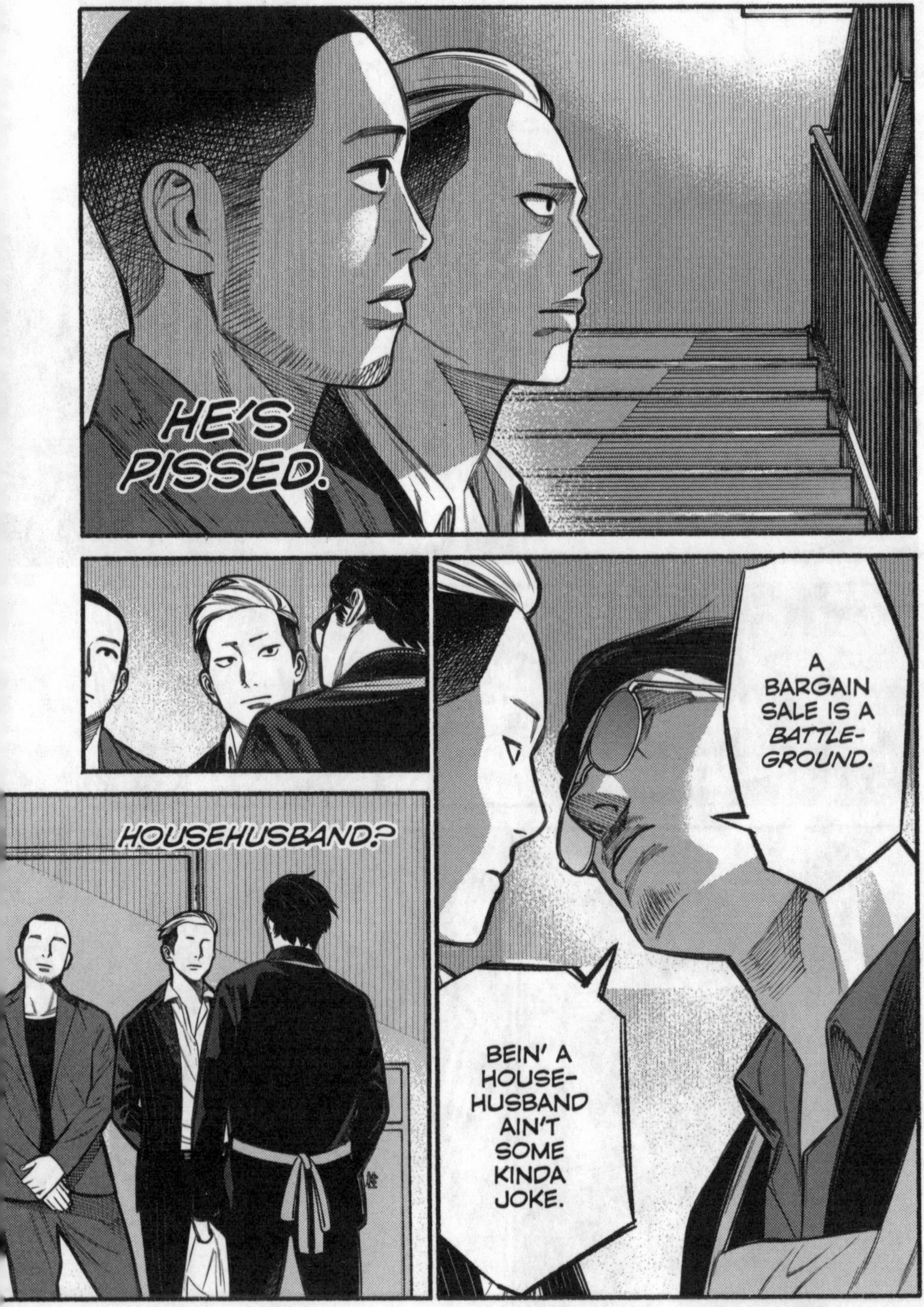
HE'S PISSED.
A BARGAIN SALE IS A *BATTLE-GROUND.*
BEIN' A HOUSE-HUSBAND AIN'T SOME KINDA JOKE.
HOUSEHUSBAND?

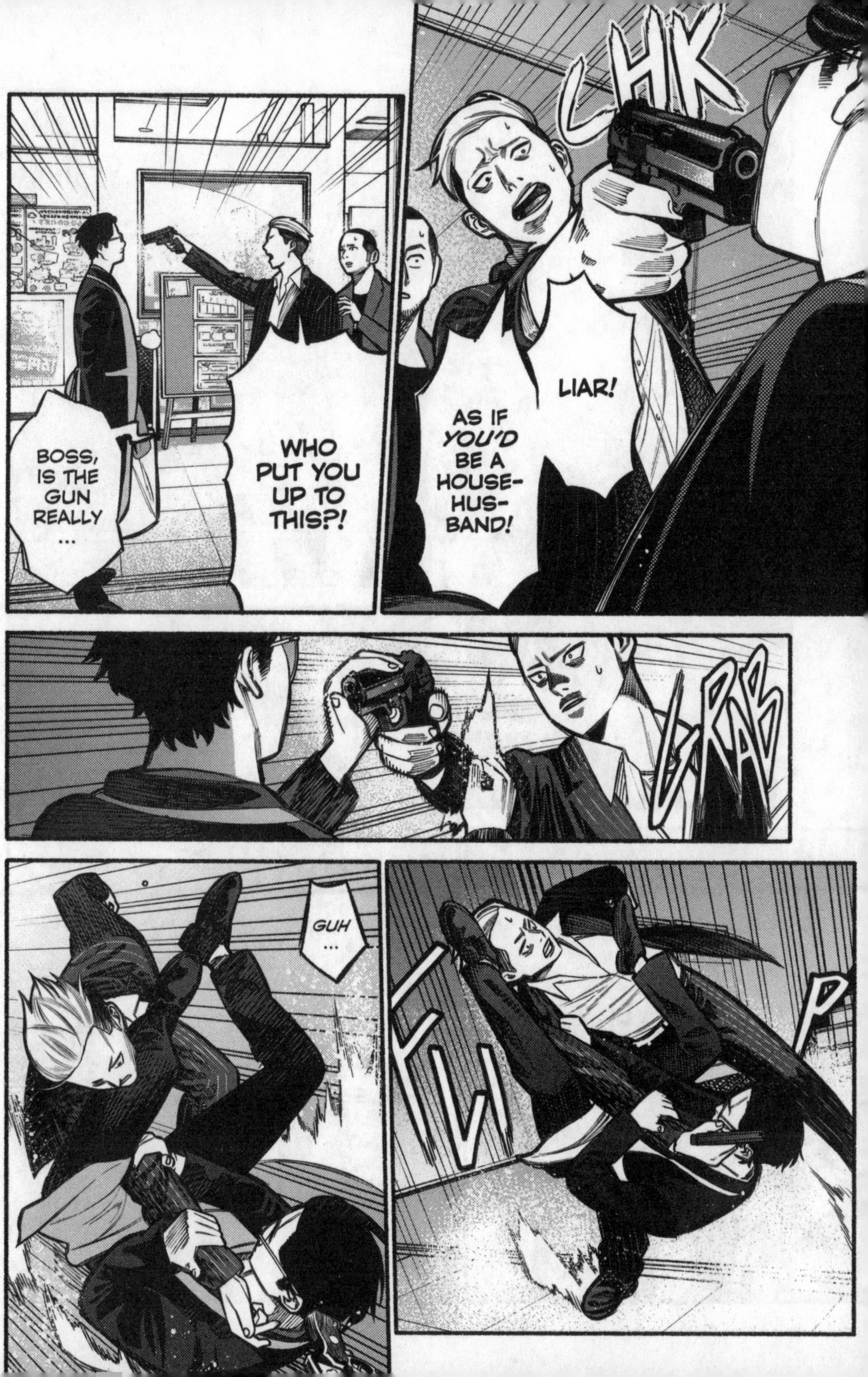
CHK
LIAR!
AS IF *YOU'D* BE A HOUSE-HUS-BAND!
WHO PUT YOU UP TO THIS?!
BOSS, IS THE GUN REALLY ...
GRAB
FW
P
GUH ...

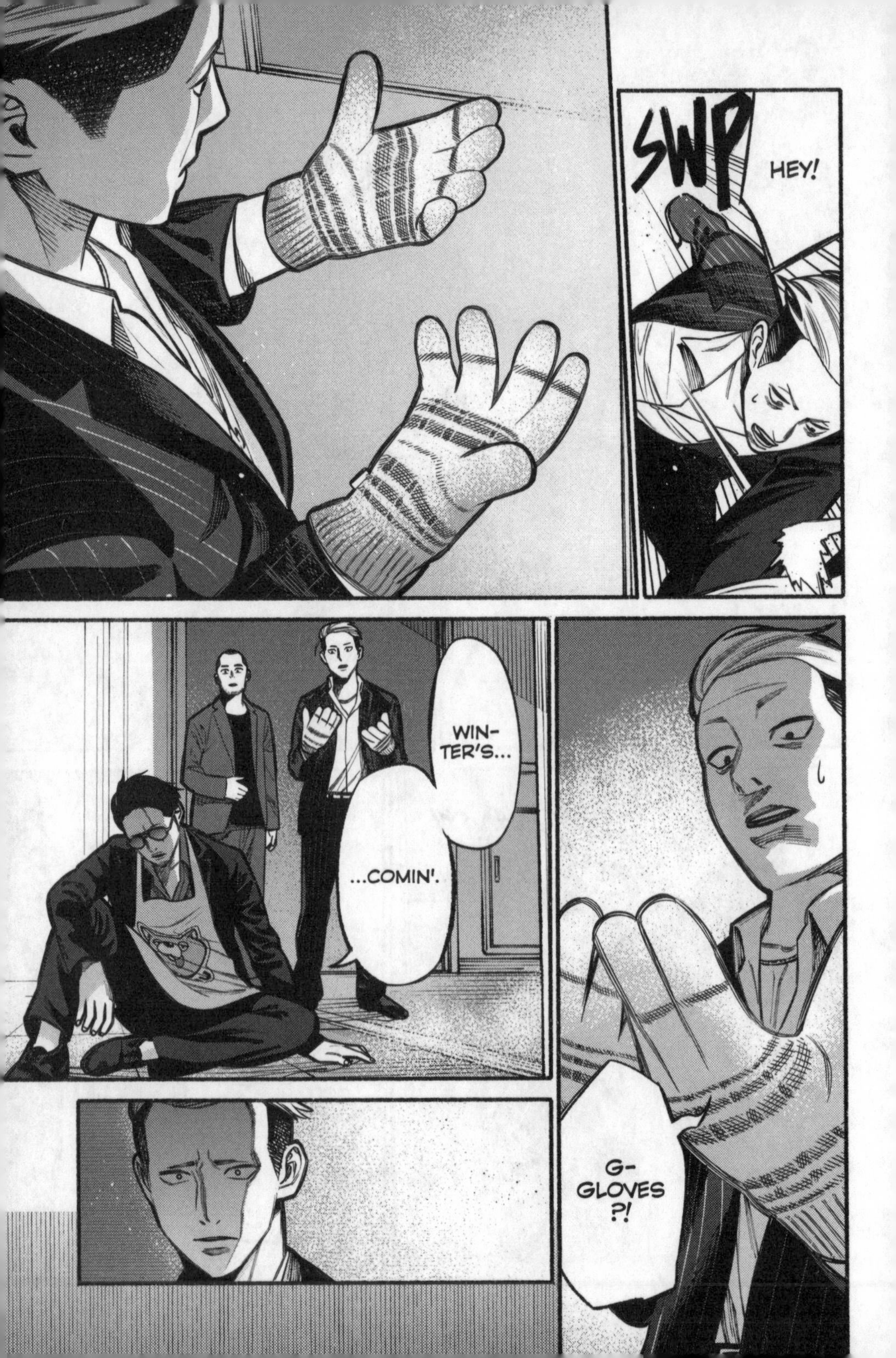
SWP
HEY!
G-GLOVES?!
WIN-TER'S...
...COMIN'.

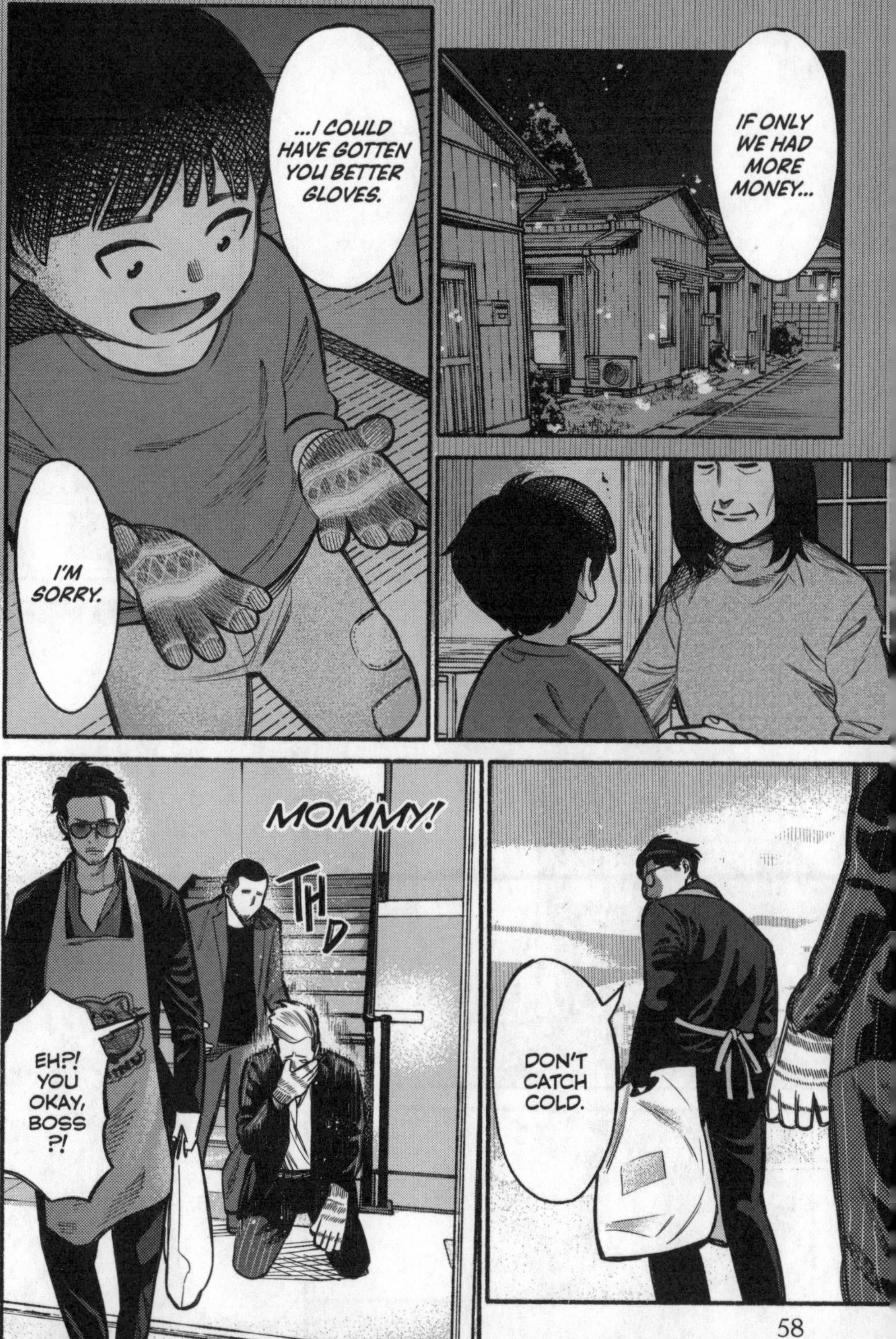
IF ONLY WE HAD MORE MONEY...
...I COULD HAVE GOTTEN YOU BETTER GLOVES.
I'M SORRY.
DON'T CATCH COLD.
MOMMY!
THD
EH?! YOU OKAY, BOSS?!

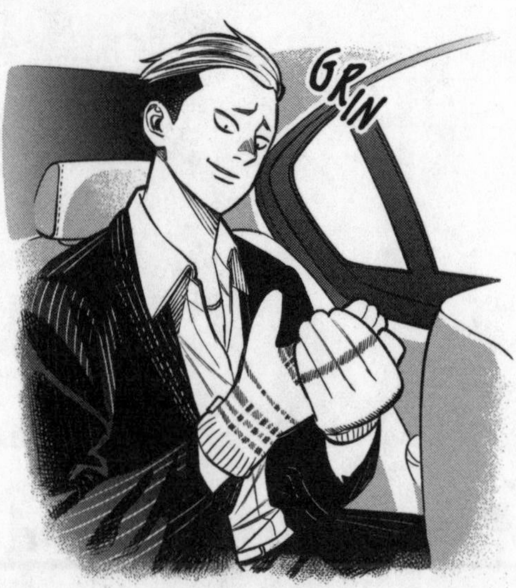
GRIN

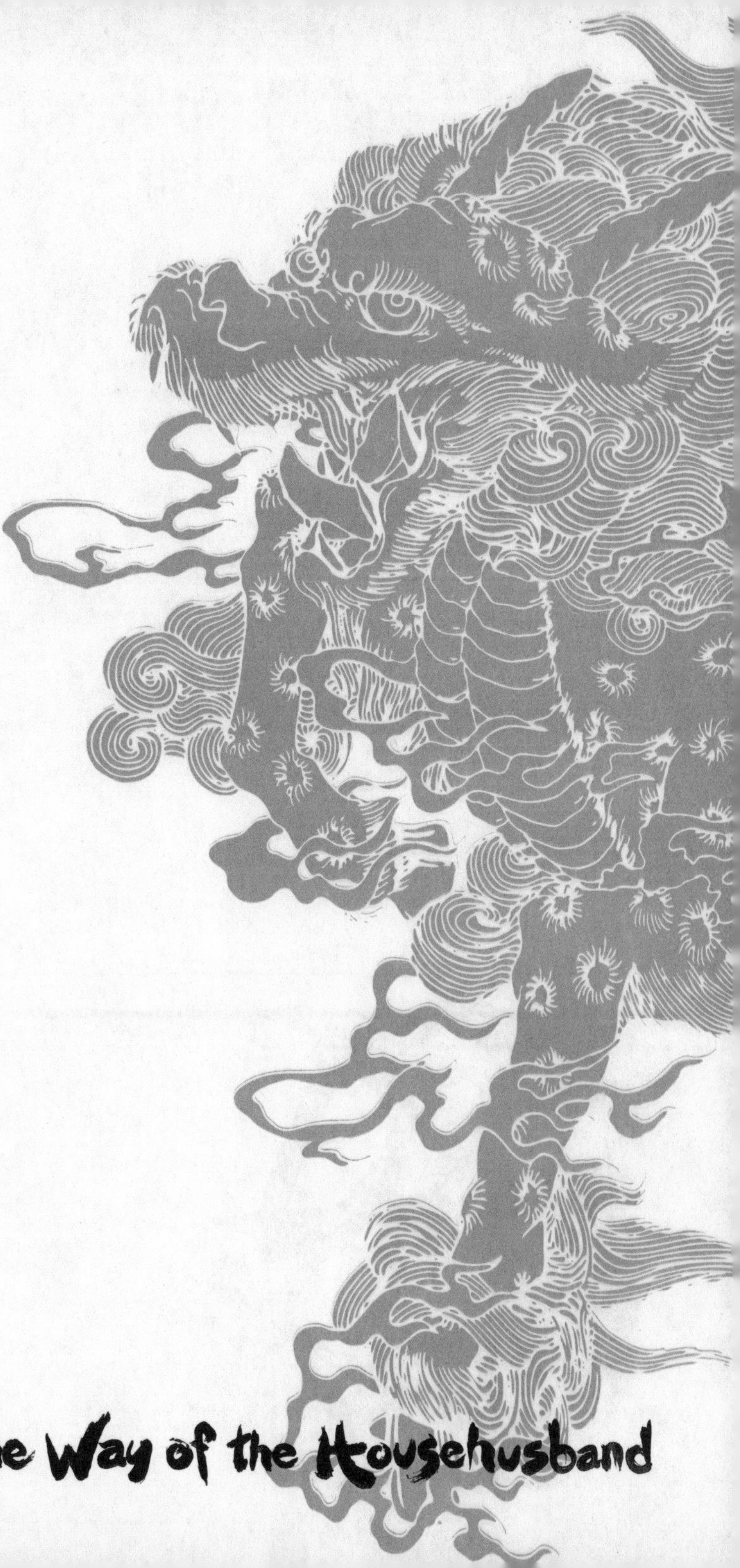

# The Way of the Househusband

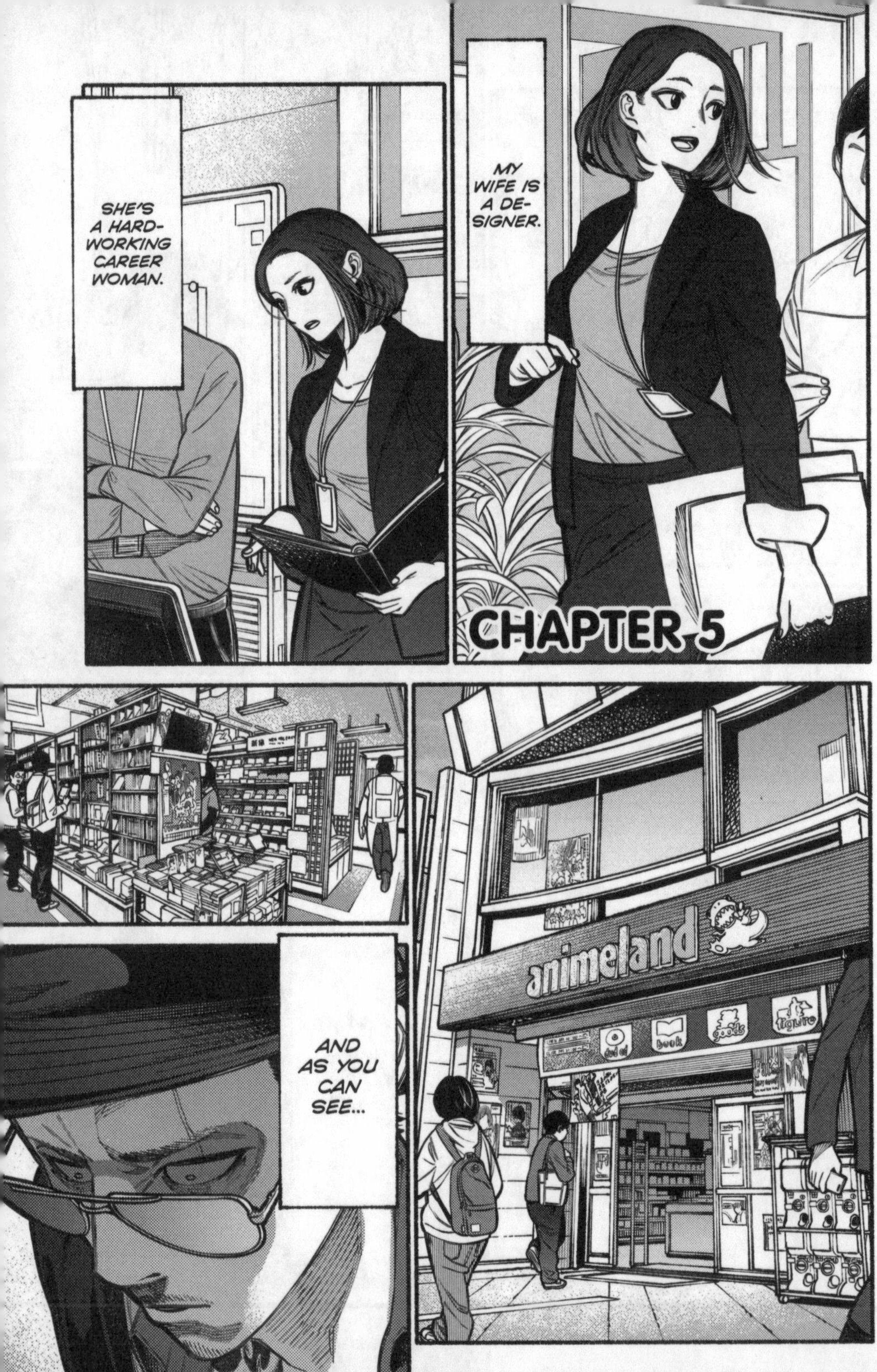
MY WIFE IS A DESIGNER.
CHAPTER 5
SHE'S A HARD-WORKING CAREER WOMAN.
animeland
figure
goods
book
dvd cd
AND AS YOU CAN SEE...

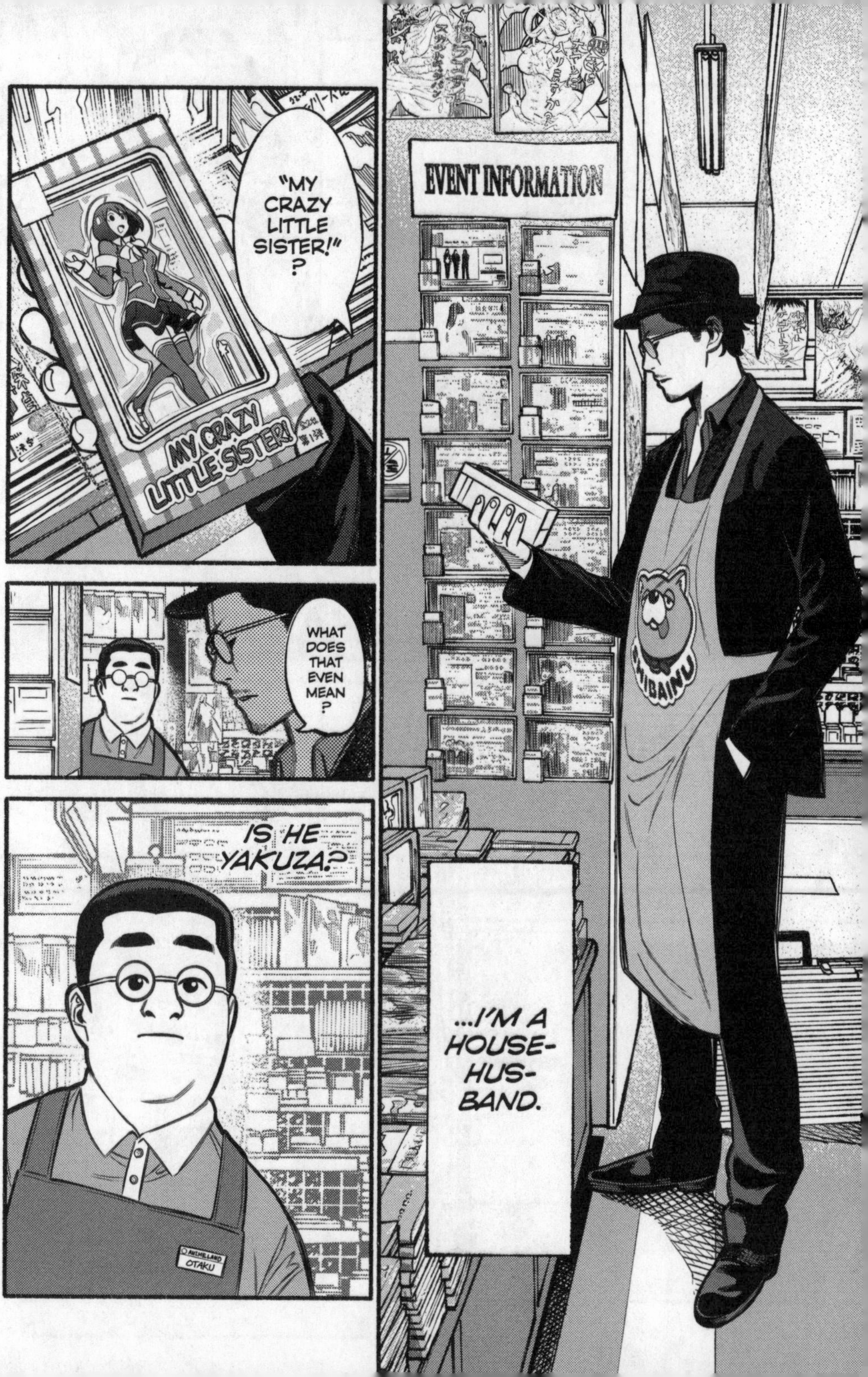
EVENT INFORMATION
SHIBAINU
...I'M A HOUSE-HUS-BAND.
"MY CRAZY LITTLE SISTER!"?
MY CRAZY LITTLE SISTER!
WHAT DOES THAT EVEN MEAN?
IS HE YAKUZA?
ANIMELAND
OTAKU

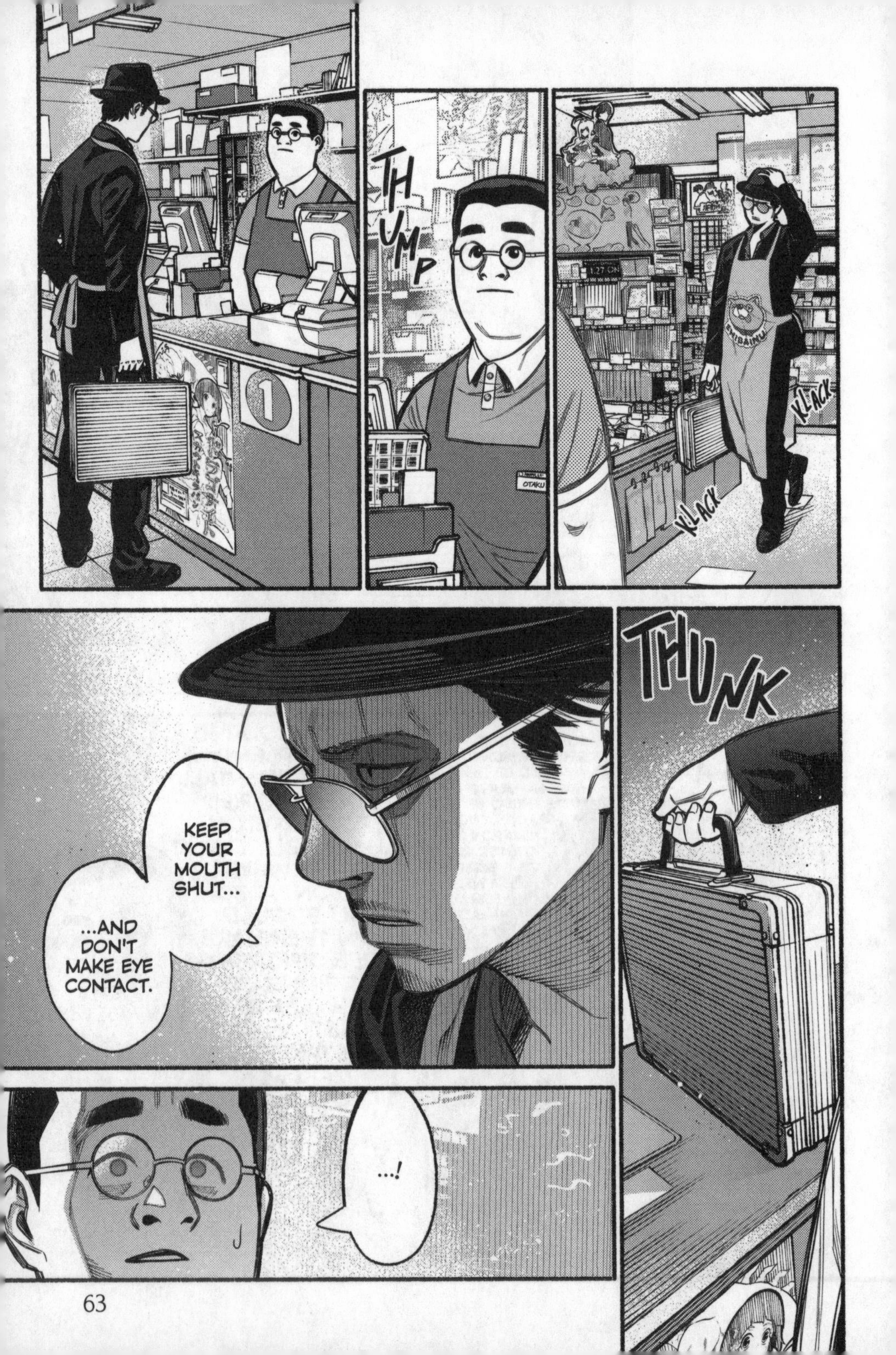
KLACK
KLACK
THUMP
OTAKU
THUNK
KEEP YOUR MOUTH SHUT...
...AND DON'T MAKE EYE CONTACT.
...!

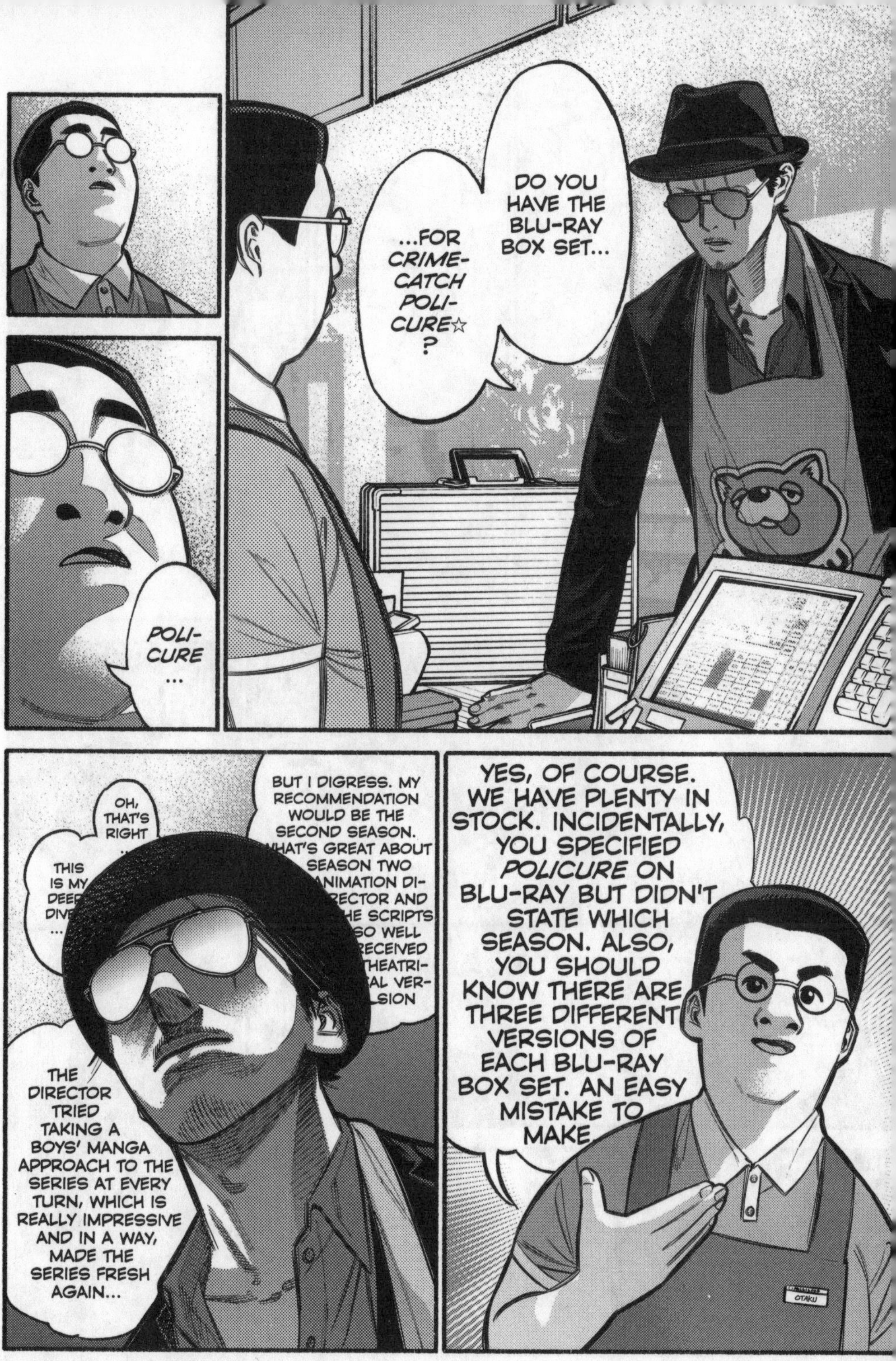
DO YOU HAVE THE BLU-RAY BOX SET...
...FOR CRIME-CATCH POLI-CURE☆?
POLI-CURE...
YES, OF COURSE. WE HAVE PLENTY IN STOCK. INCIDENTALLY, YOU SPECIFIED POLICURE ON BLU-RAY BUT DIDN'T STATE WHICH SEASON. ALSO, YOU SHOULD KNOW THERE ARE THREE DIFFERENT VERSIONS OF EACH BLU-RAY BOX SET. AN EASY MISTAKE TO MAKE
OTAKU
OH, THAT'S RIGHT
THIS IS MY DEEP DIVE...
THE DIRECTOR TRIED TAKING A BOYS' MANGA APPROACH TO THE SERIES AT EVERY TURN, WHICH IS REALLY IMPRESSIVE AND IN A WAY, MADE THE SERIES FRESH AGAIN...
BUT I DIGRESS. MY RECOMMENDATION WOULD BE THE SECOND SEASON. WHAT'S GREAT ABOUT SEASON TWO ANIMATION DI-RECTOR AND THE SCRIPTS SO WELL RECEIVED THEATRI-CAL VER-SION

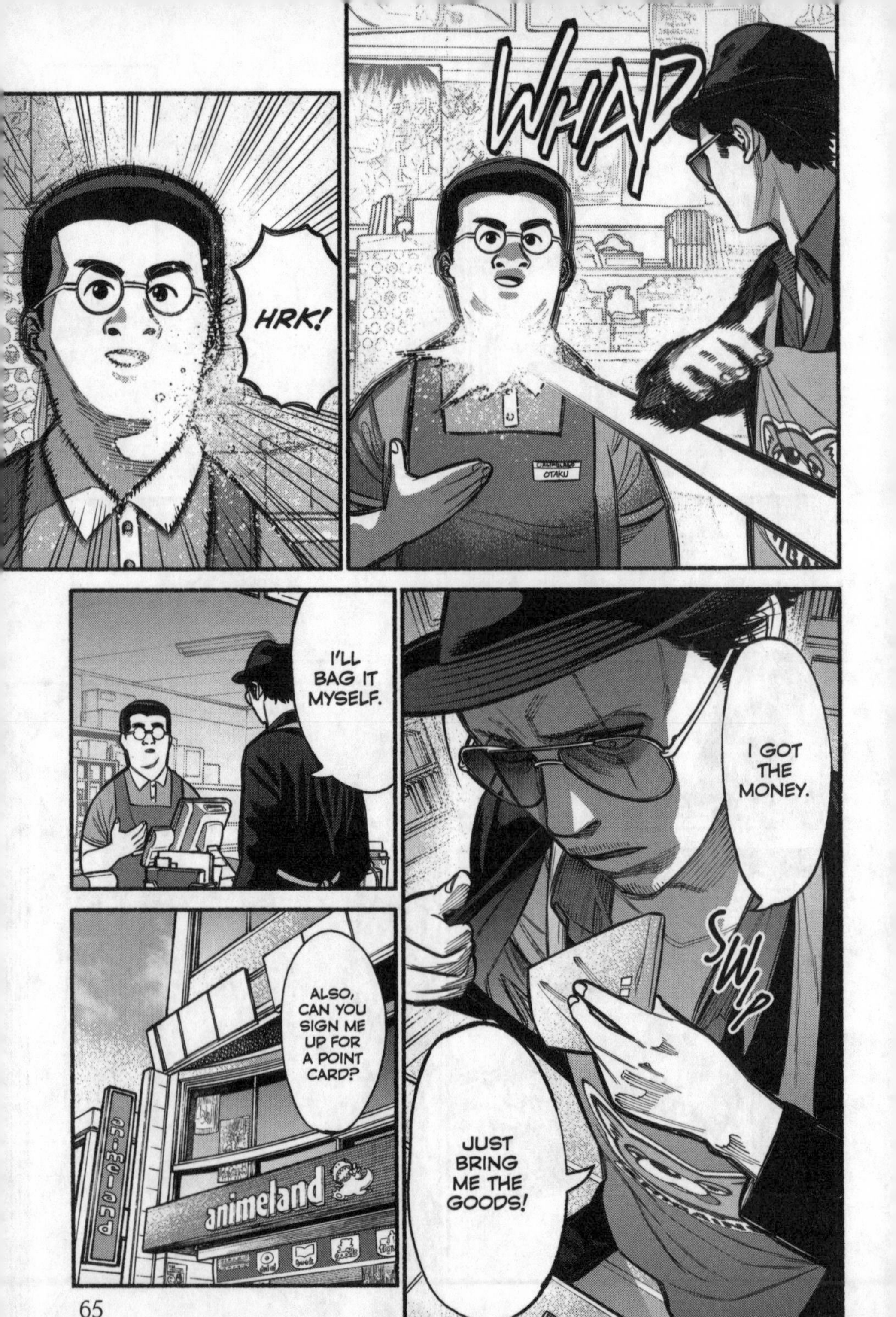
WHAP
OTAKU
HRK!
I GOT THE MONEY.
SWIP
JUST BRING ME THE GOODS!
I'LL BAG IT MYSELF.
ALSO, CAN YOU SIGN ME UP FOR A POINT CARD?
animeland
animeland

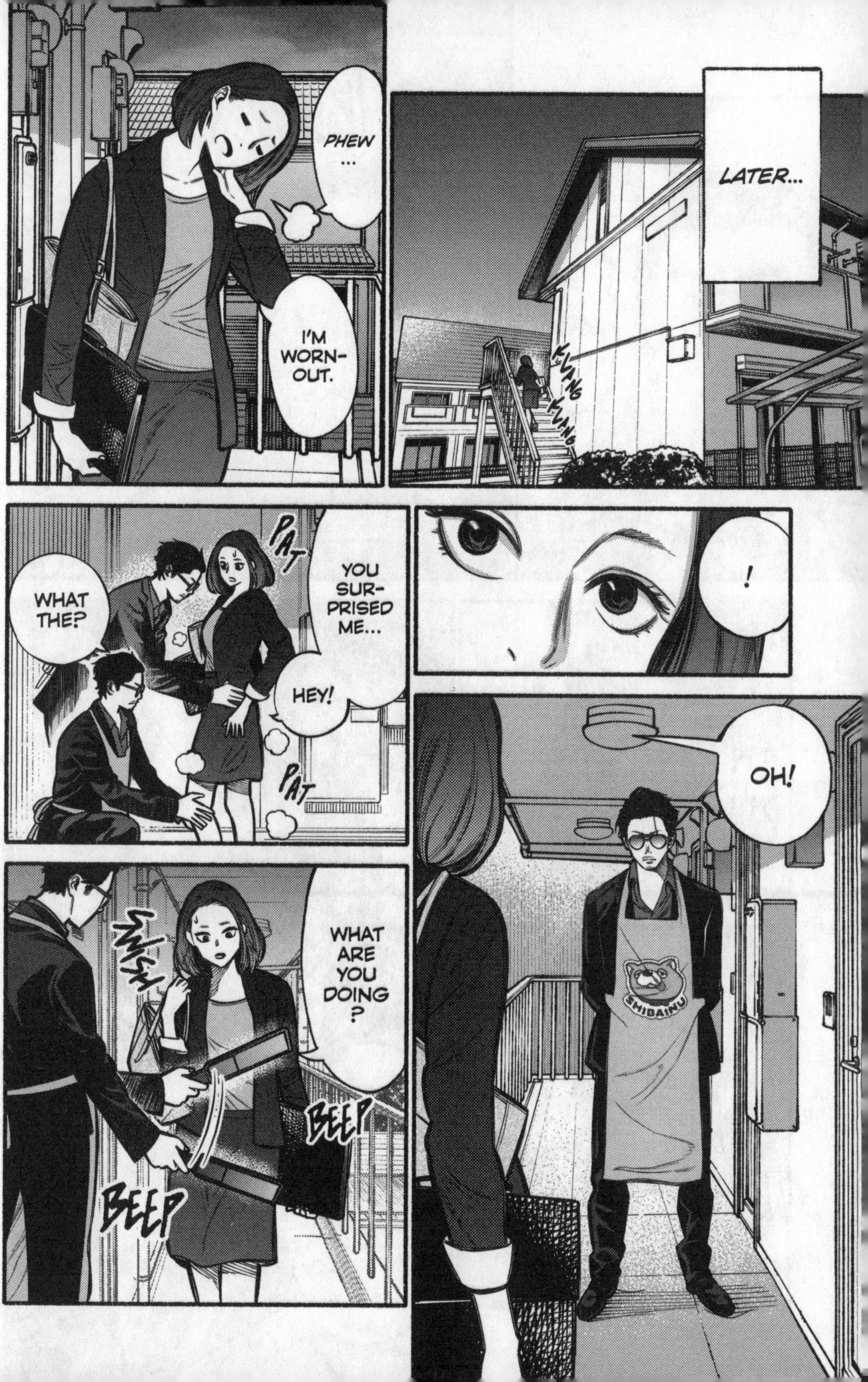

LATER...
KLANG
KLANG
PHEW...
I'M WORN-OUT.
!
OH!
PAT
YOU SURPRISED ME...
HEY!
PAT
WHAT THE?
WHAT ARE YOU DOING?
BEEP
SWISH
BEEP

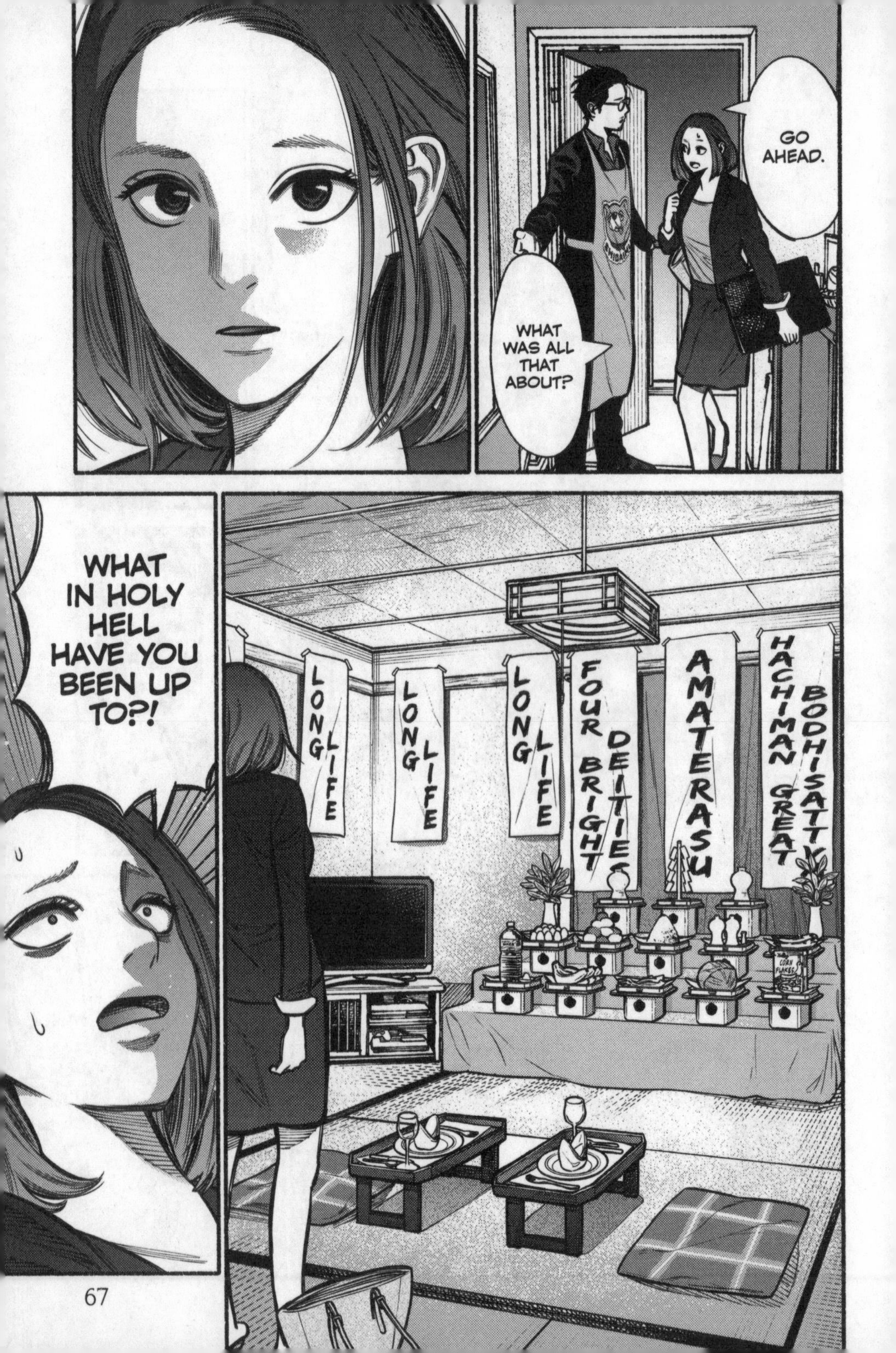
GO AHEAD.
WHAT WAS ALL THAT ABOUT?
HACHIMAN GREAT BODHISATTV
AMATERASU
FOUR BRIGHT DEITIES
LONG LIFE
LONG LIFE
LONG LIFE
CORN FLAKES
WHAT IN HOLY HELL HAVE YOU BEEN UP TO?!

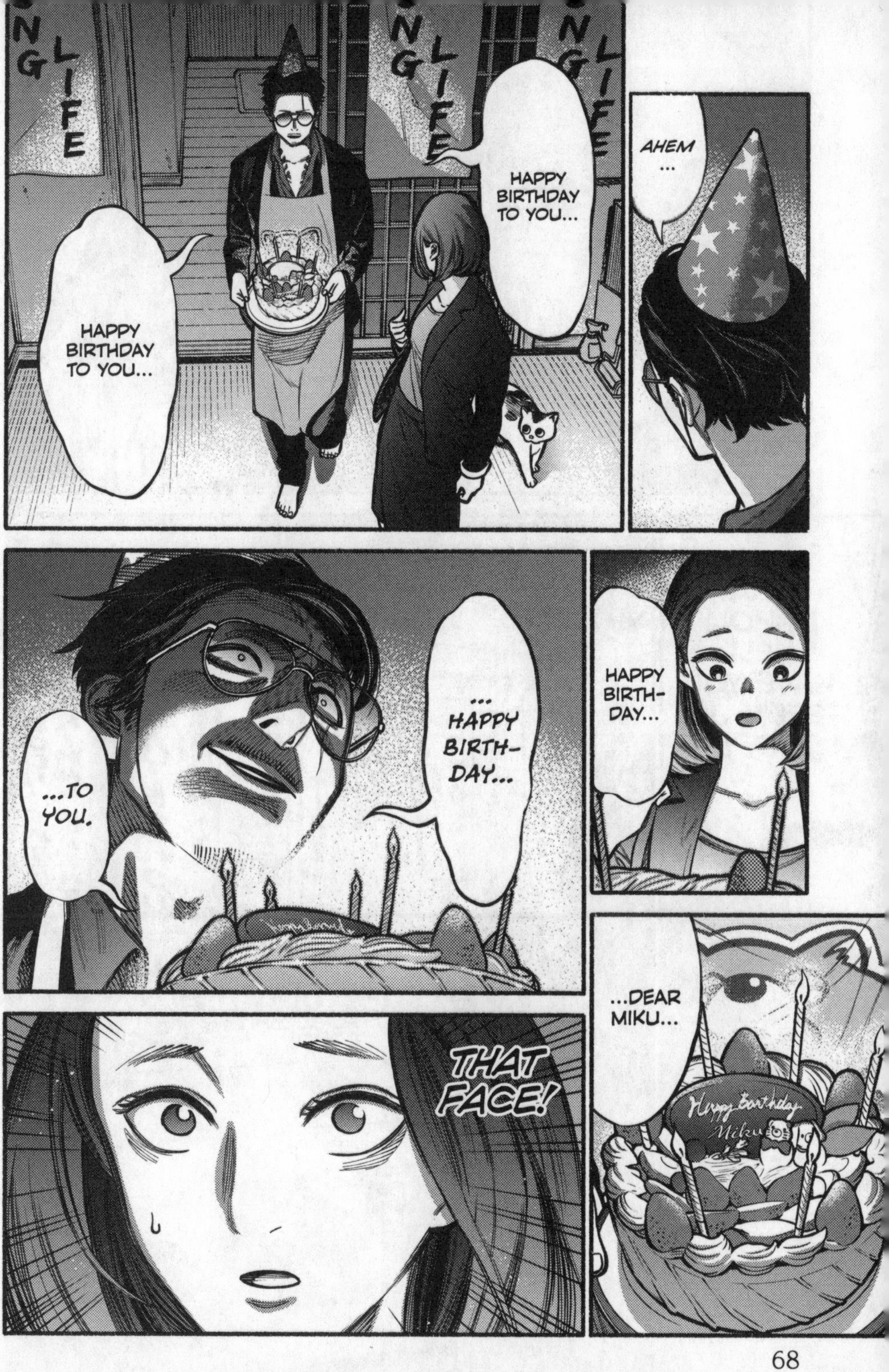
AHEM ...
NG LIFE
HAPPY BIRTHDAY TO YOU...
HAPPY BIRTHDAY TO YOU...
HAPPY BIRTH-DAY...
... HAPPY BIRTH-DAY...
...TO YOU.
...DEAR MIKU...
Happy Birthday Miku
THAT FACE!

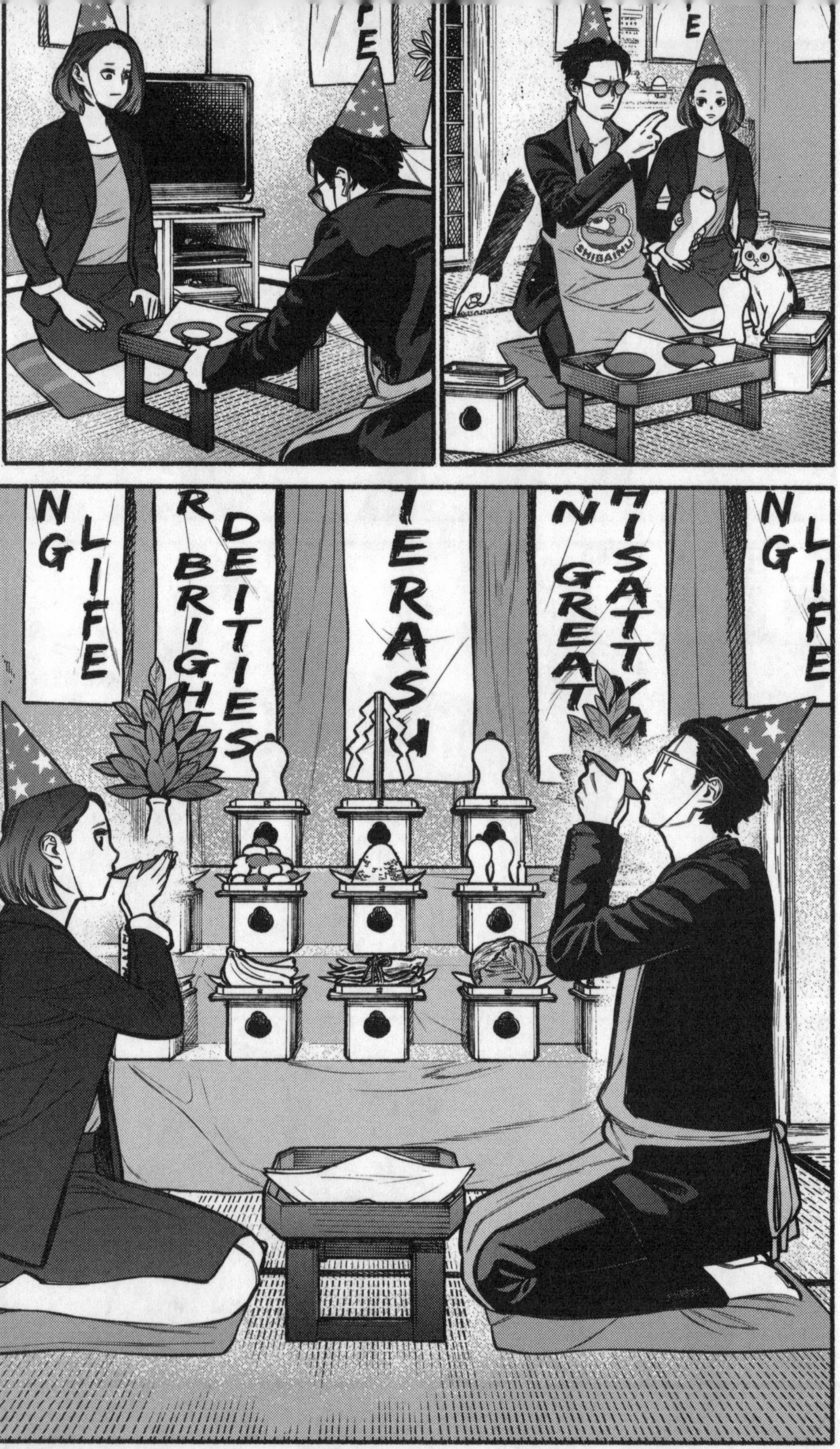
SHIBAINU
NG LIFE
HISATT
N GREAT
TERAS
DEITIES
R BRIGH
LIFE
NG

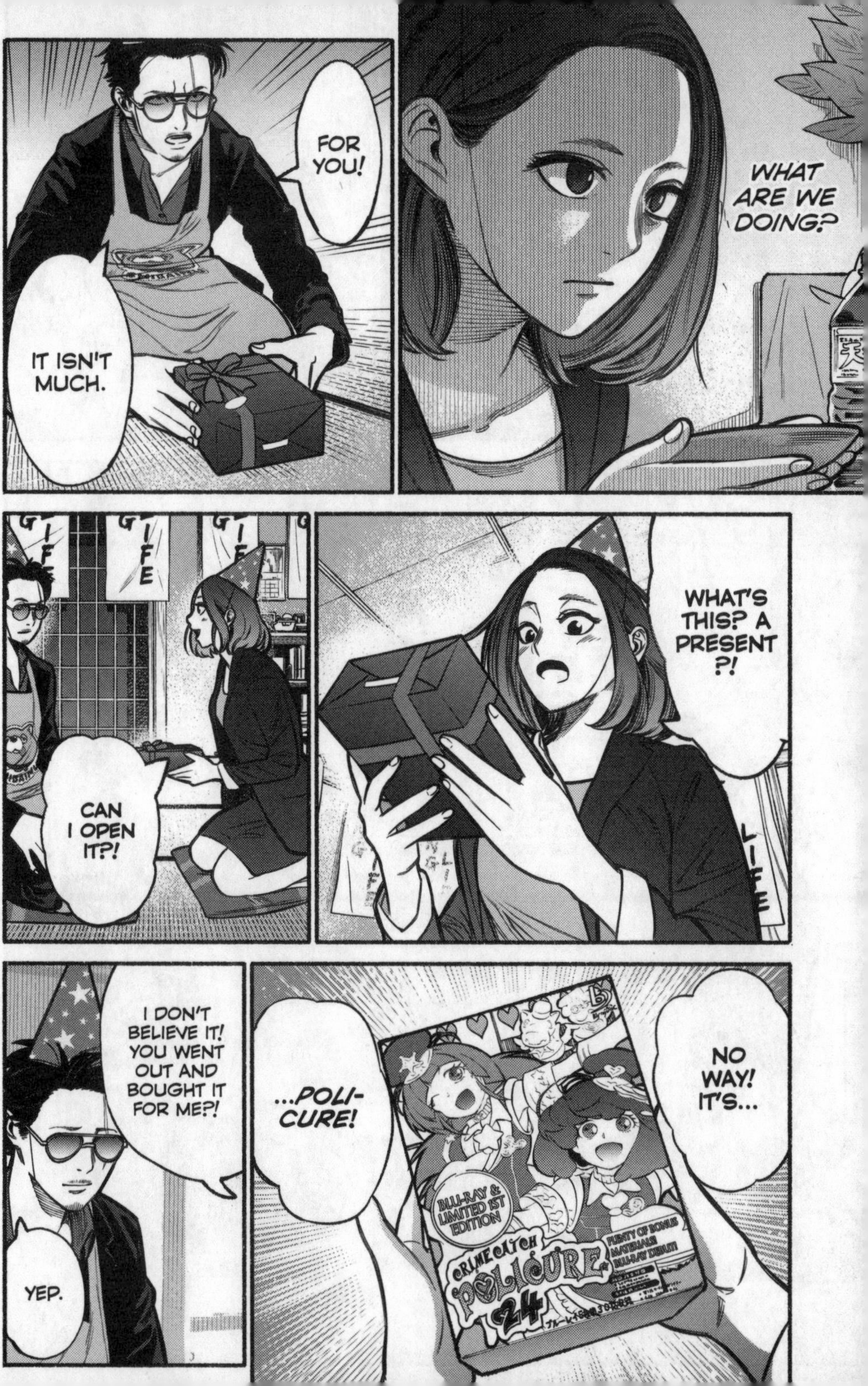
WHAT ARE WE DOING?
FOR YOU!
IT ISN'T MUCH.
WHAT'S THIS? A PRESENT?!
CAN I OPEN IT?!
NO WAY! IT'S...
...POLI-CURE!
BLU-RAY & LIMITED 1ST EDITION
PLENTY OF BONUS MATERIALS BLU-RAY DEBUT!
CRIME CATCH POLICURE 24
I DON'T BELIEVE IT! YOU WENT OUT AND BOUGHT IT FOR ME?!
YEP.

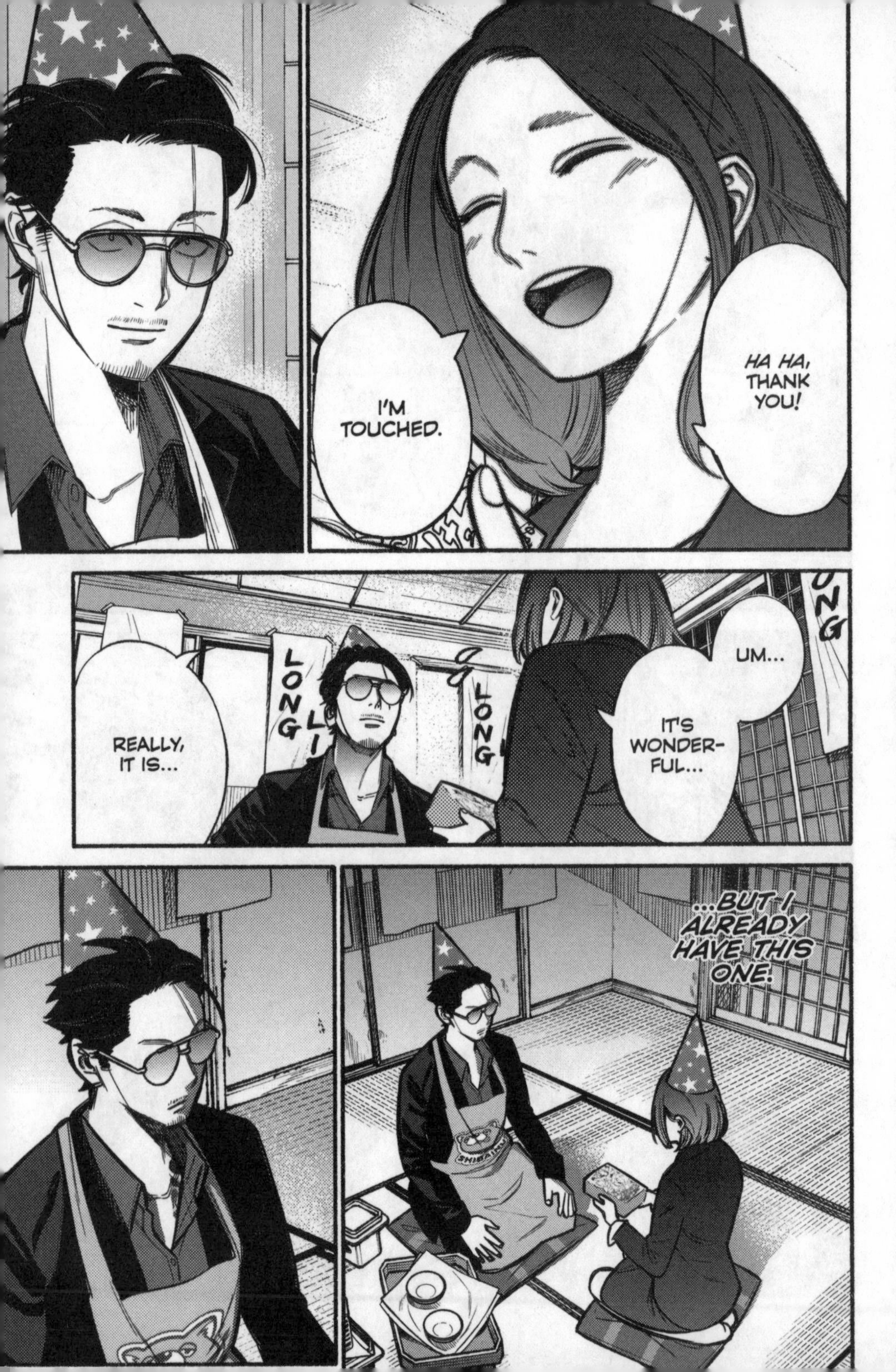

HA HA, THANK YOU!
I'M TOUCHED.
UM...
IT'S WONDERFUL...
LONG
LONG
REALLY, IT IS...
...BUT I ALREADY HAVE THIS ONE.

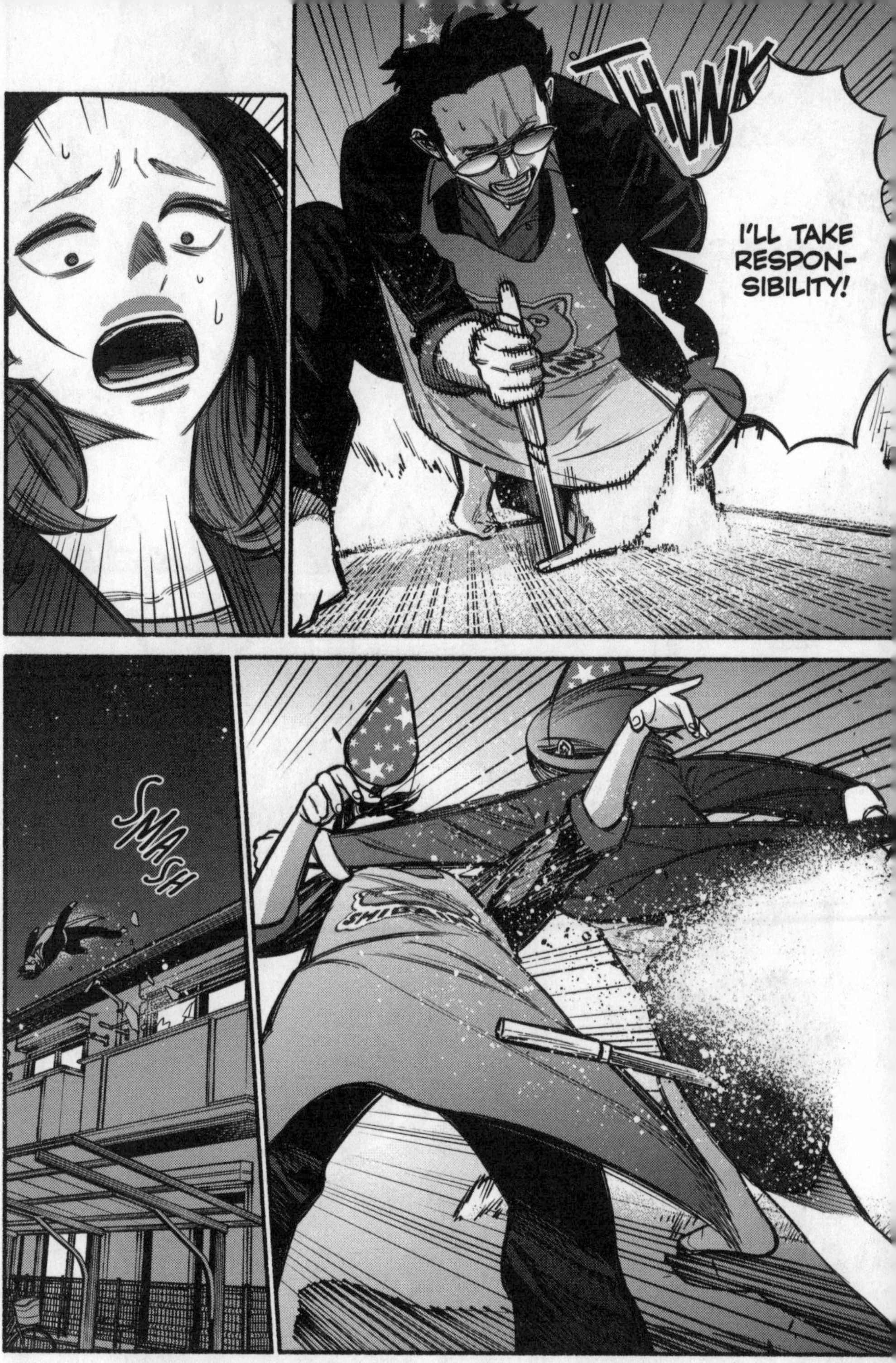
THUNK
I'LL TAKE RESPON-SIBILITY!
SMASH

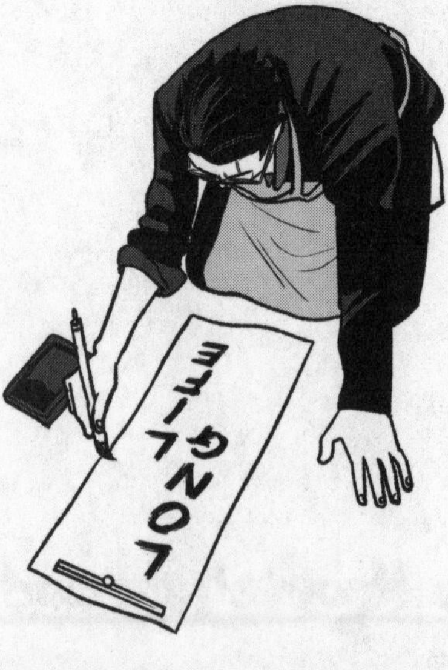
LONG
LIFE

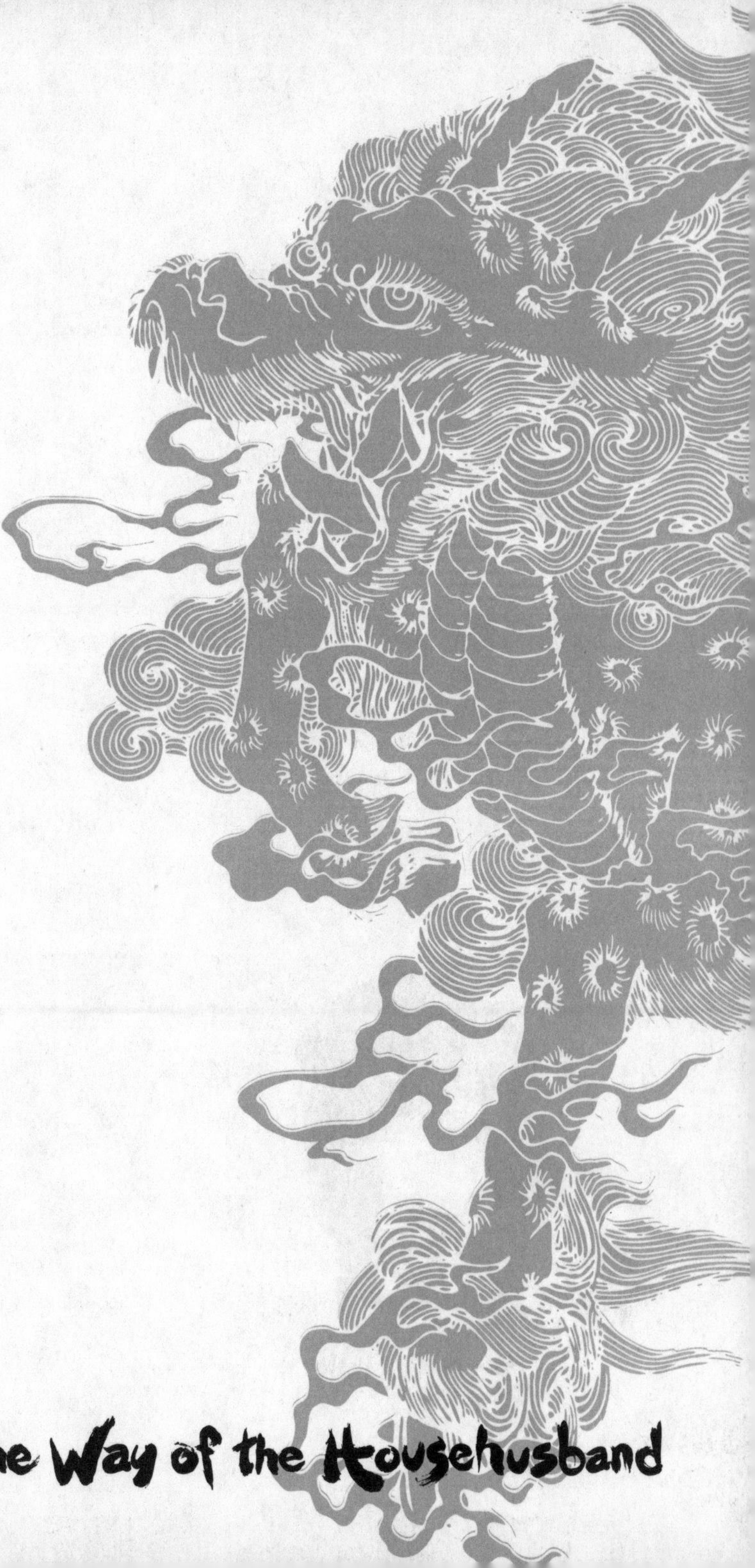

# The Way of the Househusband

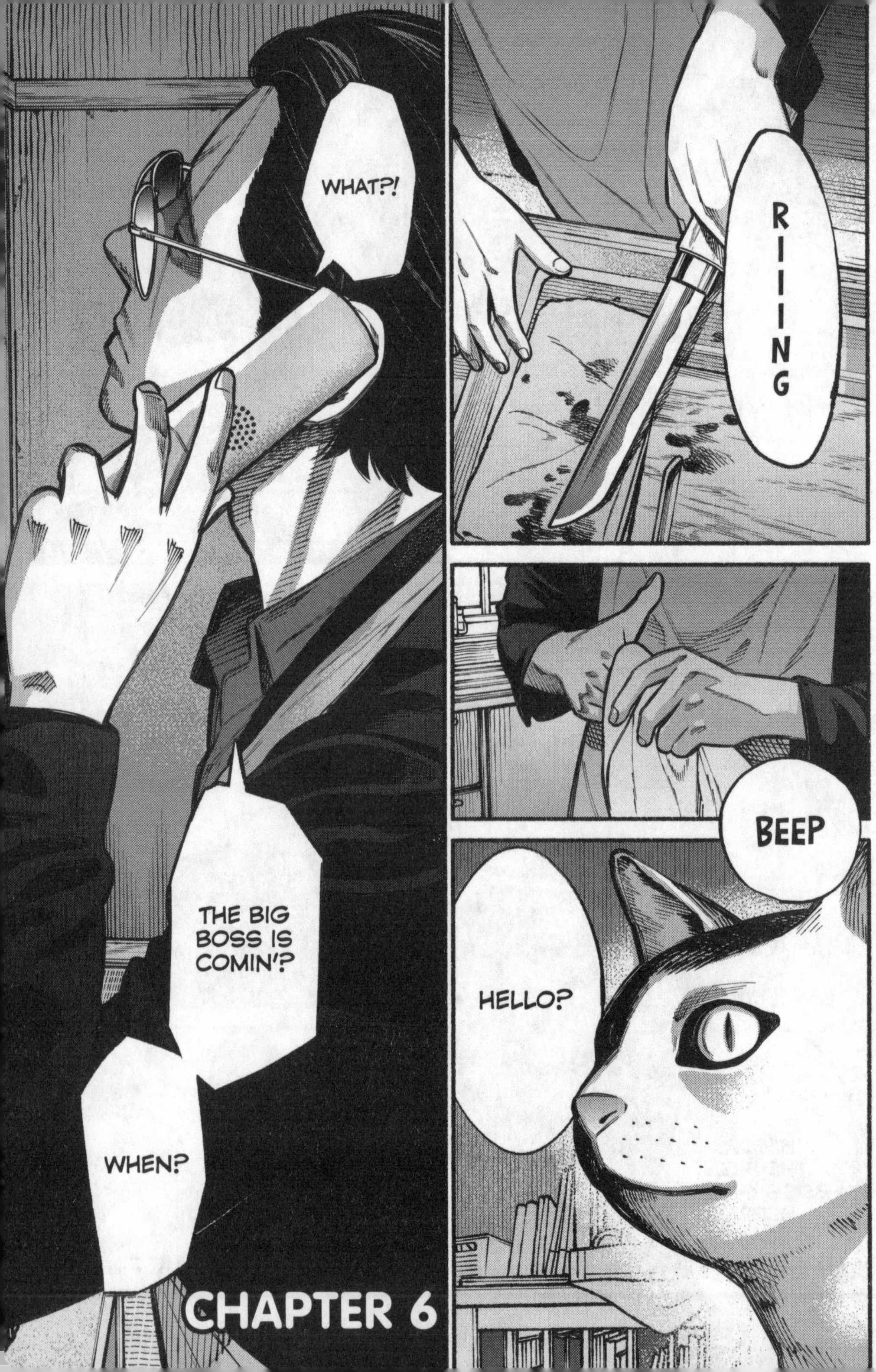
RIIING
BEEP
HELLO?
WHAT?!
THE BIG BOSS IS COMIN'?
WHEN?
CHAPTER 6

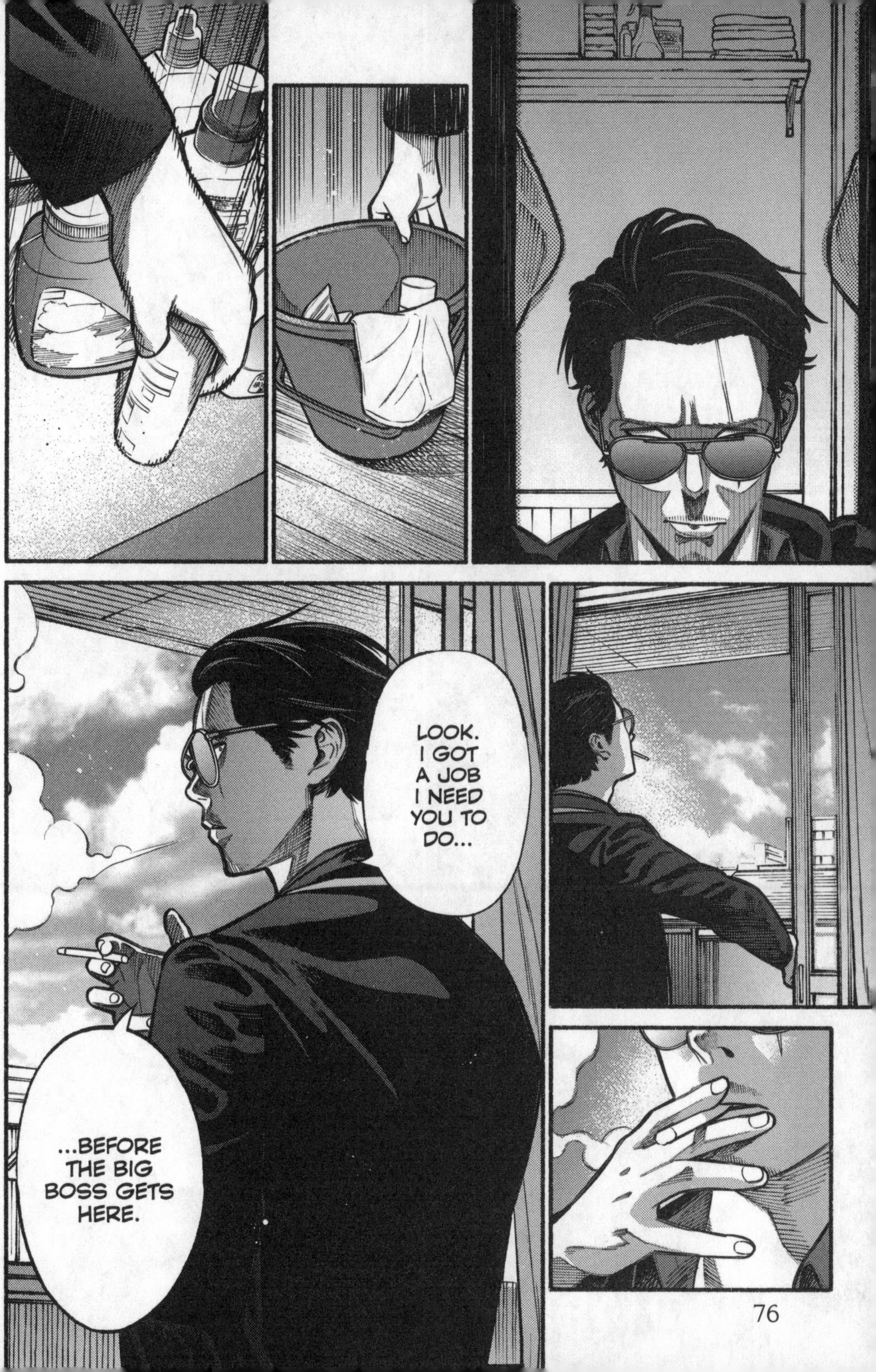
LOOK. I GOT A JOB I NEED YOU TO DO...
...BEFORE THE BIG BOSS GETS HERE.

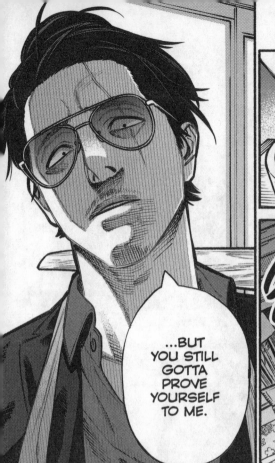

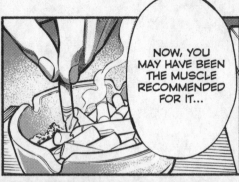

NOW, YOU MAY HAVE BEEN THE MUSCLE RECOMMENDED FOR IT...

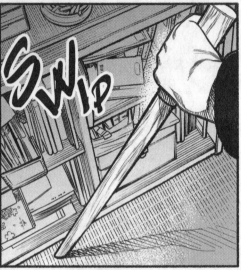

SWIP

...BUT YOU STILL GOTTA PROVE YOURSELF TO ME.

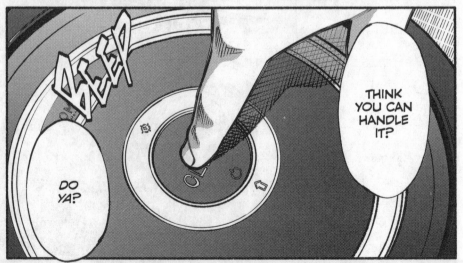

BEEP

DO YA?

THINK YOU CAN HANDLE IT?

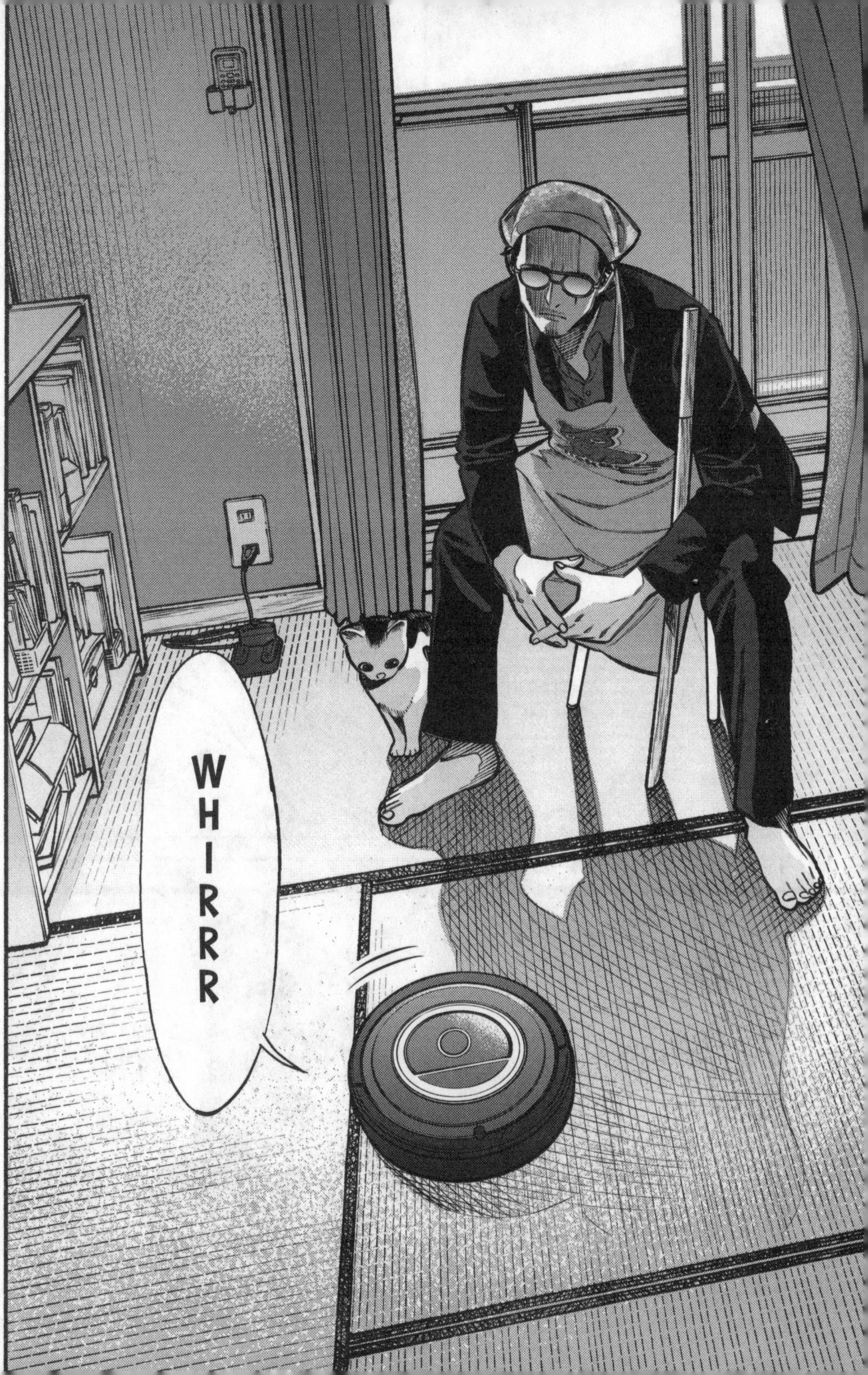
WHIRRR

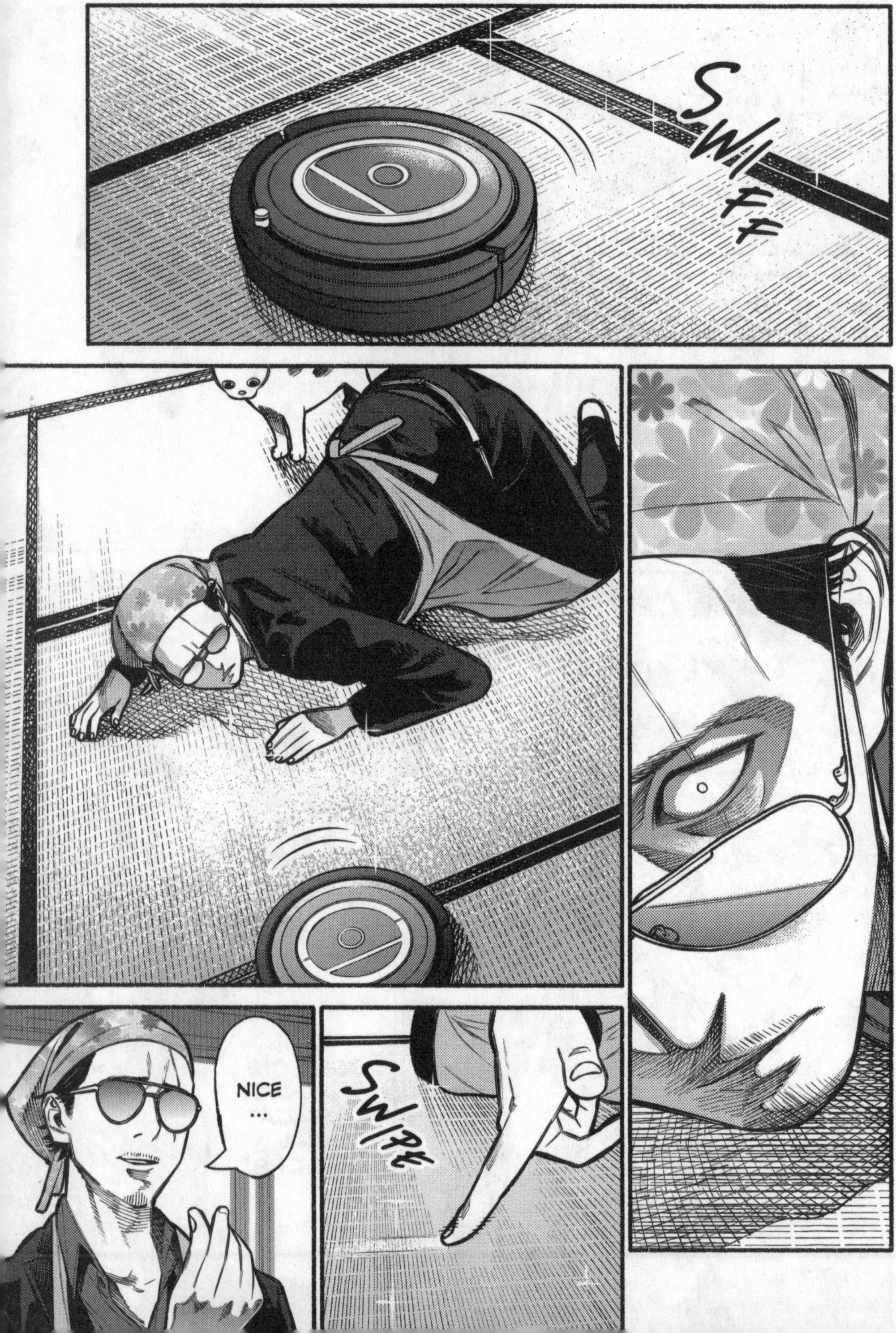
SWIFF
SWIPE
NICE ...

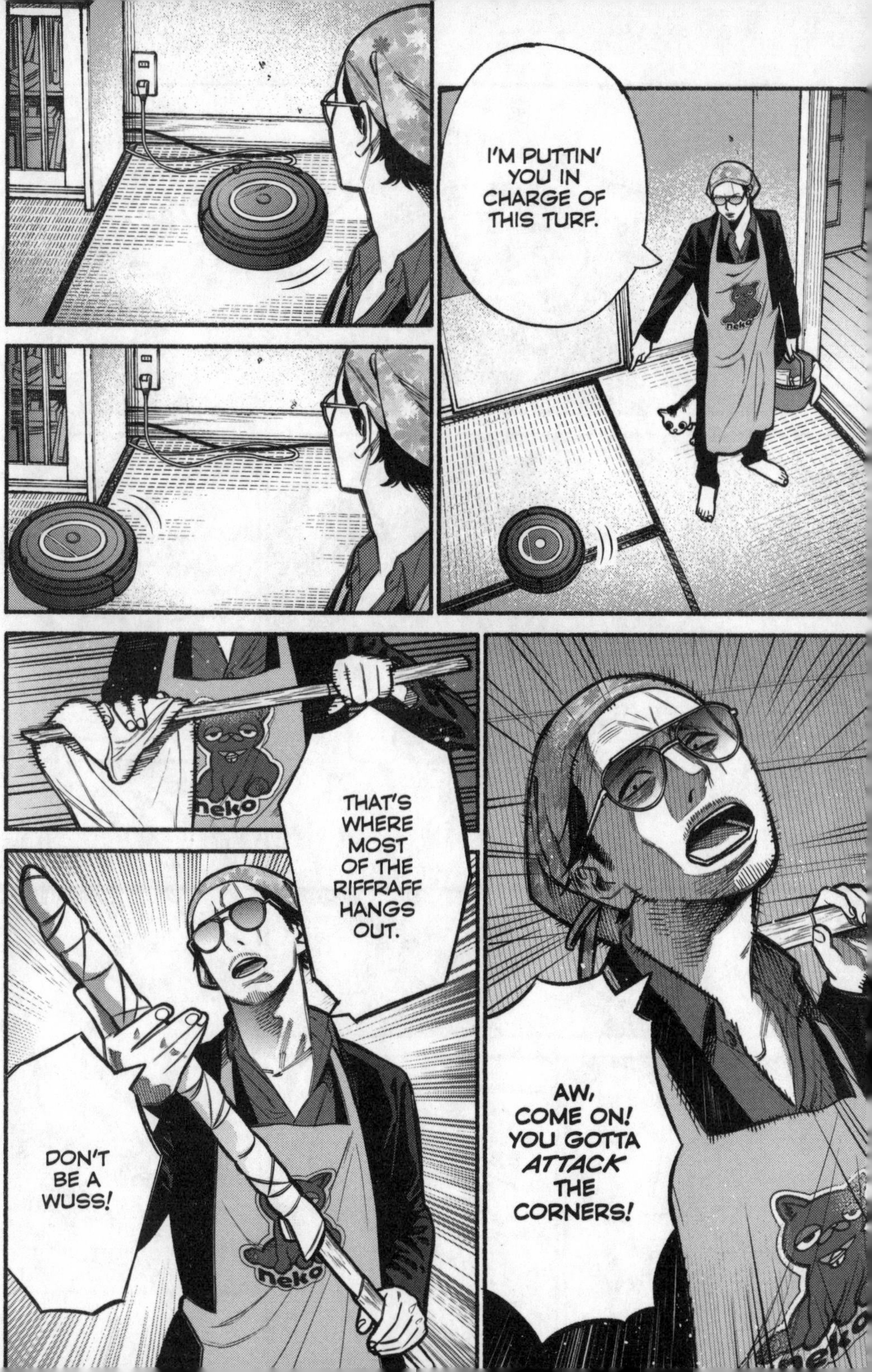
I'M PUTTIN' YOU IN CHARGE OF THIS TURF.
AW, COME ON! YOU GOTTA *ATTACK* THE CORNERS!
THAT'S WHERE MOST OF THE RIFFRAFF HANGS OUT.
DON'T BE A WUSS!

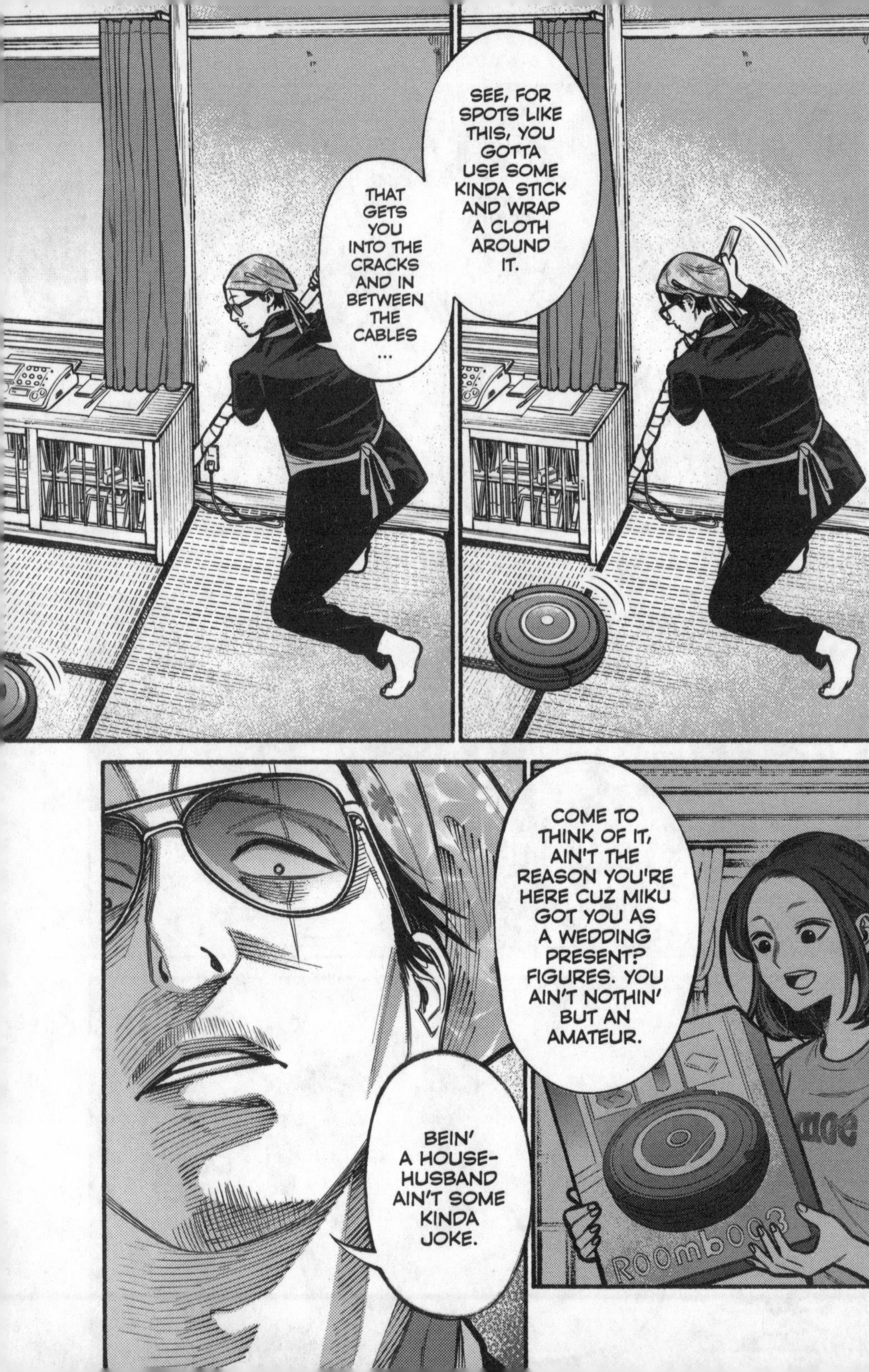
SEE, FOR SPOTS LIKE THIS, YOU GOTTA USE SOME KINDA STICK AND WRAP A CLOTH AROUND IT.
THAT GETS YOU INTO THE CRACKS AND IN BETWEEN THE CABLES ...
COME TO THINK OF IT, AIN'T THE REASON YOU'RE HERE CUZ MIKU GOT YOU AS A WEDDING PRESENT? FIGURES. YOU AIN'T NOTHIN' BUT AN AMATEUR.
BEIN' A HOUSE-HUSBAND AIN'T SOME KINDA JOKE.

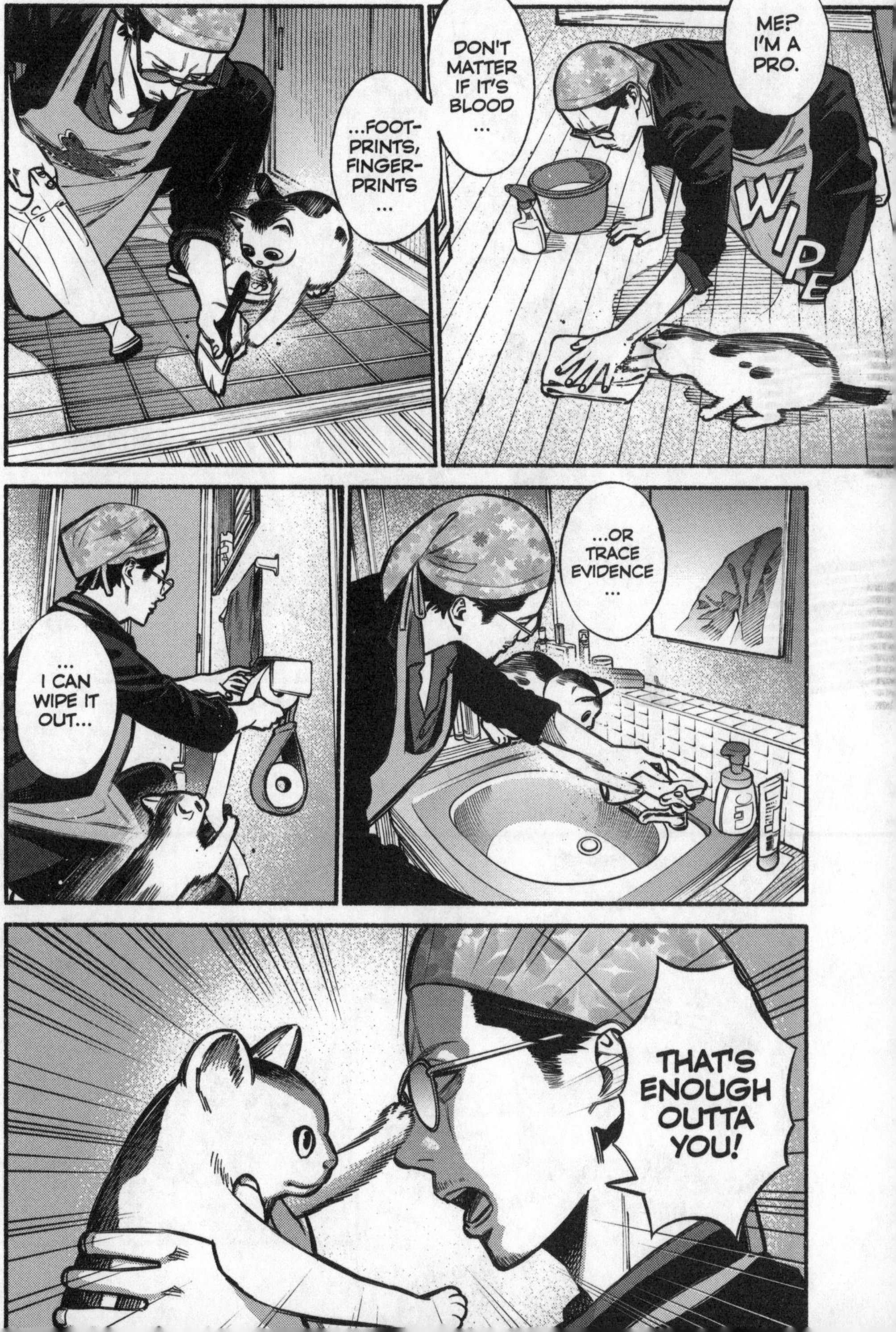
ME? I'M A PRO.
WIPE
DON'T MATTER IF IT'S BLOOD...
...FOOT-PRINTS, FINGER-PRINTS...
...OR TRACE EVIDENCE...
...I CAN WIPE IT OUT...
THAT'S ENOUGH OUTTA YOU!

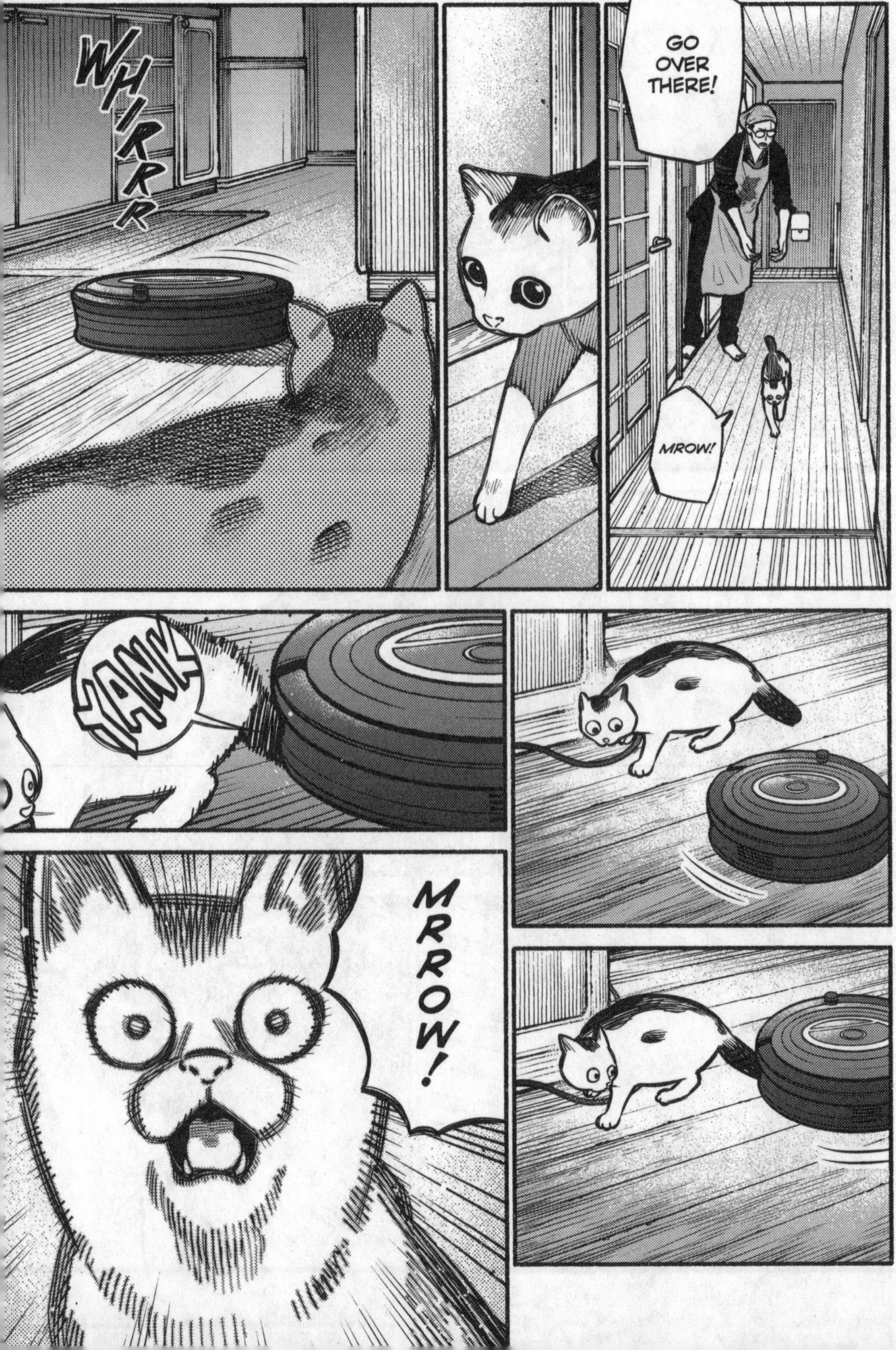
GO OVER THERE!
MROW!
WHIRRR
YANK
MRROW!

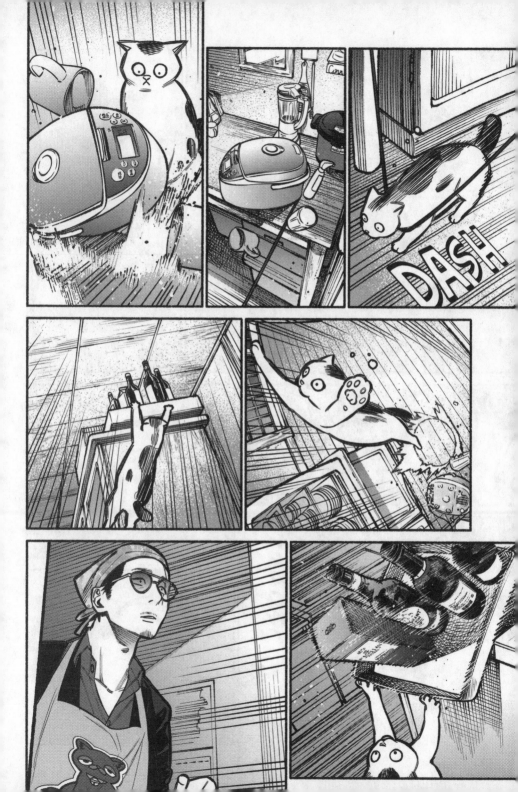

DASH

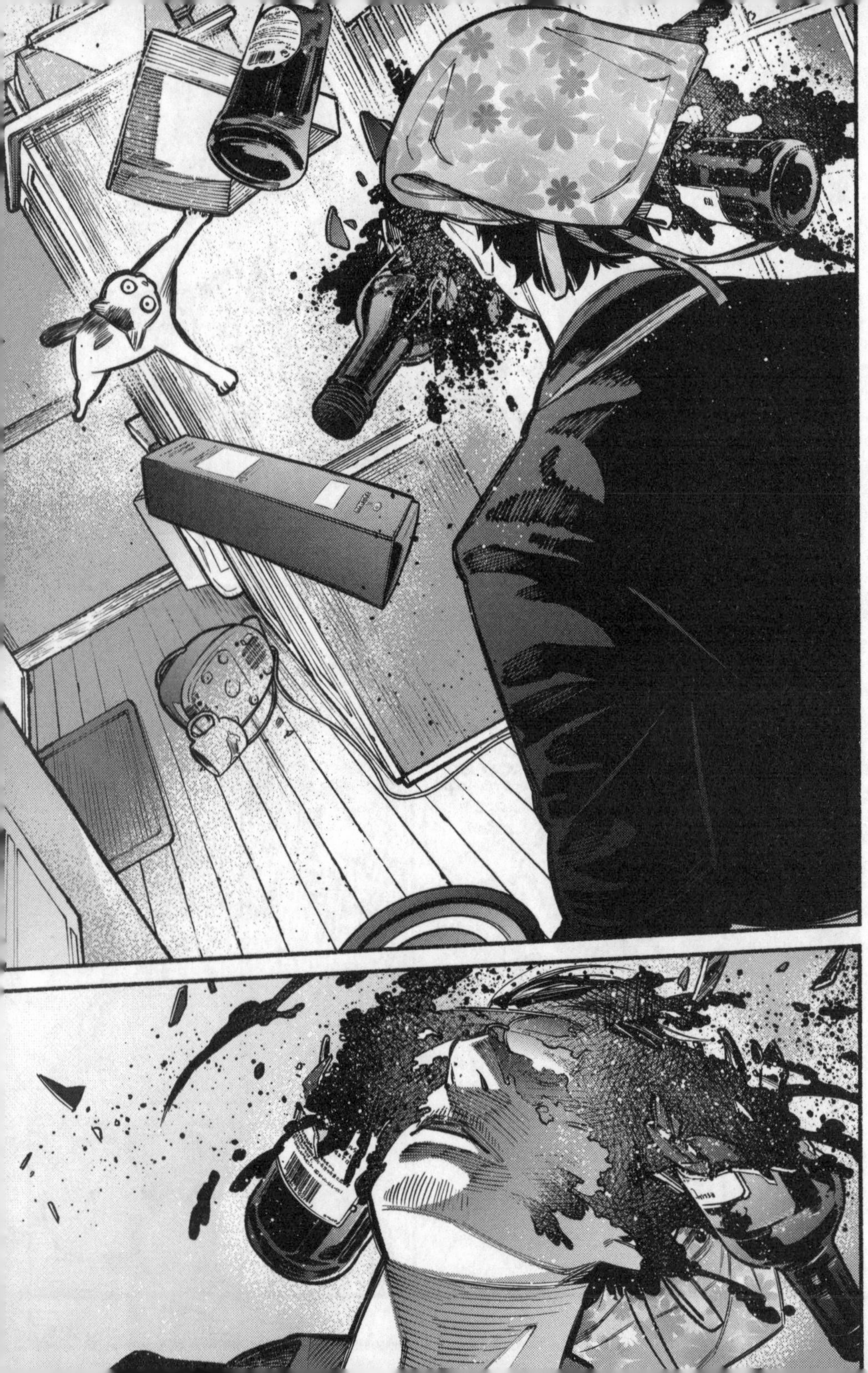

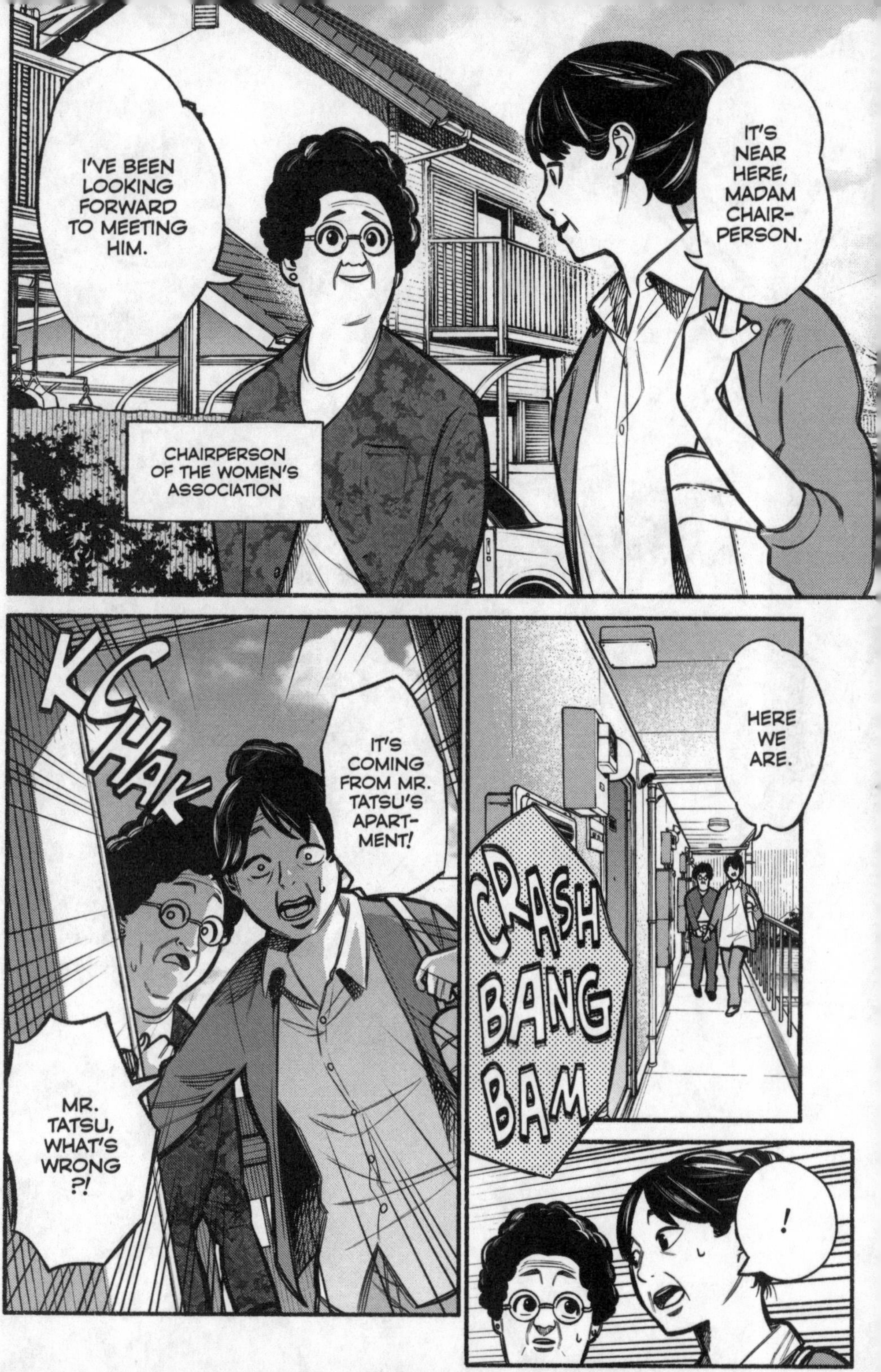
IT'S NEAR HERE, MADAM CHAIR-PERSON.
I'VE BEEN LOOKING FORWARD TO MEETING HIM.
CHAIRPERSON OF THE WOMEN'S ASSOCIATION
HERE WE ARE.
CRASH BANG BAM
!
KCHAK
IT'S COMING FROM MR. TATSU'S APART-MENT!
MR. TATSU, WHAT'S WRONG?!

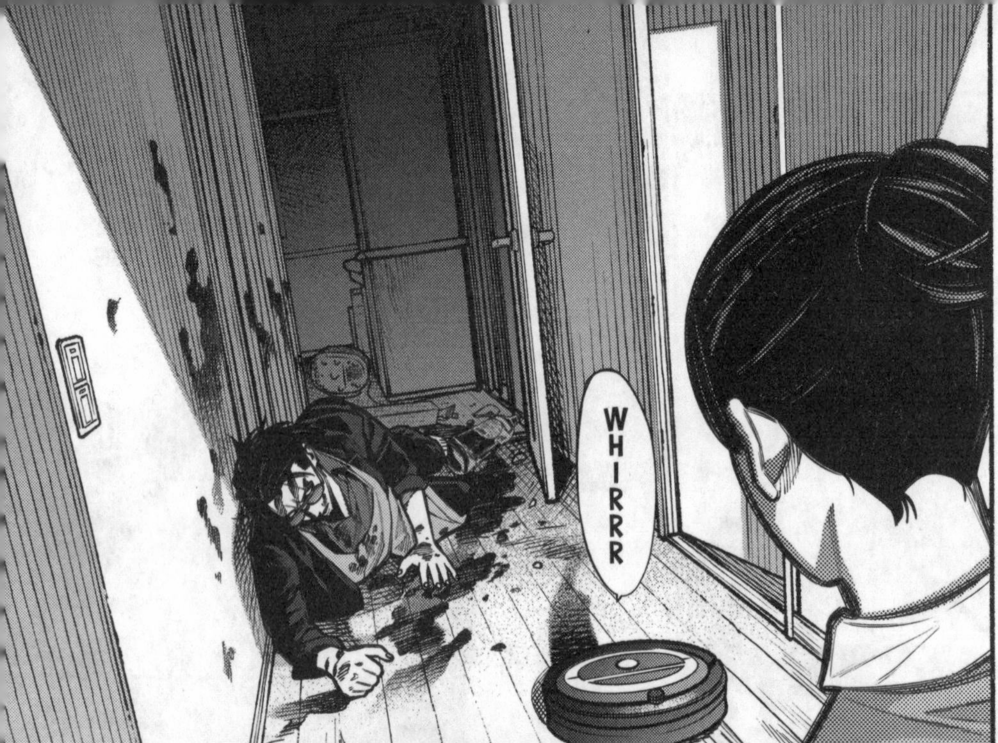
WHIRRR
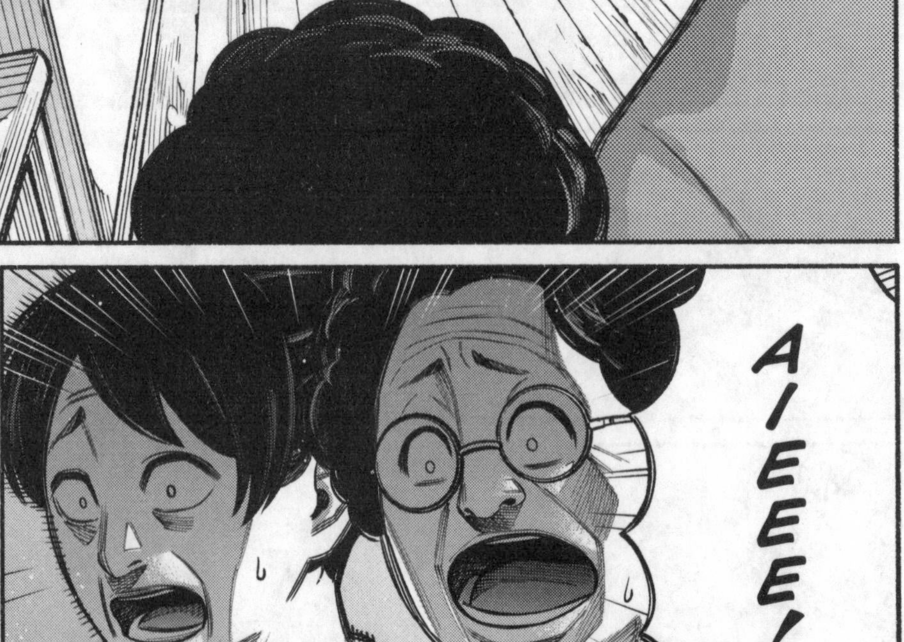
AIEEE!

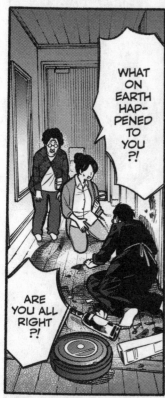

WHAT ON EARTH HAP- PENED TO YOU?!

ARE YOU ALL RIGHT?!

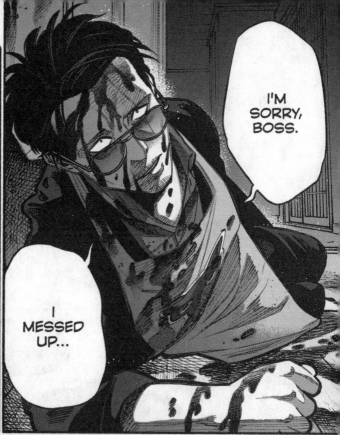

I'M SORRY, BOSS.

I MESSED UP...

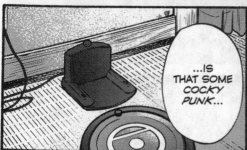

...IS THAT SOME *COCKY PUNK*...

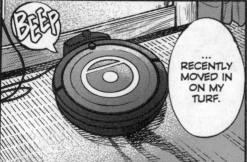

BEEP

...RECENTLY MOVED IN ON MY TURF.

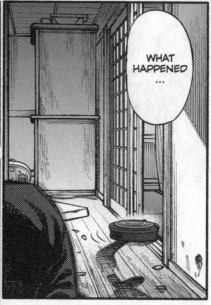

WHAT HAPPENED...

88

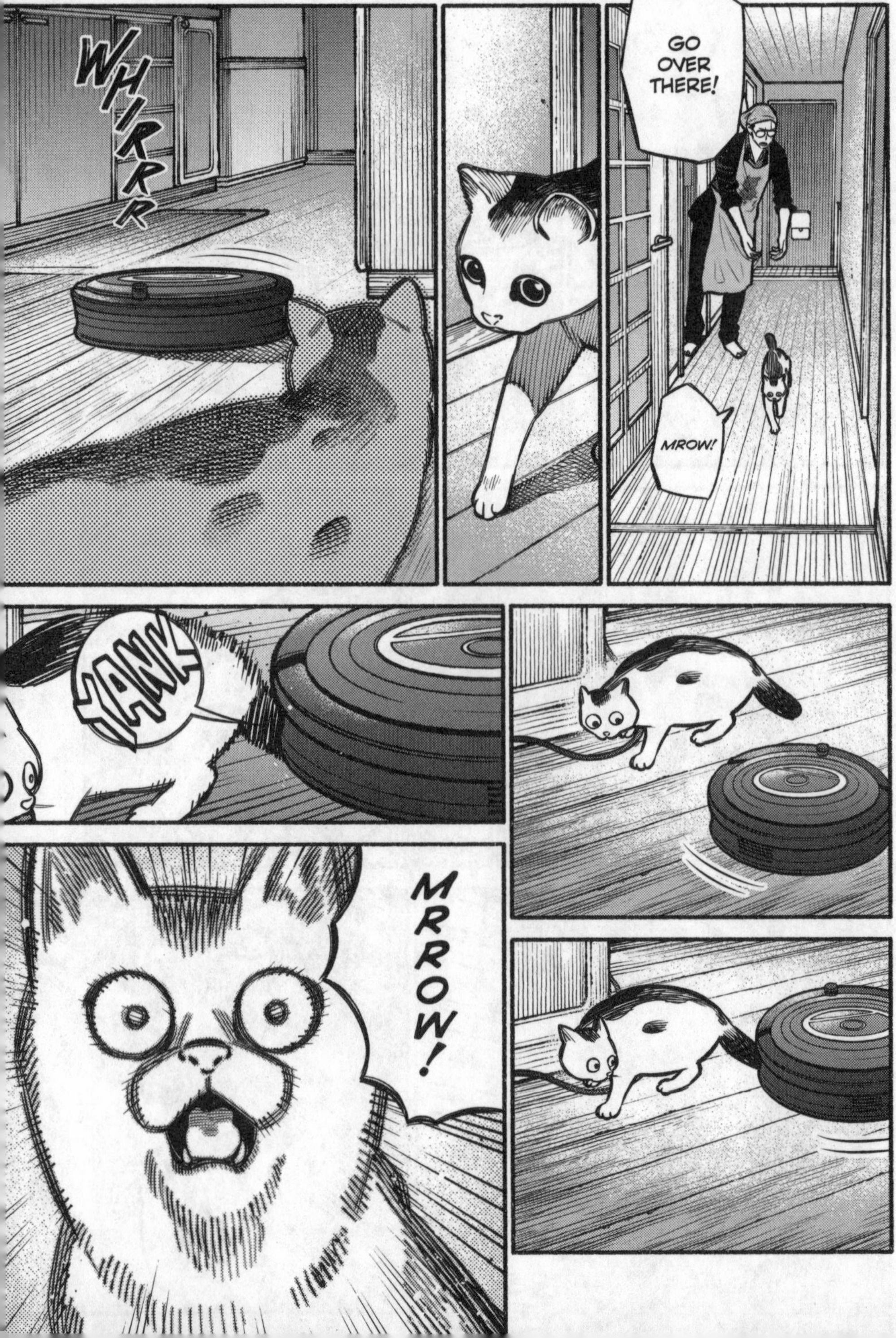
GO OVER THERE!
MROW!
WHIRRR
YANK
MRROW!

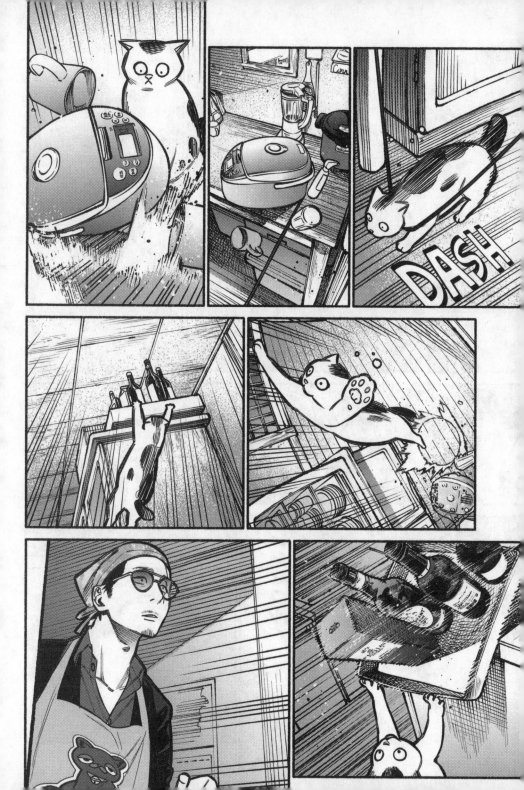

DASH

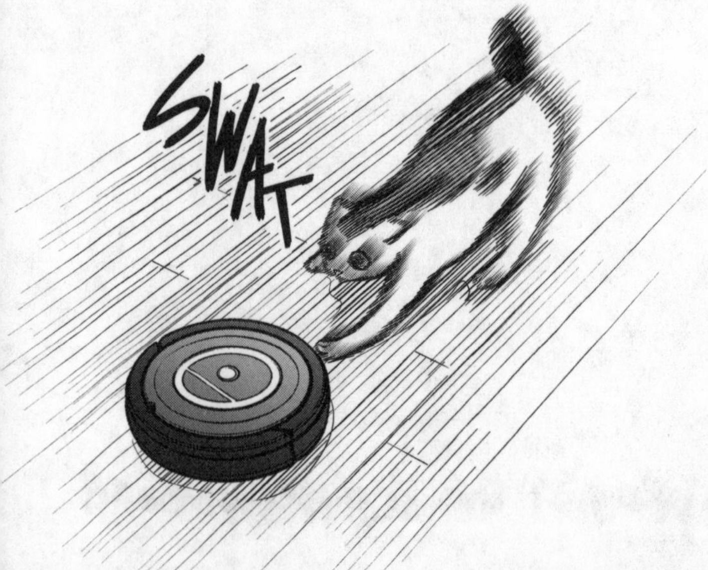
SWAT

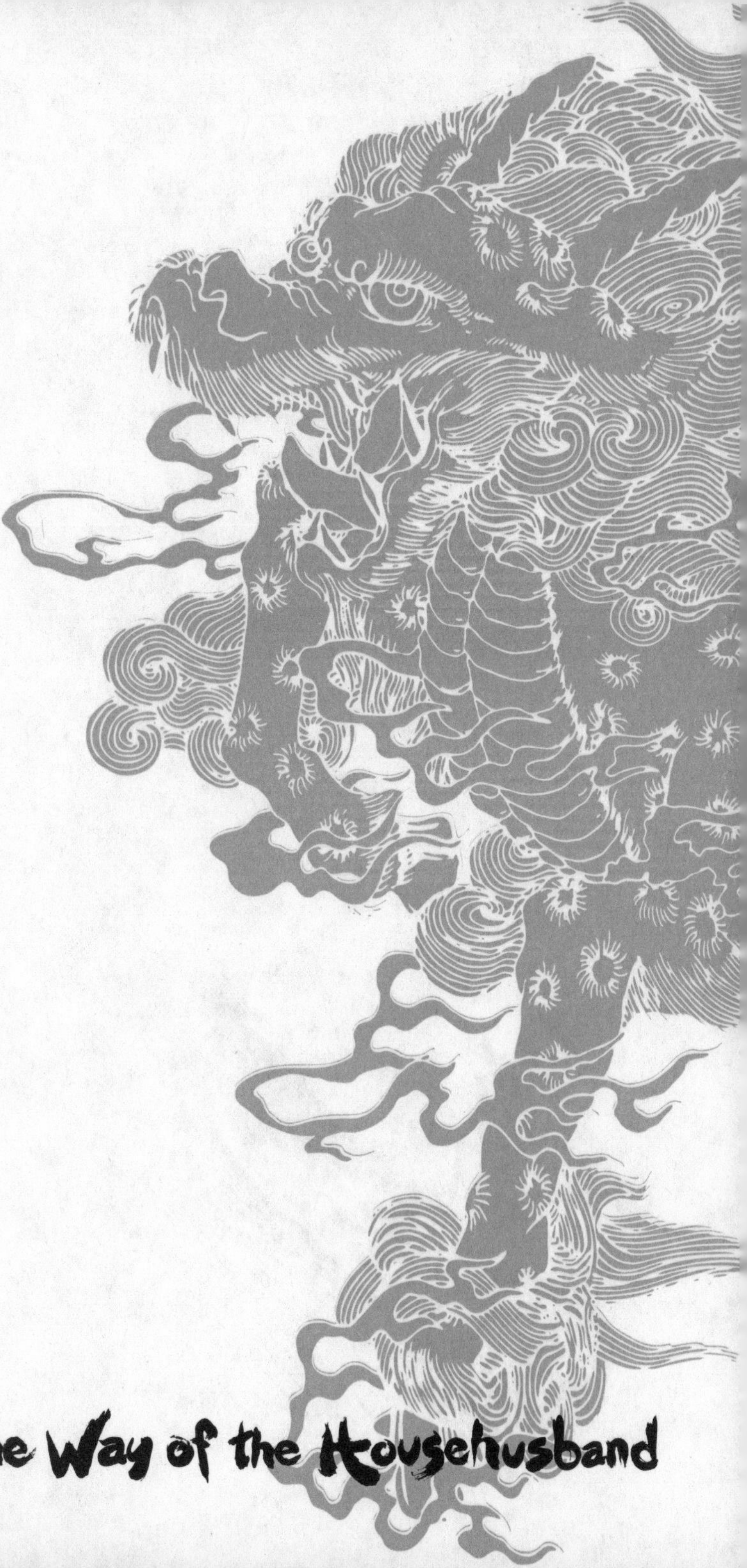

The Way of the Househusband

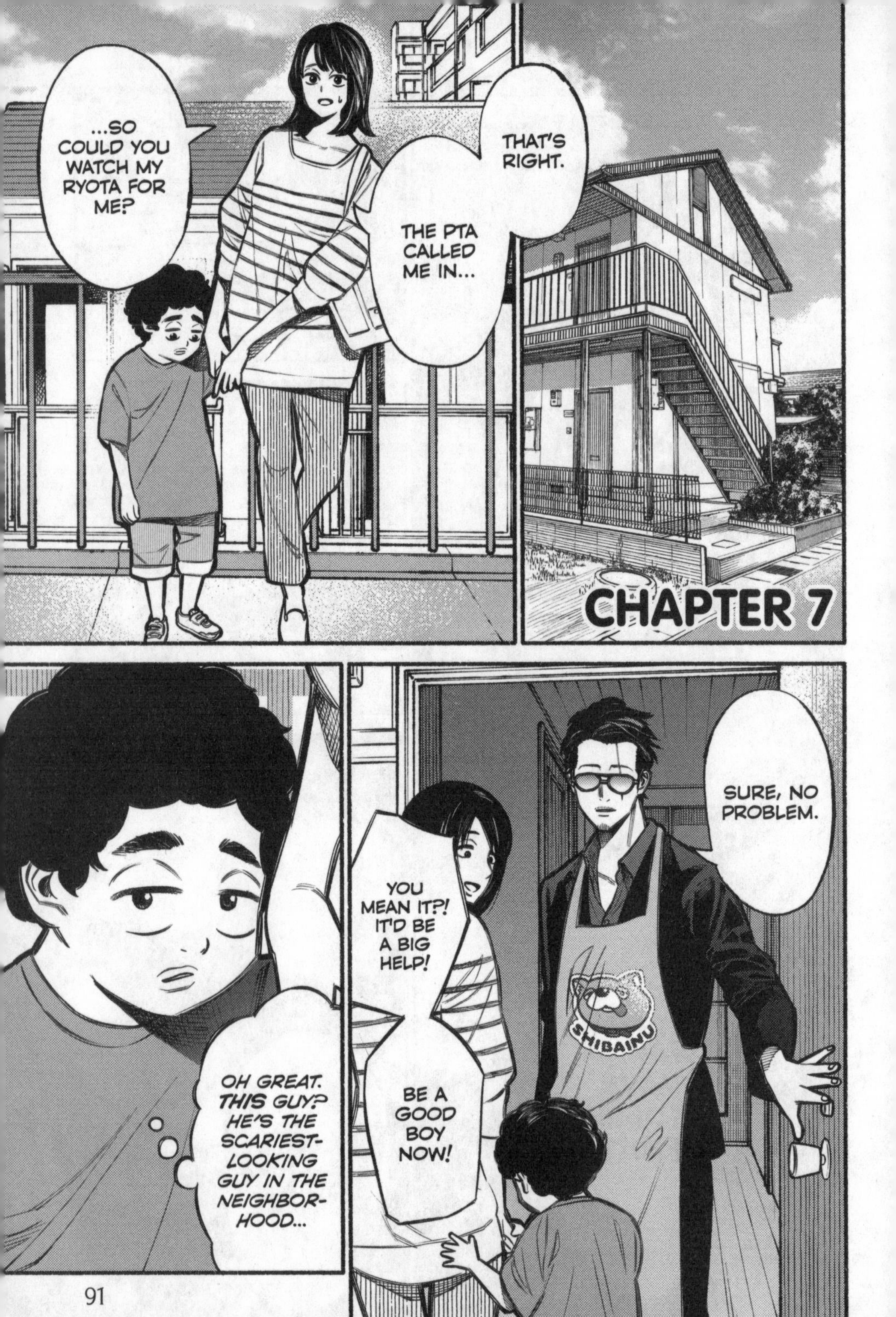
CHAPTER 7
THAT'S RIGHT.
THE PTA CALLED ME IN...
...SO COULD YOU WATCH MY RYOTA FOR ME?
SURE, NO PROBLEM.
YOU MEAN IT?! IT'D BE A BIG HELP!
SHIBAINU
BE A GOOD BOY NOW!
OH GREAT. THIS GUY? HE'S THE SCARIEST-LOOKING GUY IN THE NEIGHBOR-HOOD...

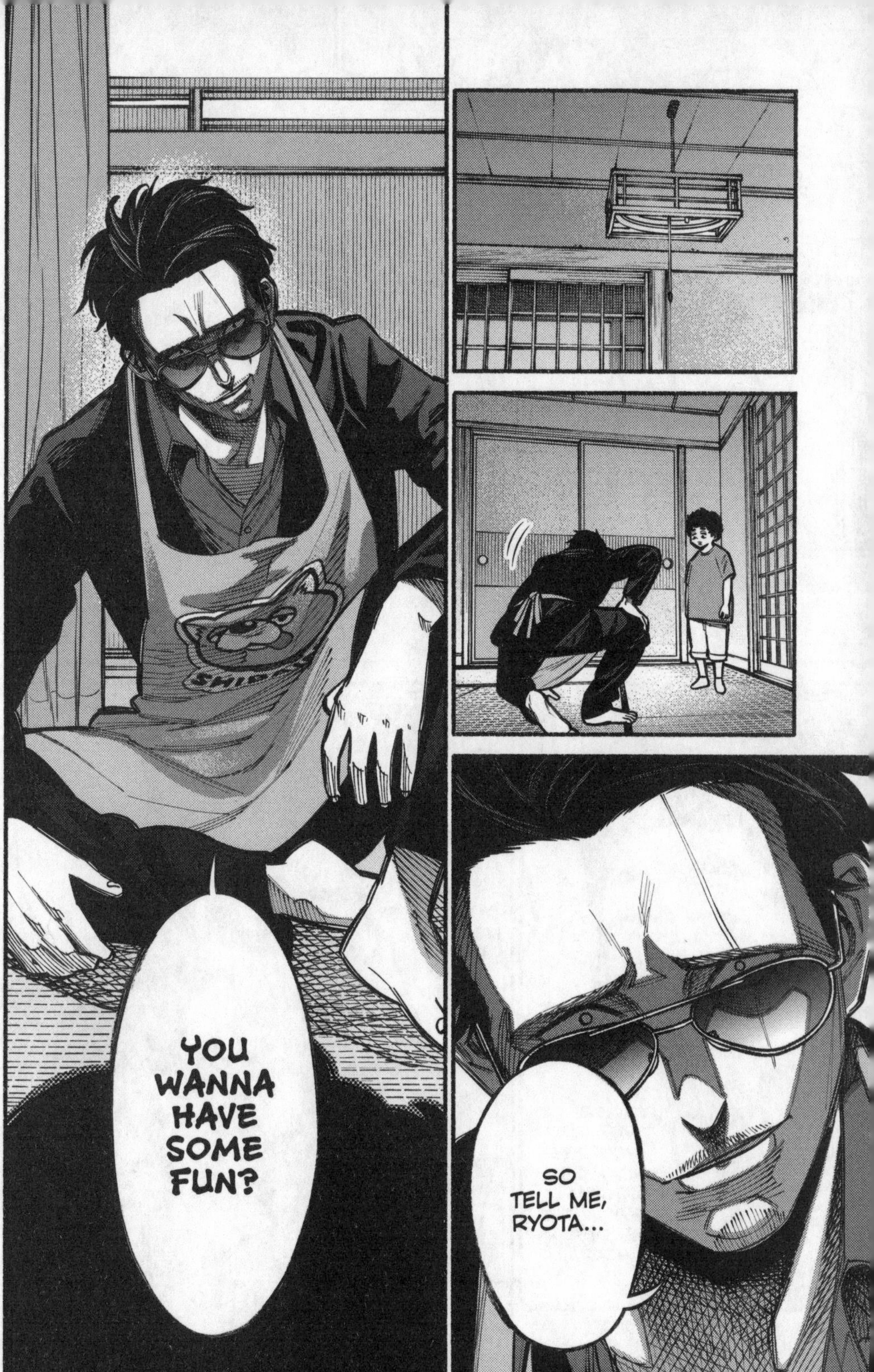
SO TELL ME, RYOTA...
YOU WANNA HAVE SOME FUN?

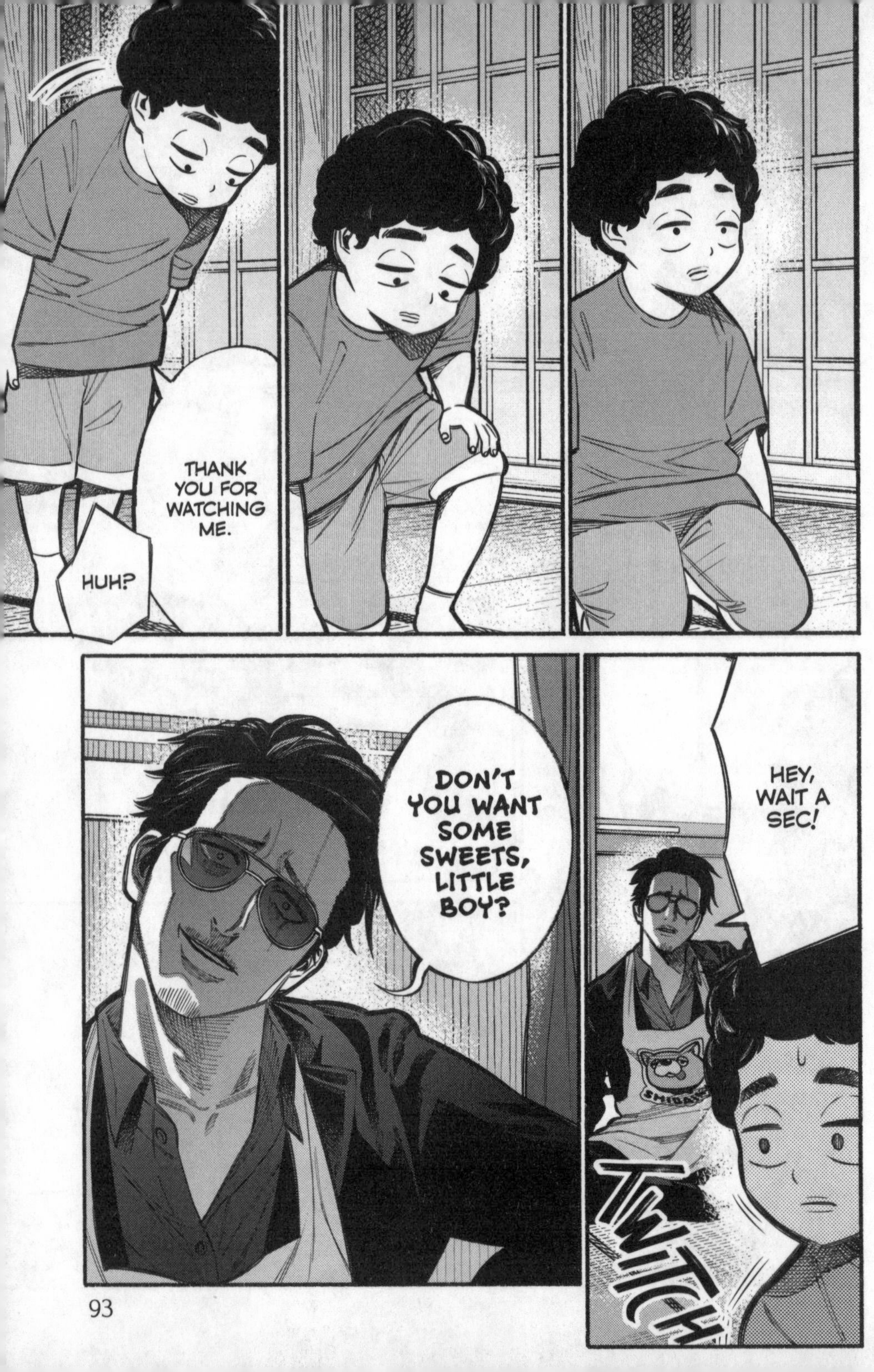
THANK YOU FOR WATCHING ME.
HUH?
HEY, WAIT A SEC!
TWITCH
DON'T YOU WANT SOME SWEETS, LITTLE BOY?

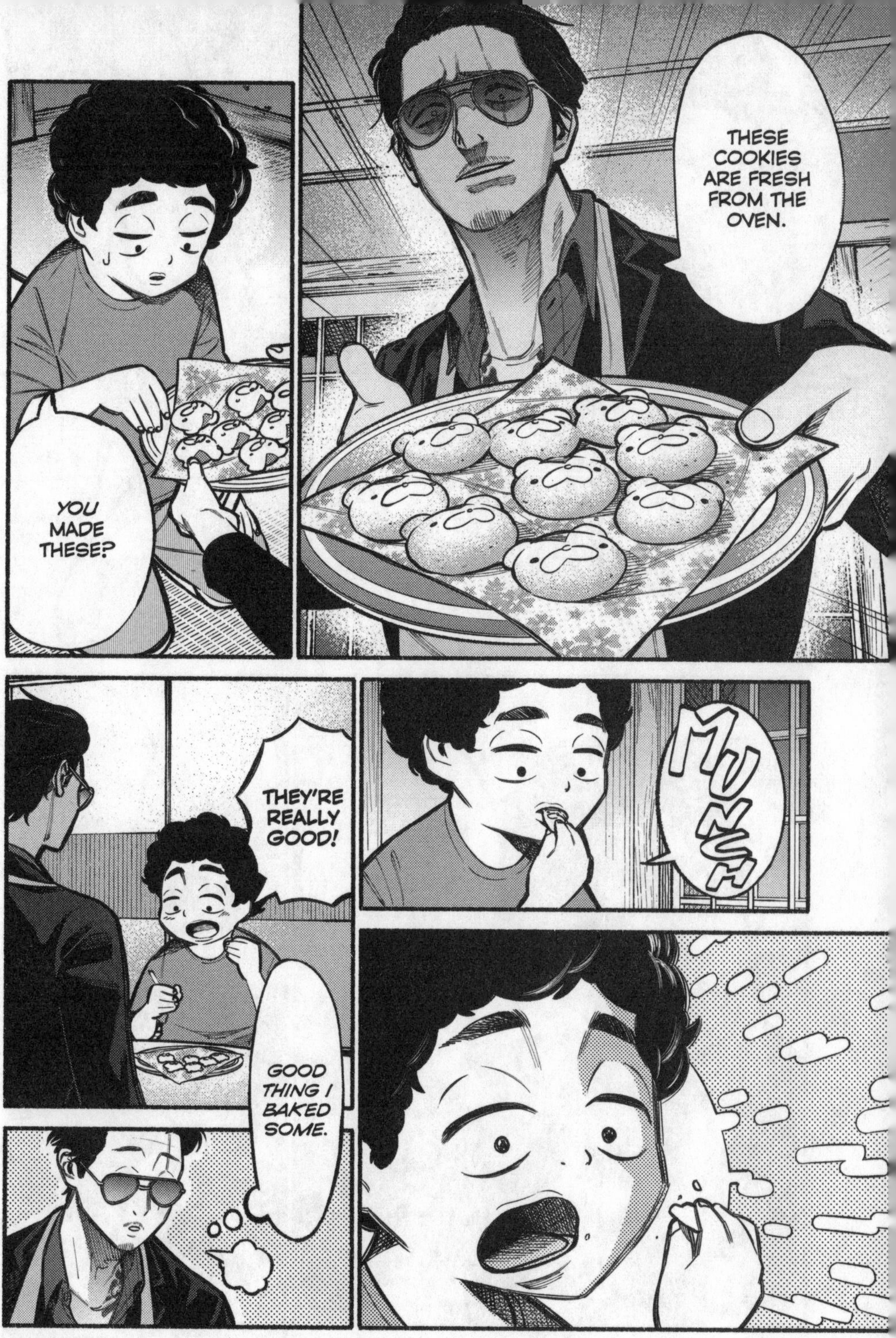
THESE COOKIES ARE FRESH FROM THE OVEN.
YOU MADE THESE?
MUNCH
THEY'RE REALLY GOOD!
GOOD THING I BAKED SOME.

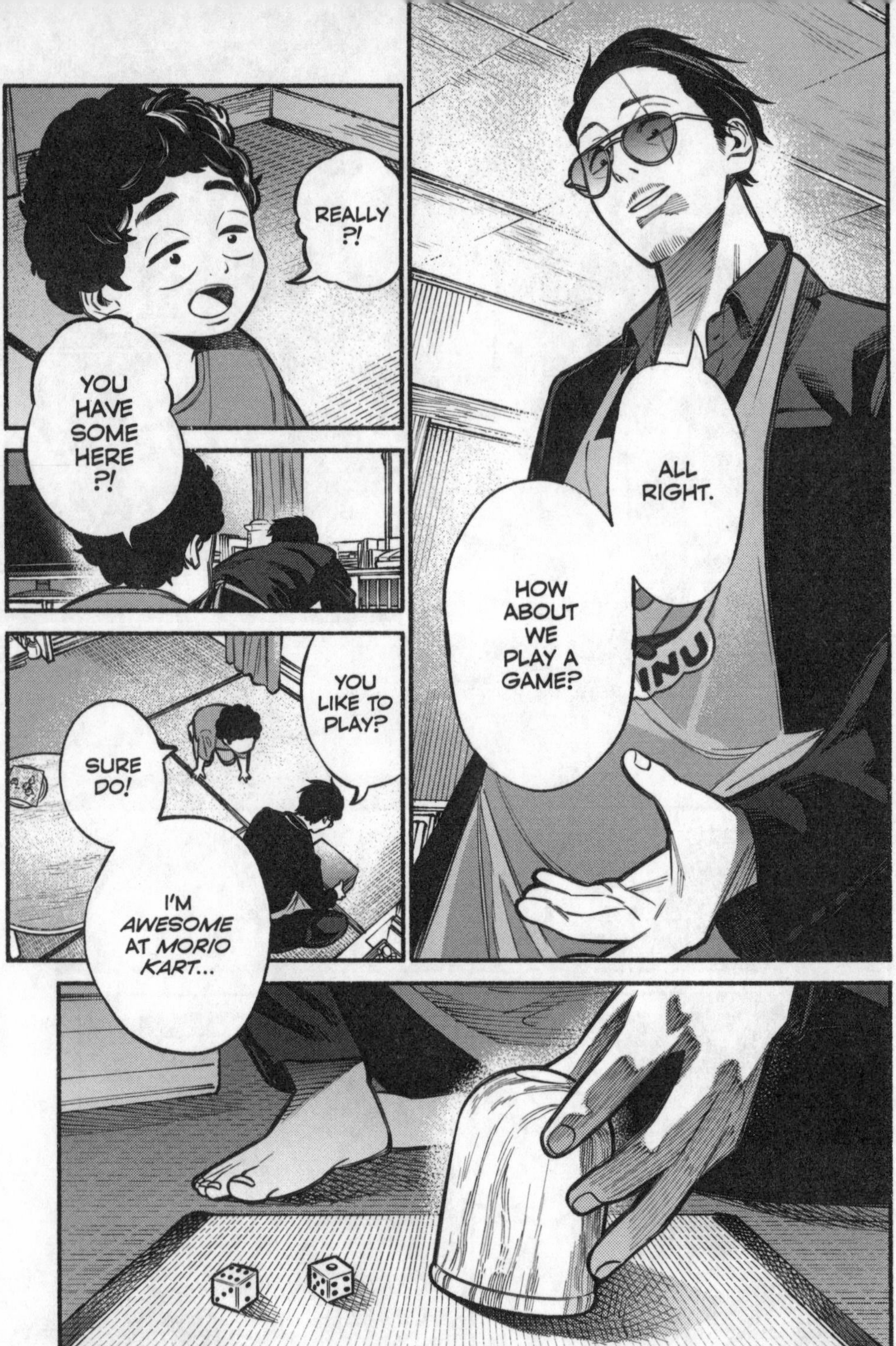
ALL RIGHT.
HOW ABOUT WE PLAY A GAME?
INU
REALLY ?!
YOU HAVE SOME HERE ?!
YOU LIKE TO PLAY?
SURE DO!
I'M *AWESOME* AT *MORIO KART*...

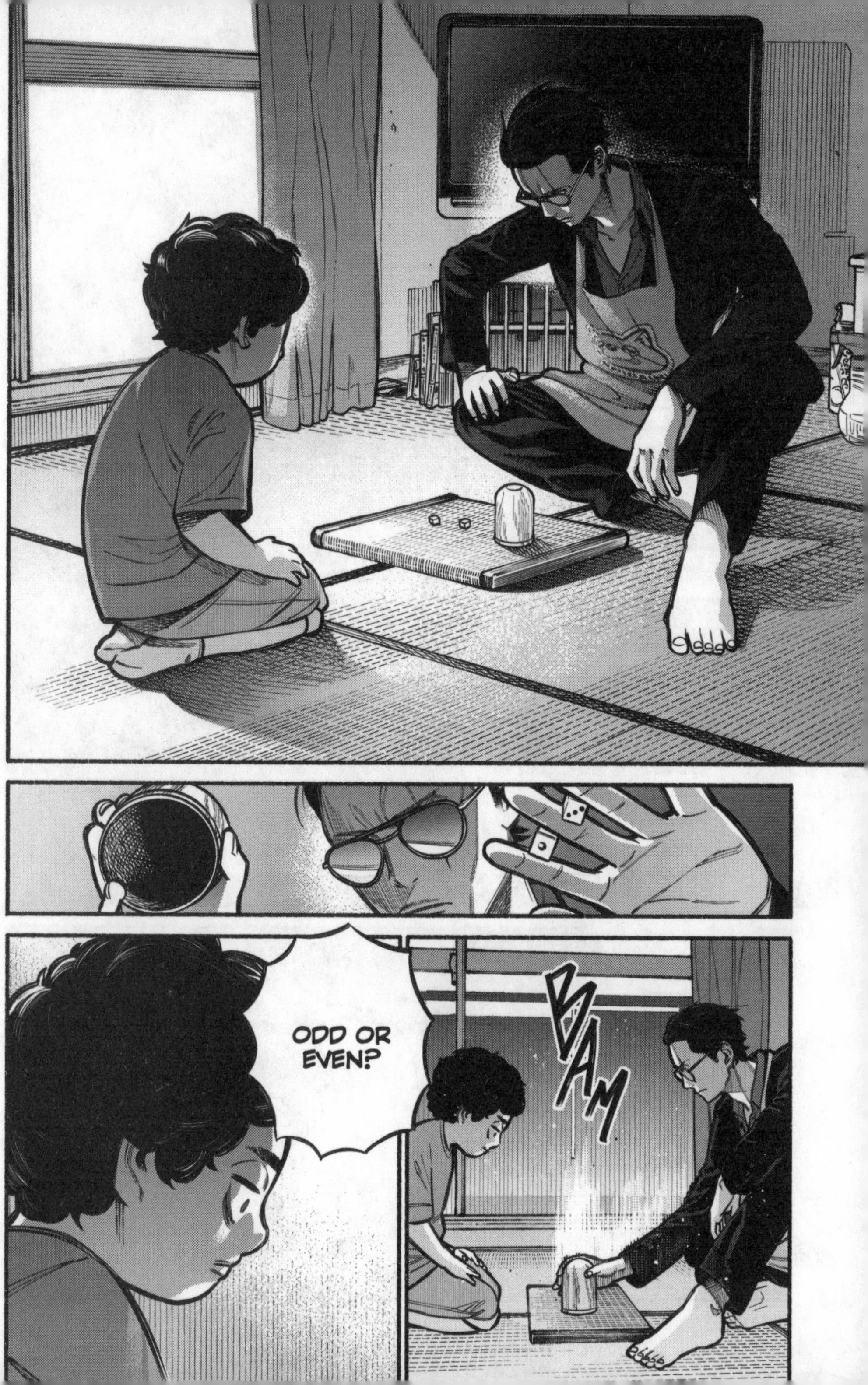
BAM
ODD OR EVEN?

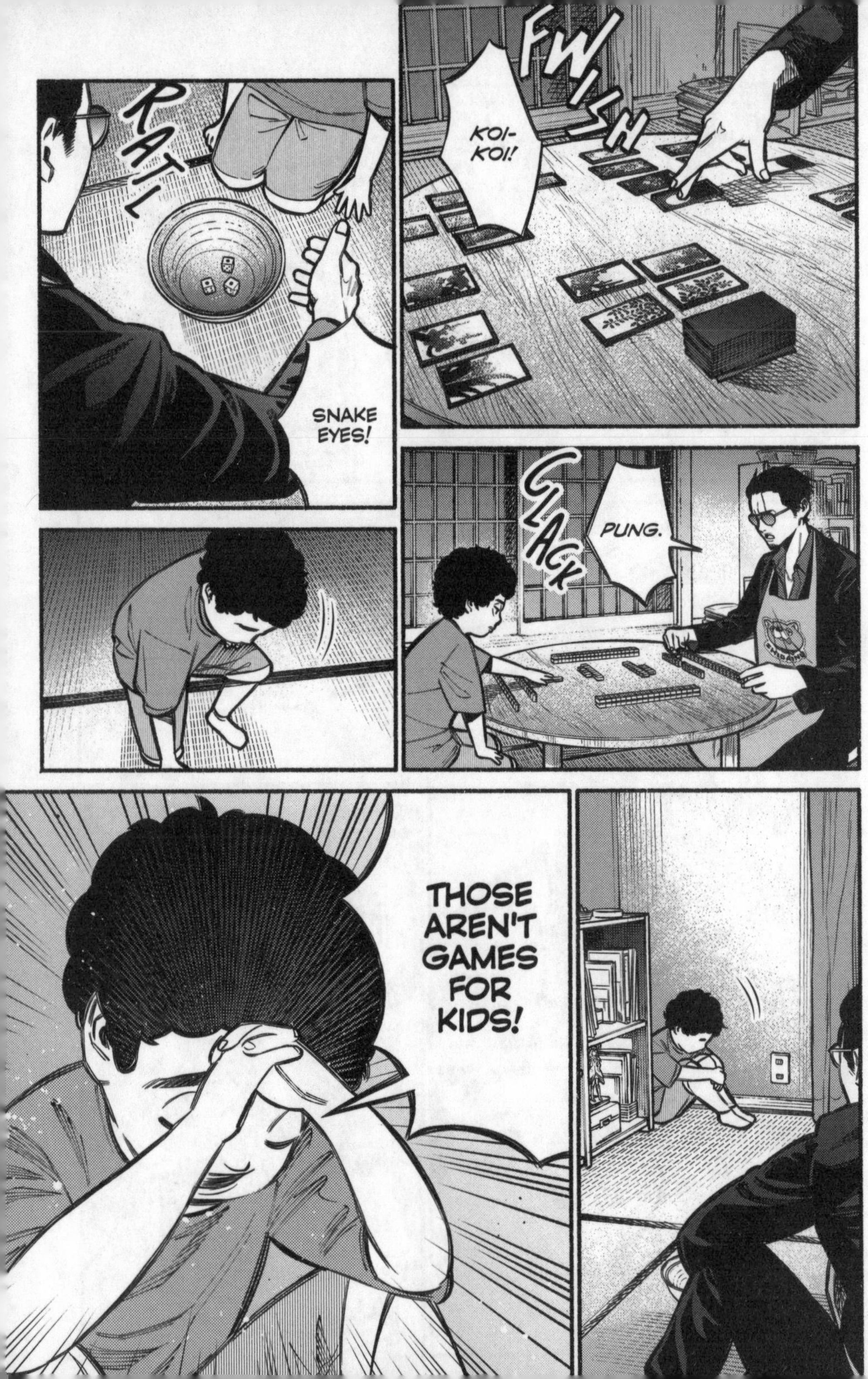
FWISH
KOI-KOI!
RATTL
SNAKE EYES!
CLACK
PUNG.
THOSE AREN'T GAMES FOR KIDS!

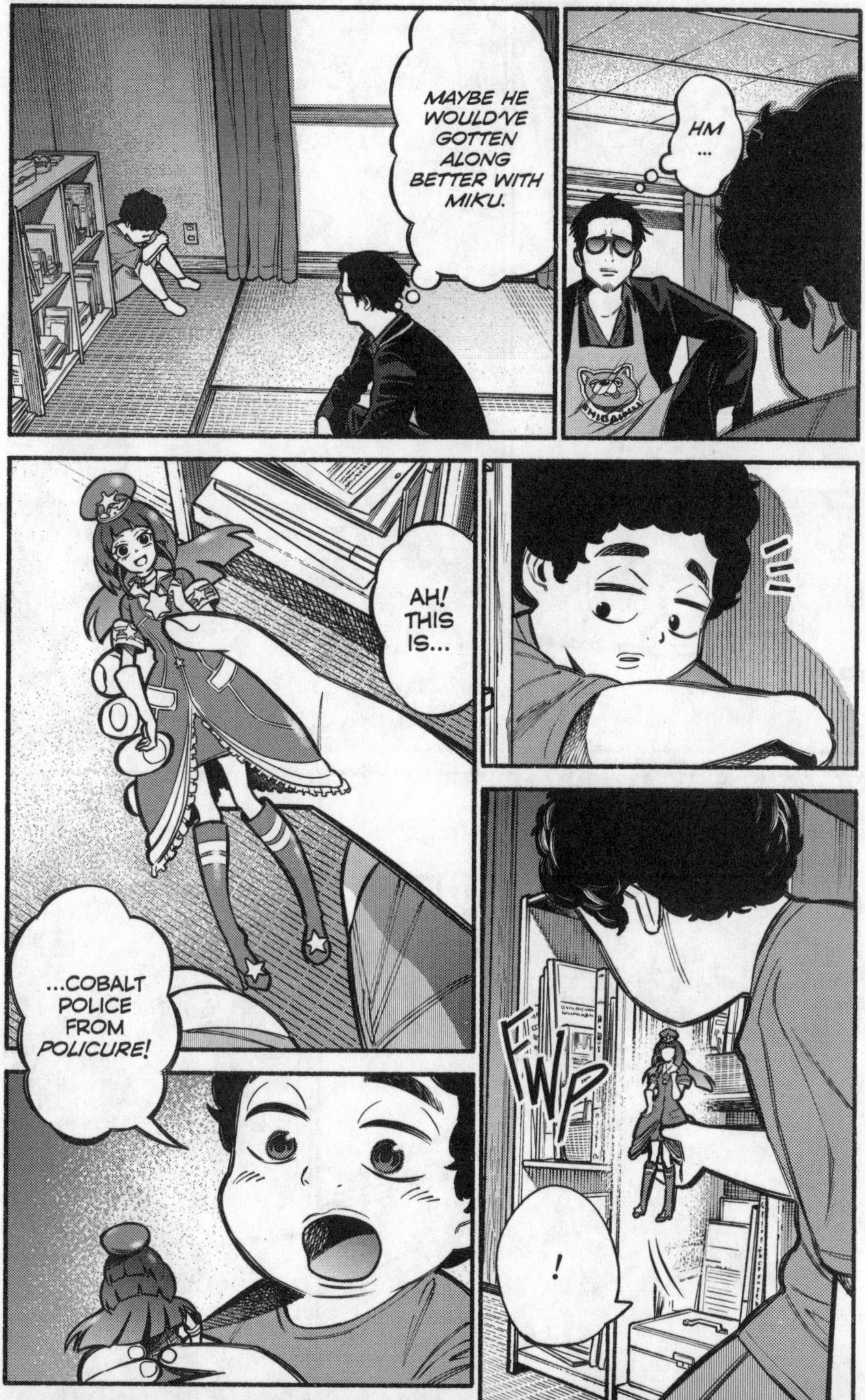
HM ...
MAYBE HE WOULD'VE GOTTEN ALONG BETTER WITH MIKU.
AH! THIS IS...
FWP
!
...COBALT POLICE FROM POLICURE!

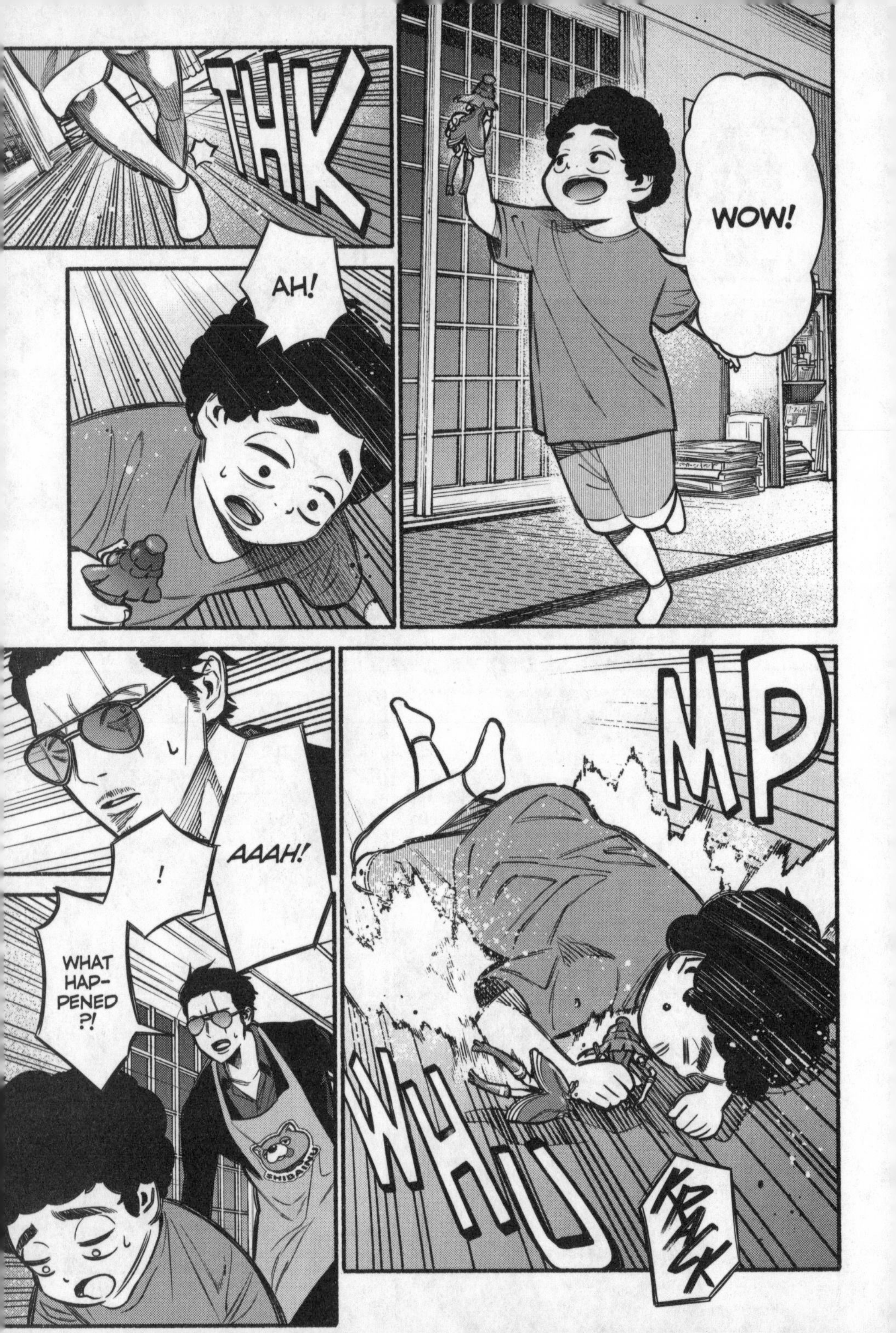
WOW!
THK
AH!
WHU
MP
AAAH!
!
WHAT HAP-PENED?!

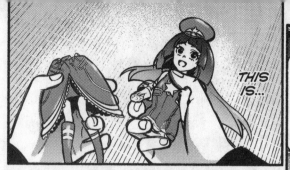

THIS IS...

ARE YOU HURT, RYOTA?!

I-I'M SORRY...

IT BROKE...

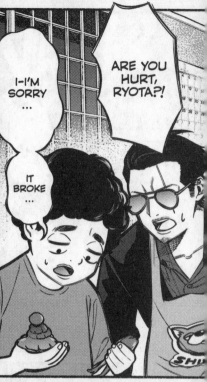

...MIKU'S PRECIOUS...

...POLICURE THING!

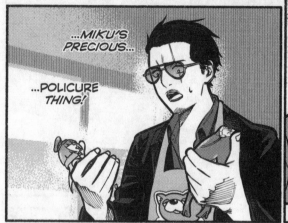

PULL YOURSELF TOGETH-ER...

...POLI-CURE BLUE ONE!

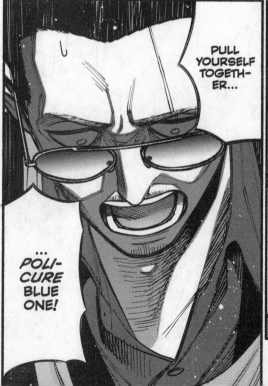

HEY! HEY!

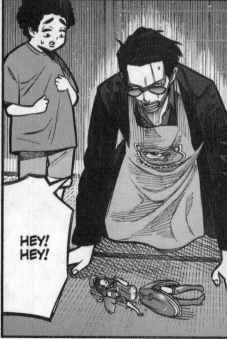

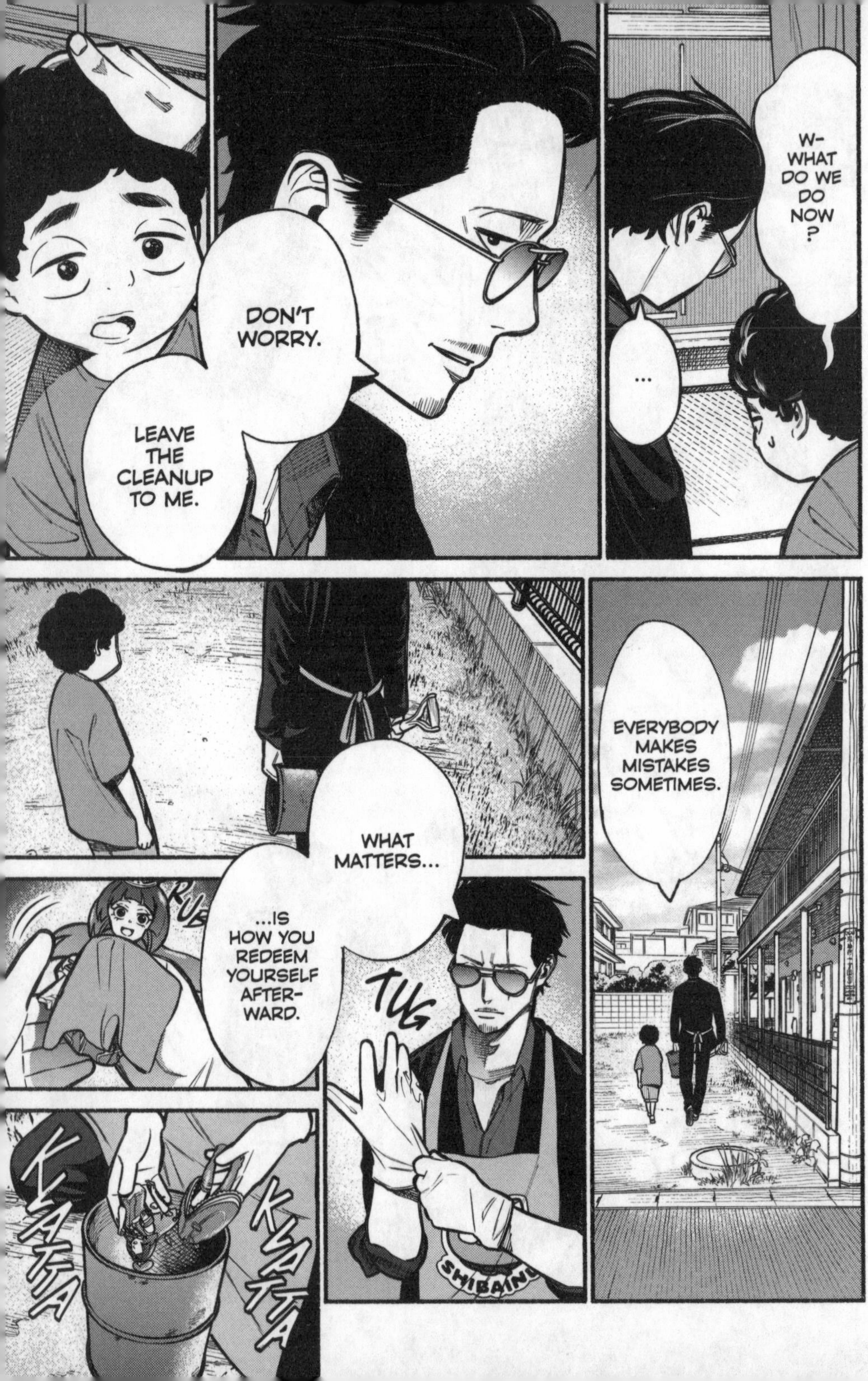
W-WHAT DO WE DO NOW?
...
DON'T WORRY.
LEAVE THE CLEANUP TO ME.
EVERYBODY MAKES MISTAKES SOMETIMES.
WHAT MATTERS...
TUG
RUB
...IS HOW YOU REDEEM YOURSELF AFTER-WARD.

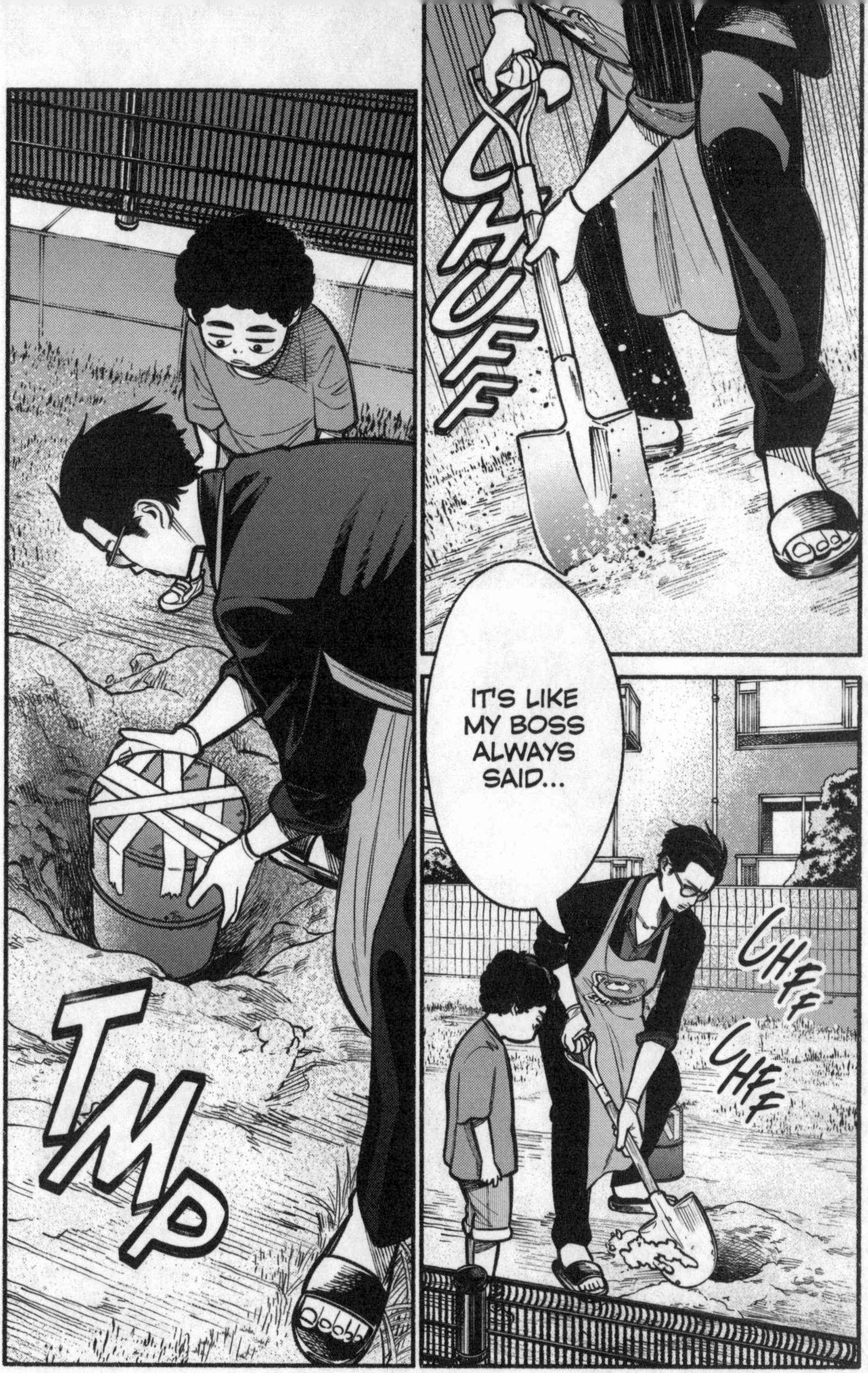
CHUFF
IT'S LIKE MY BOSS ALWAYS SAID...
CHFF CHFF
TMP

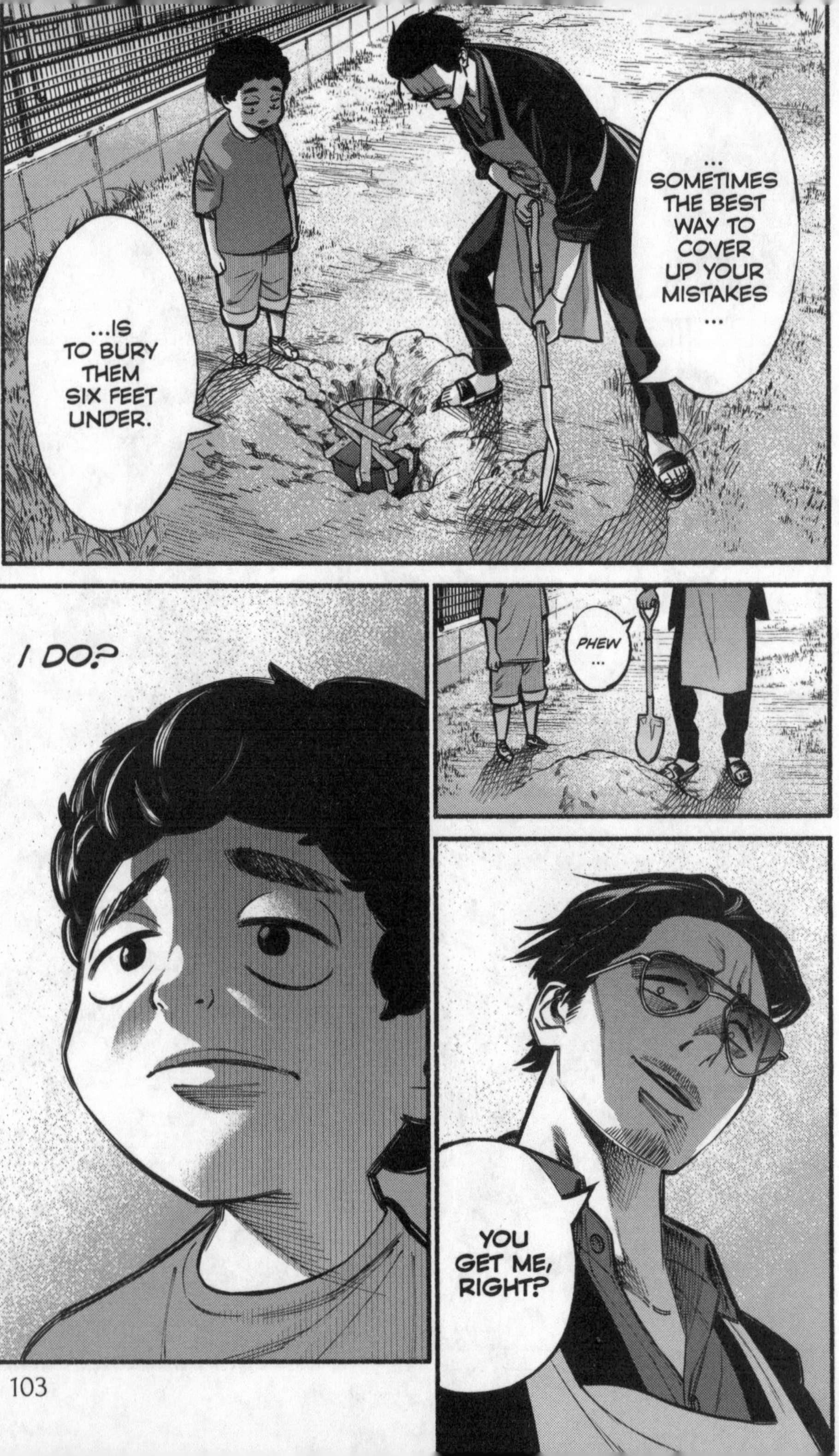
... SOMETIMES THE BEST WAY TO COVER UP YOUR MISTAKES ...
...IS TO BURY THEM SIX FEET UNDER.
PHEW ...
YOU GET ME, RIGHT?
I DO?

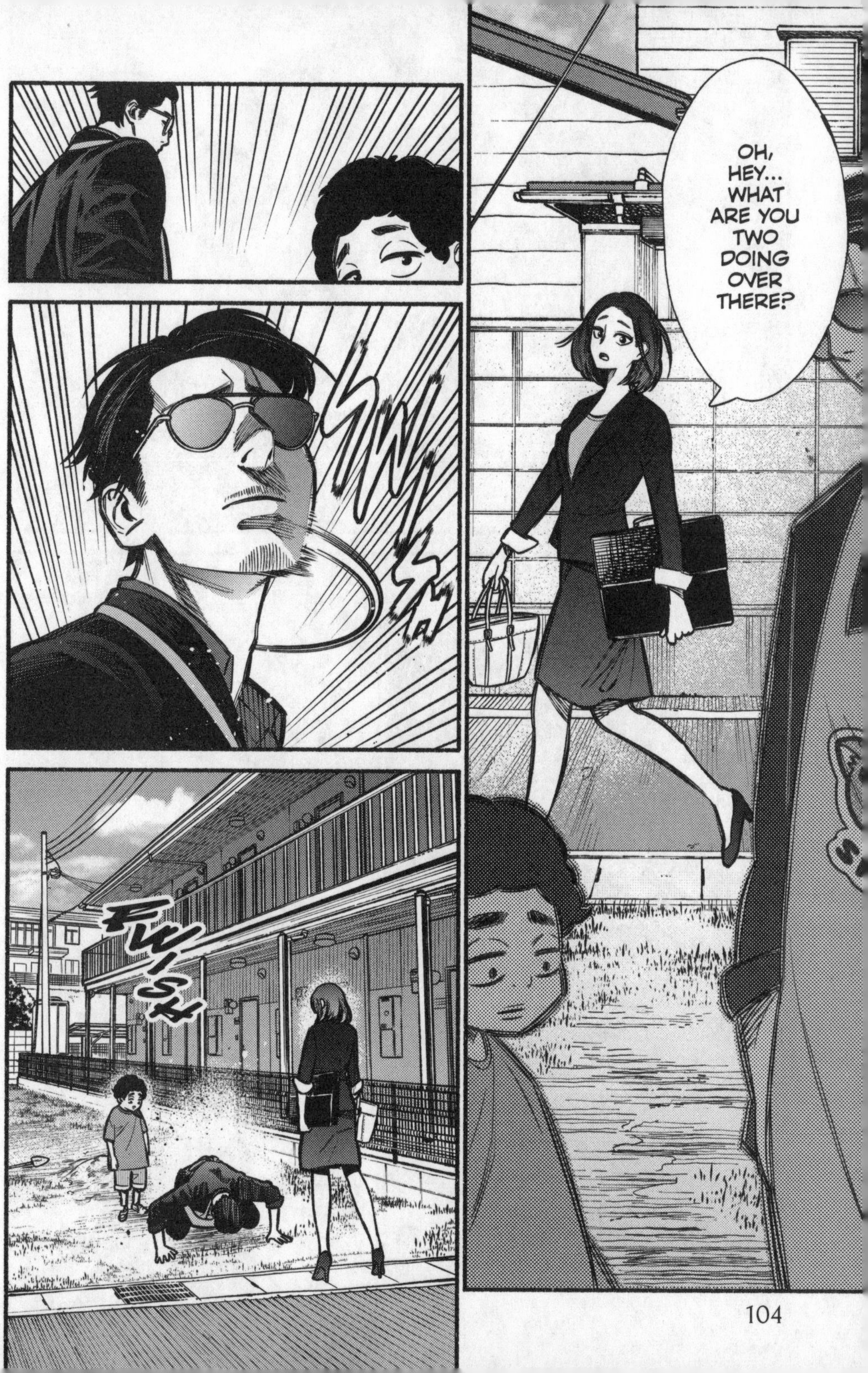
OH, HEY... WHAT ARE YOU TWO DOING OVER THERE?
FWISH

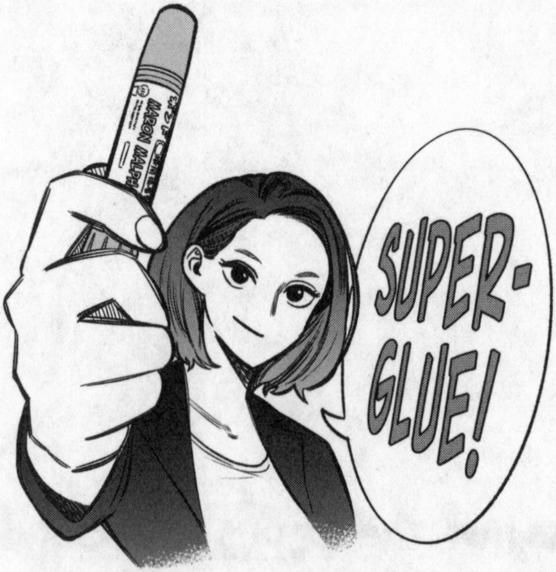
SUPER-GLUE!

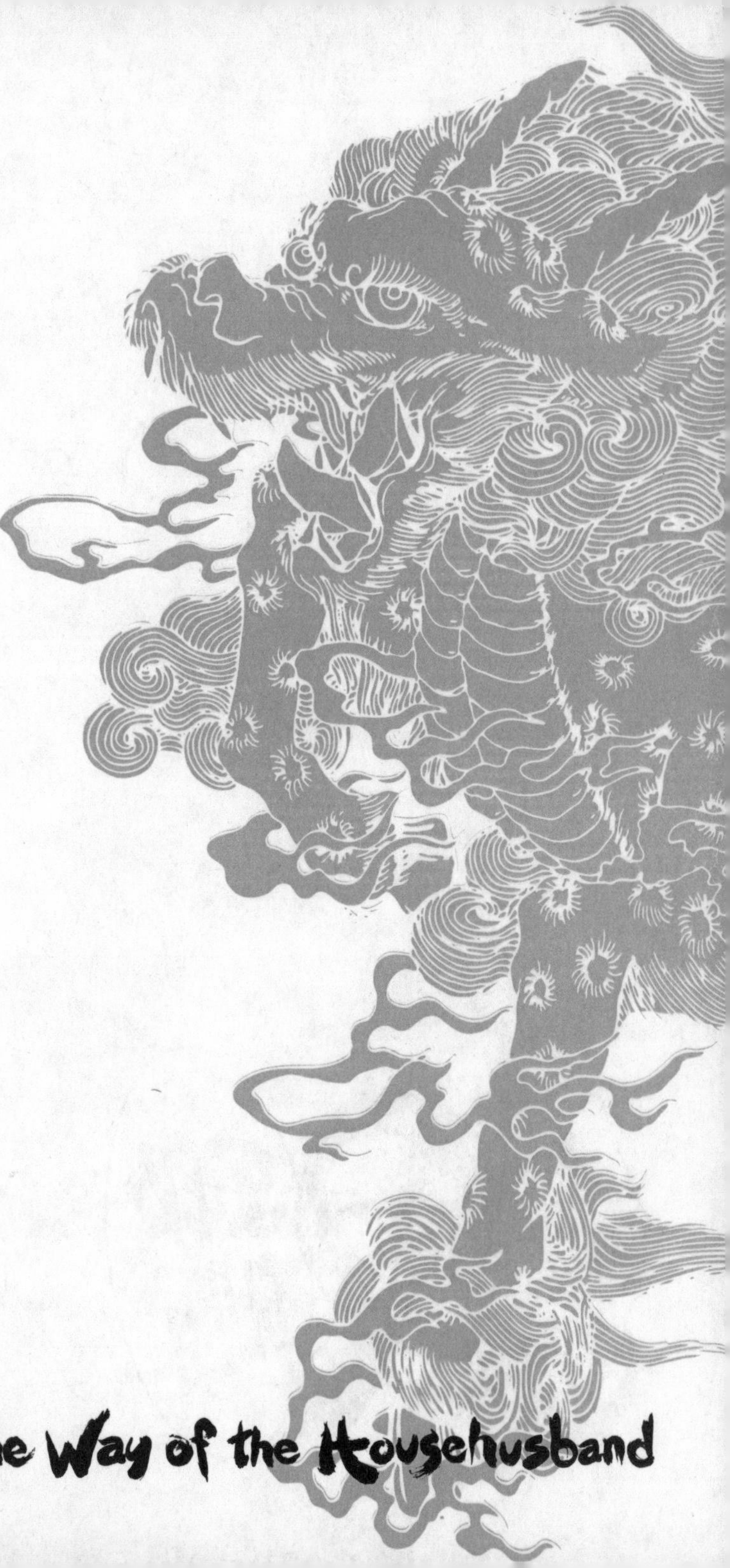

# The Way of the Househusband

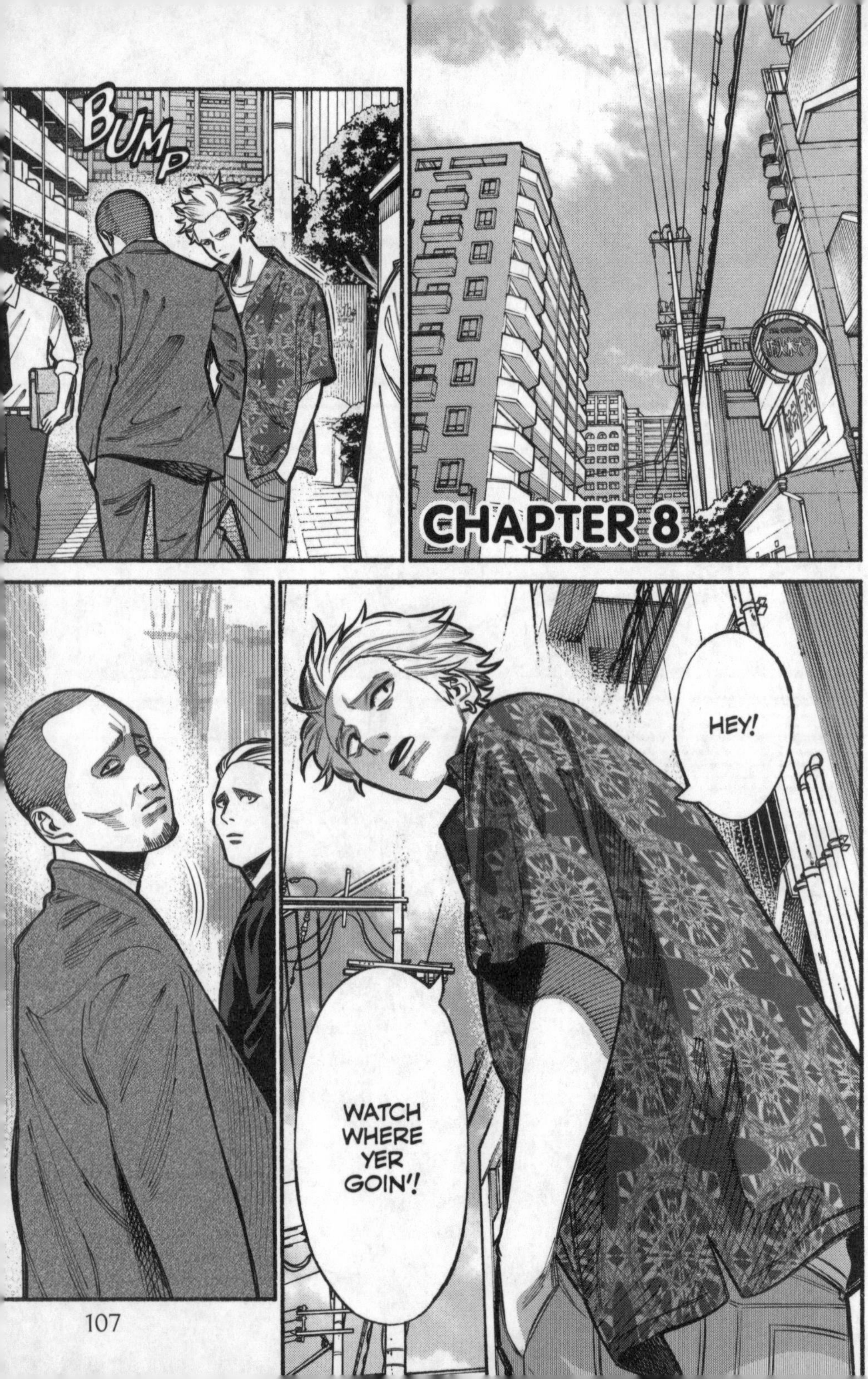
CHAPTER 8
BUMP
HEY!
WATCH WHERE YER GOIN'!

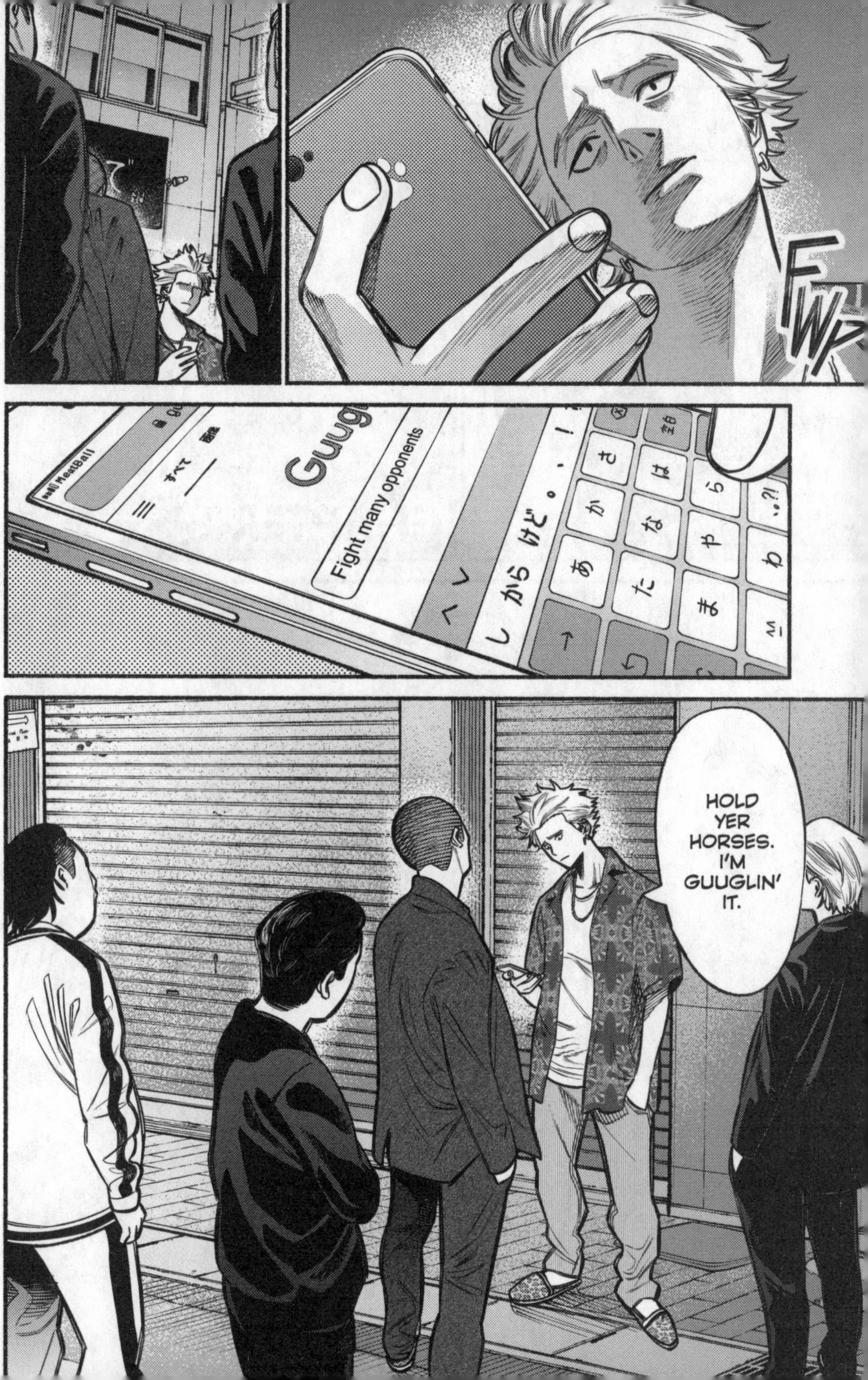
FWP
Fight many opponents
HOLD YER HORSES. I'M GUUGLIN' IT.

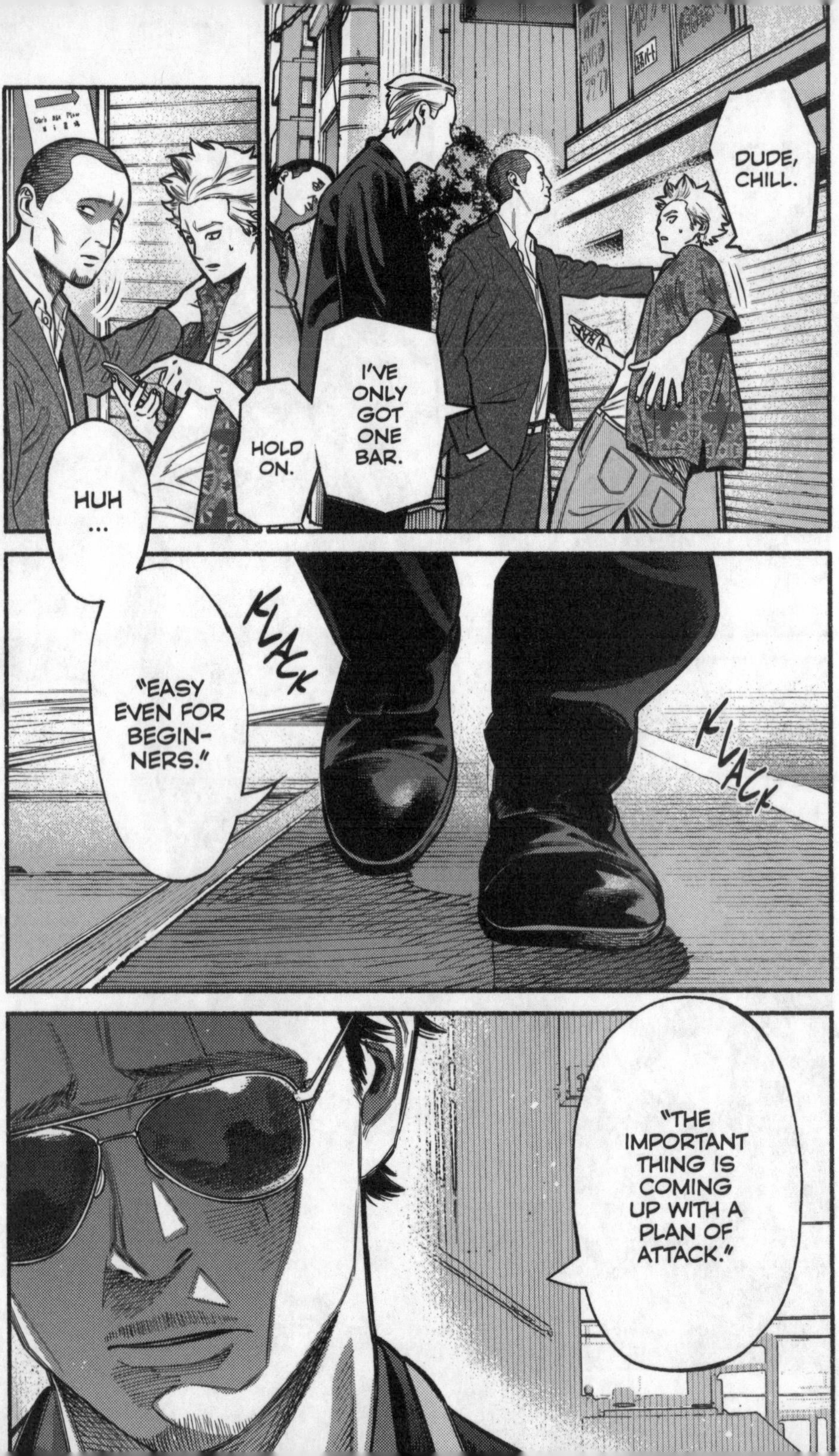
DUDE, CHILL.
I'VE ONLY GOT ONE BAR.
HOLD ON.
HUH ...
"EASY EVEN FOR BEGIN-NERS."
KLACK
KLACK
"THE IMPORTANT THING IS COMING UP WITH A PLAN OF ATTACK."

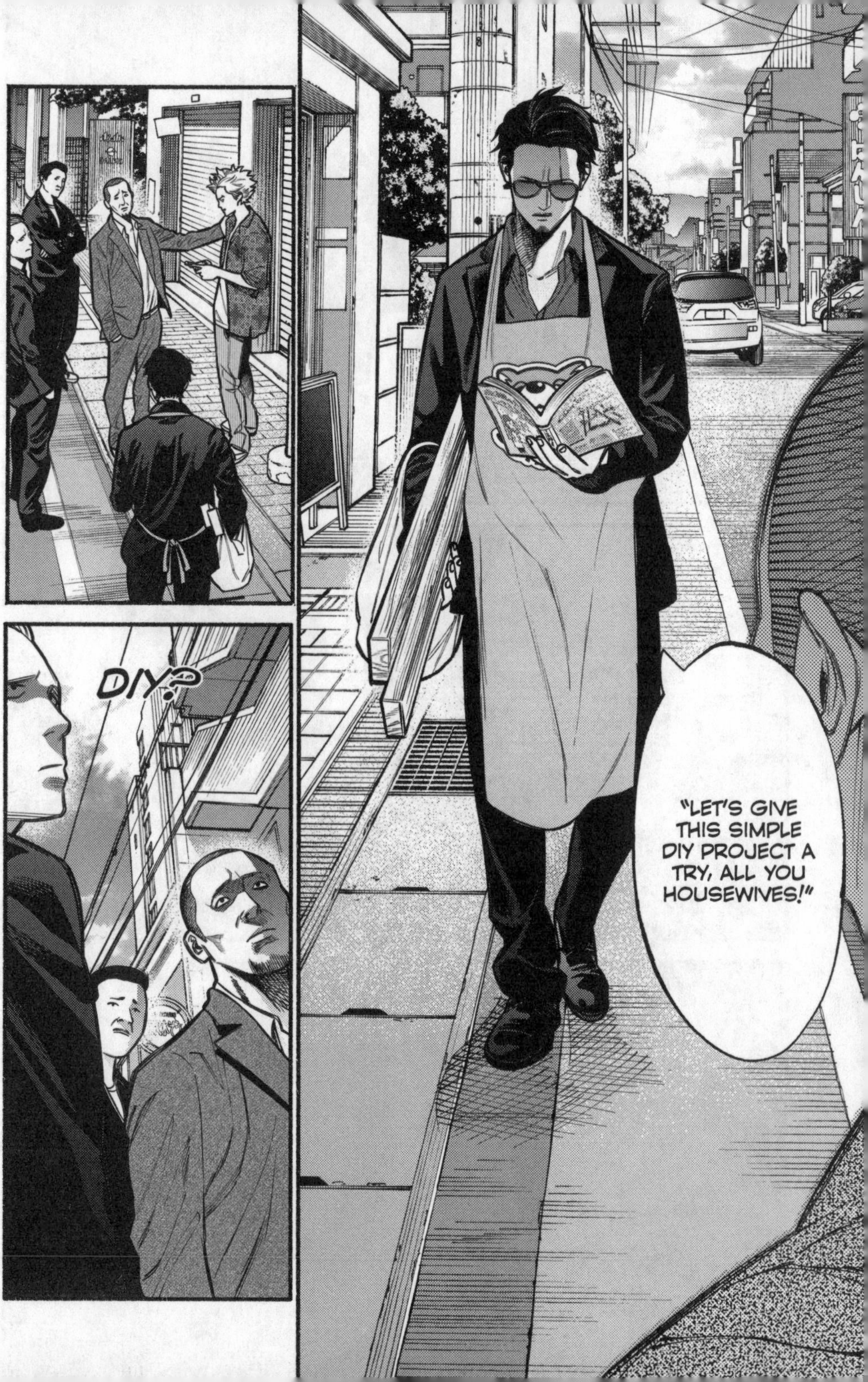
"LET'S GIVE THIS SIMPLE DIY PROJECT A TRY, ALL YOU HOUSEWIVES!"
DIY?

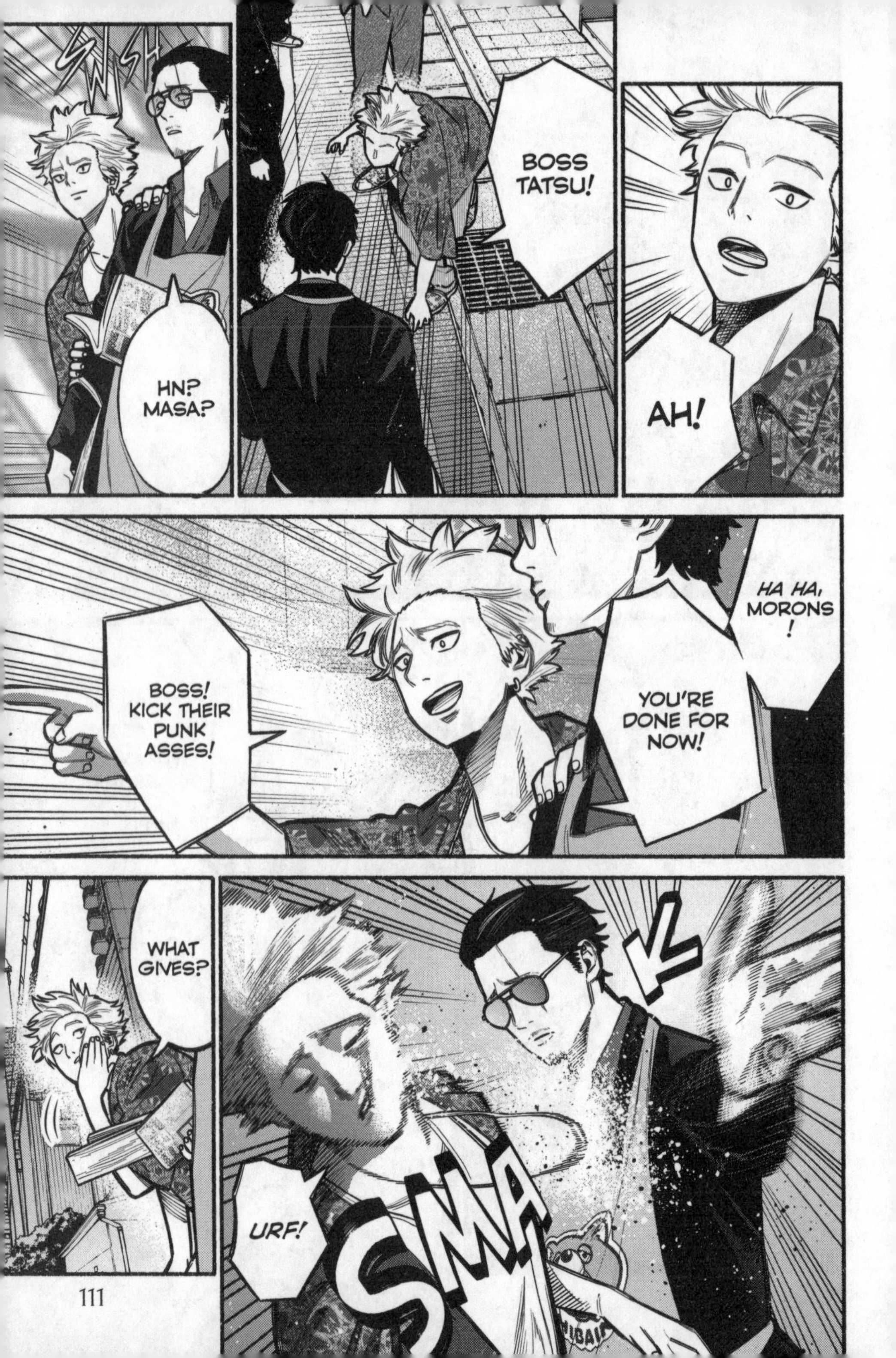

AH!
BOSS TATSU!
SWISH
HN? MASA?
HA HA, MORONS!
YOU'RE DONE FOR NOW!
BOSS! KICK THEIR PUNK ASSES!
K
SMA
URF!
WHAT GIVES?

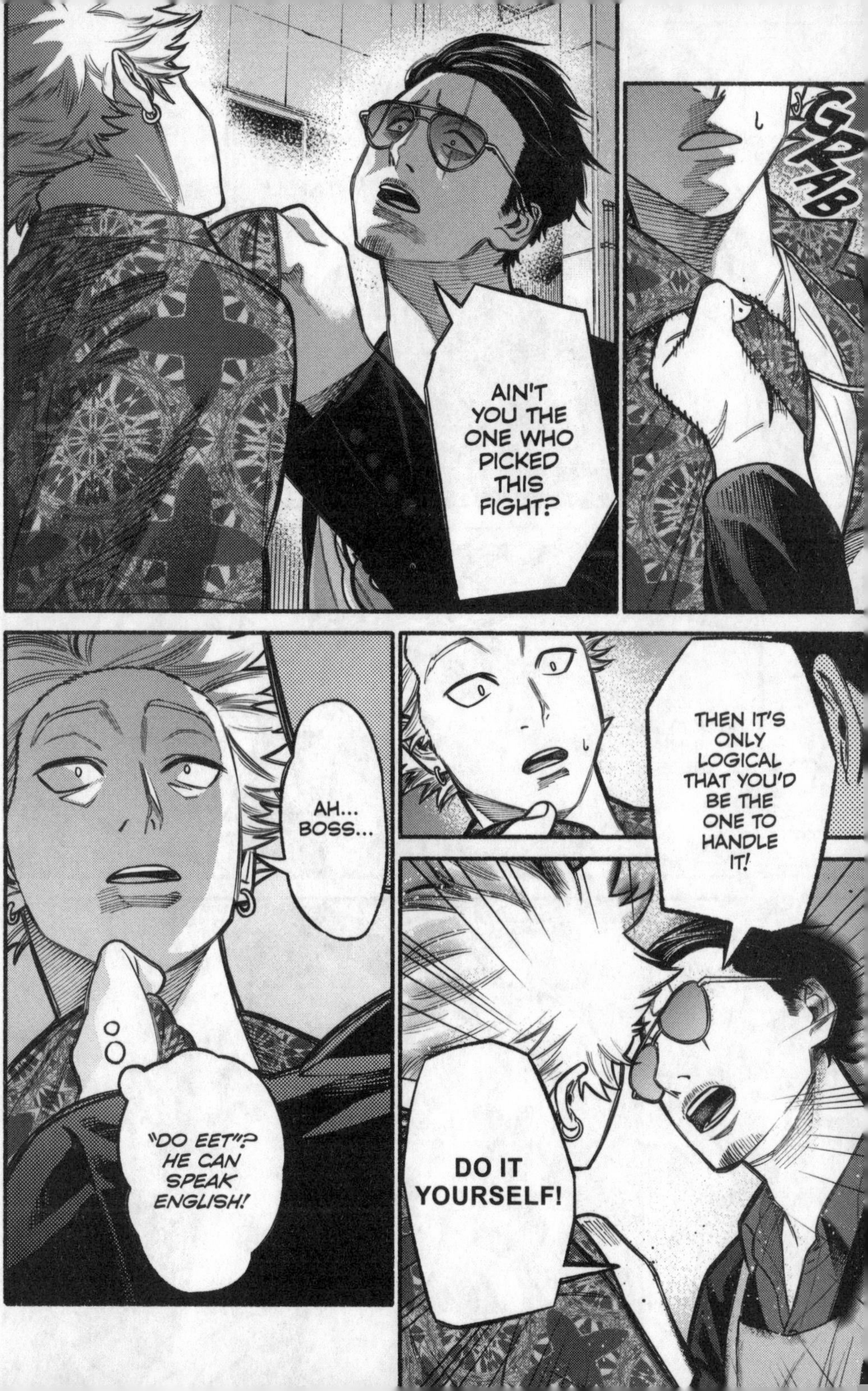
GRAB
AIN'T YOU THE ONE WHO PICKED THIS FIGHT?
THEN IT'S ONLY LOGICAL THAT YOU'D BE THE ONE TO HANDLE IT!
DO IT YOURSELF!
AH... BOSS...
"DO EET"!? HE CAN SPEAK ENGLISH!

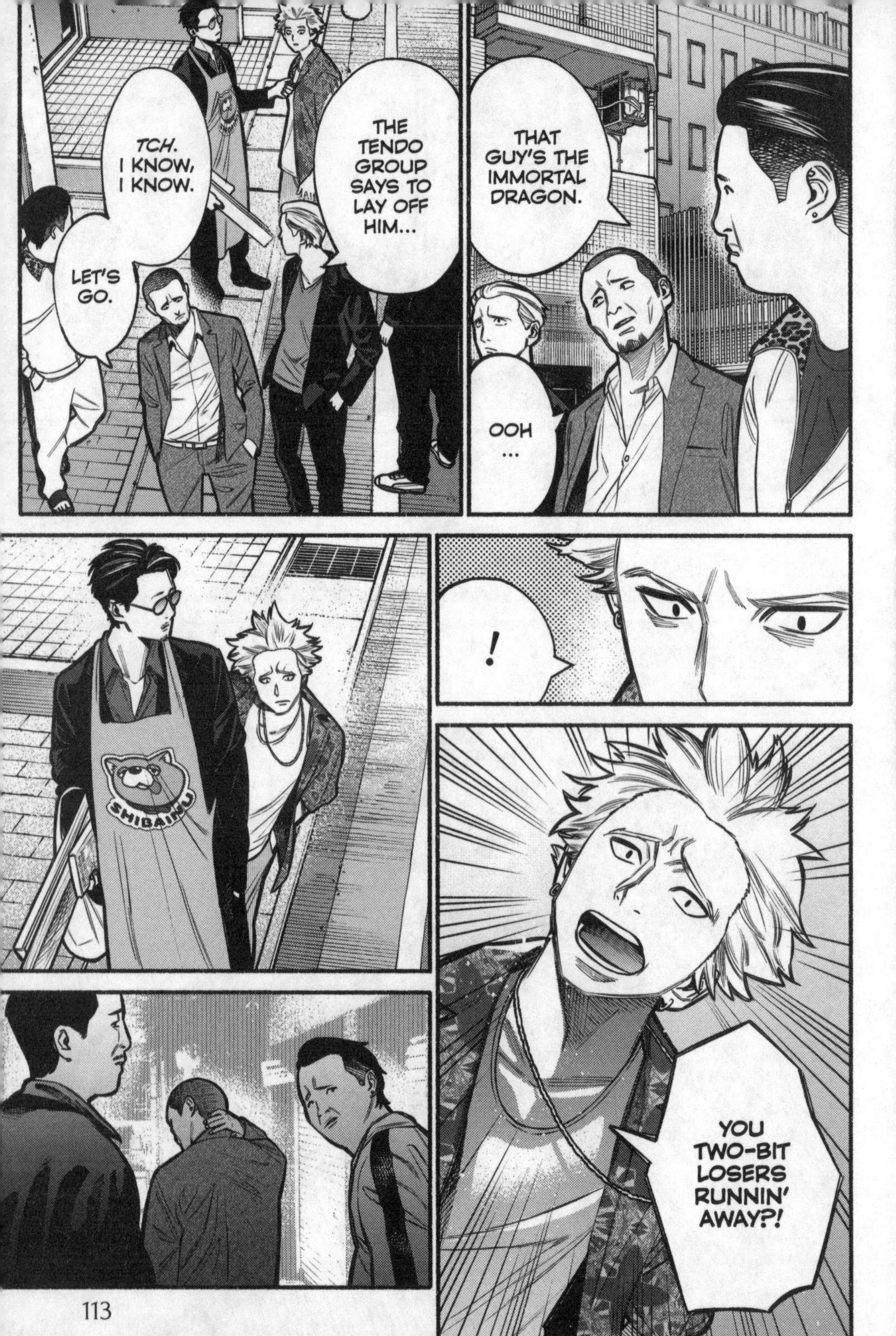
THAT GUY'S THE IMMORTAL DRAGON.
OOH...
THE TENDO GROUP SAYS TO LAY OFF HIM...
*TCH*. I KNOW, I KNOW.
LET'S GO.
!
YOU TWO-BIT LOSERS RUNNIN' AWAY?!

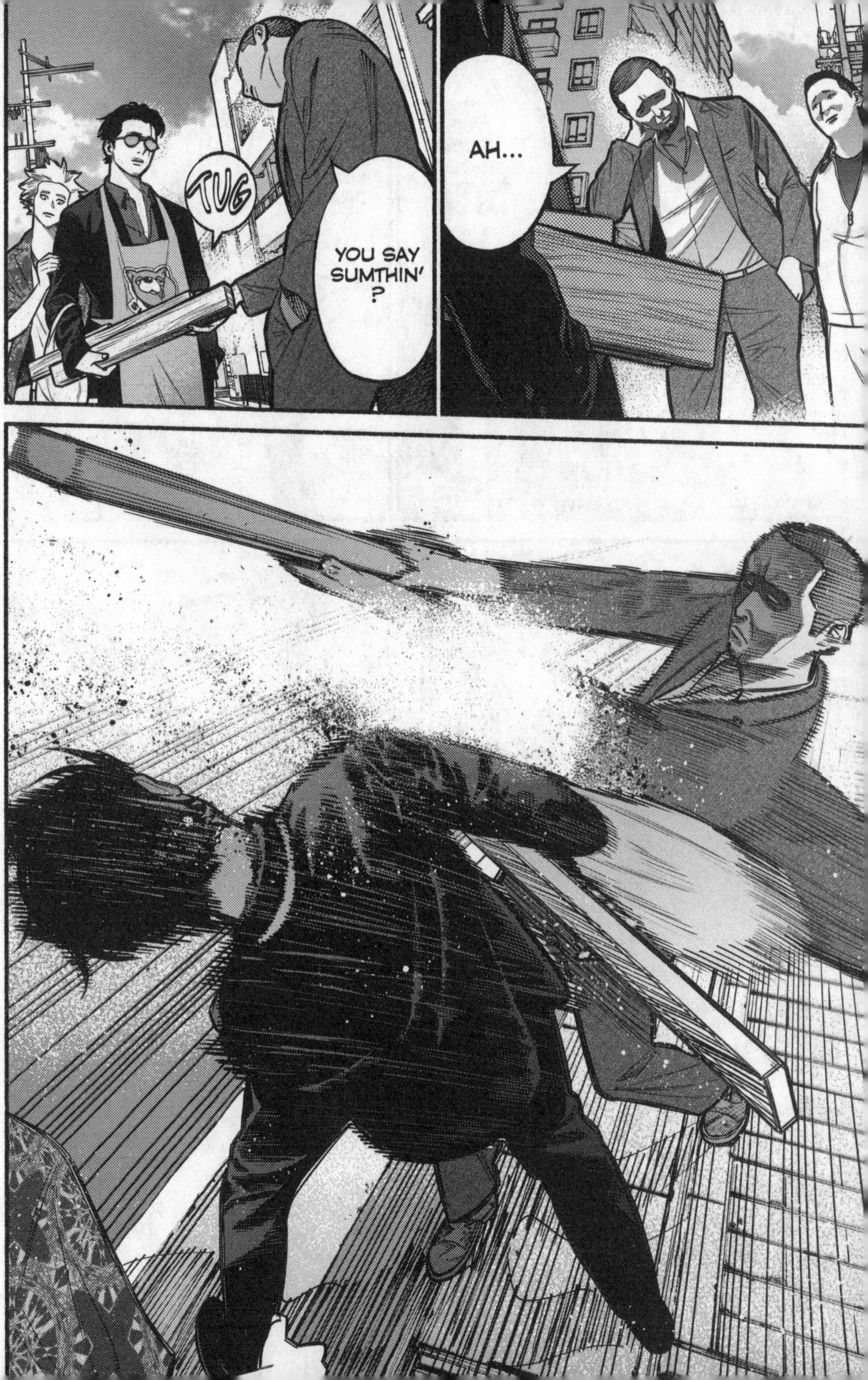
AH...
YOU SAY SUMTHIN' ?
TUG

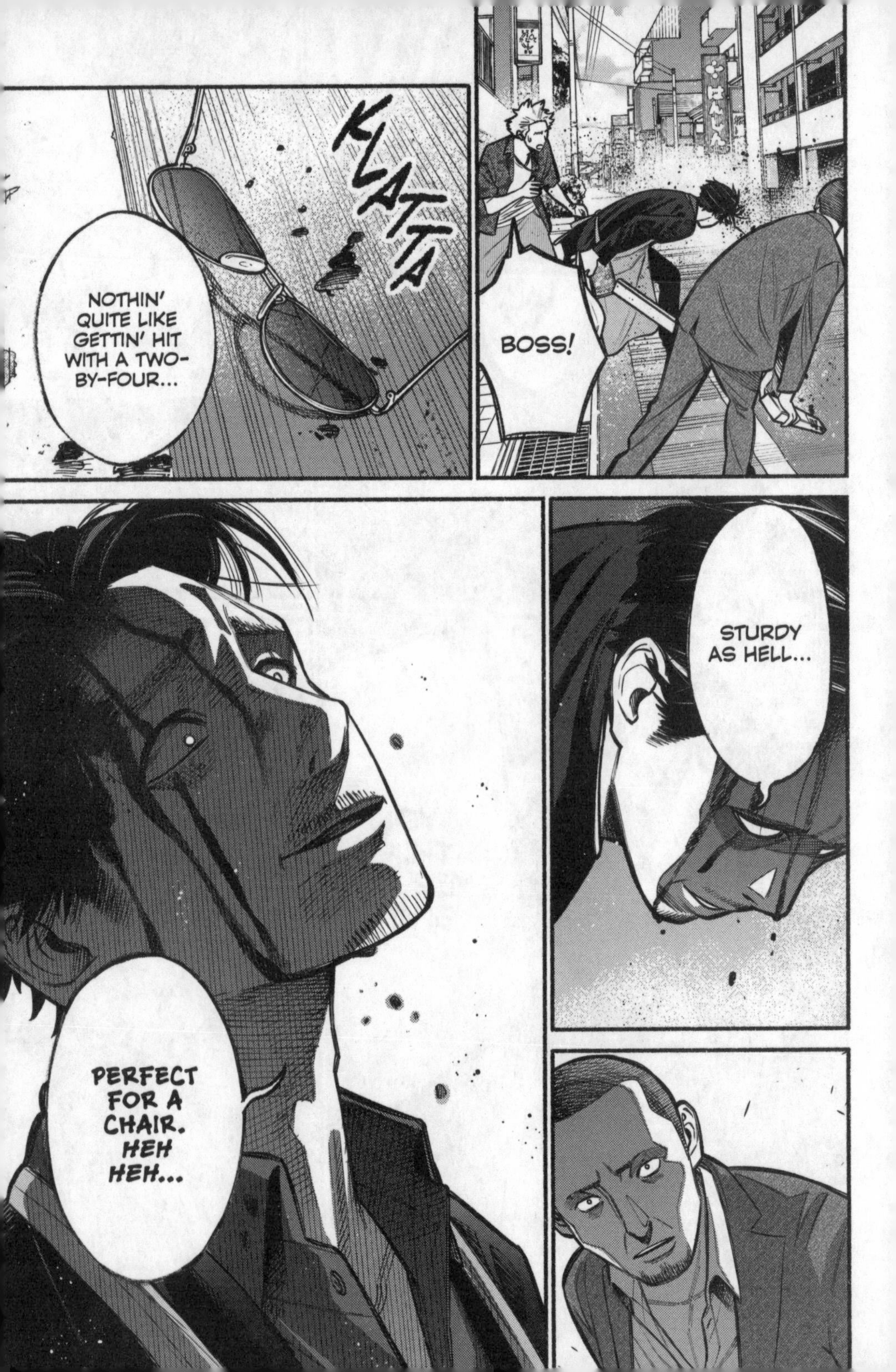

はんしん
BOSS!
KLATTA
NOTHIN' QUITE LIKE GETTIN' HIT WITH A TWO-BY-FOUR...
STURDY AS HELL...
PERFECT FOR A CHAIR. HEH HEH...

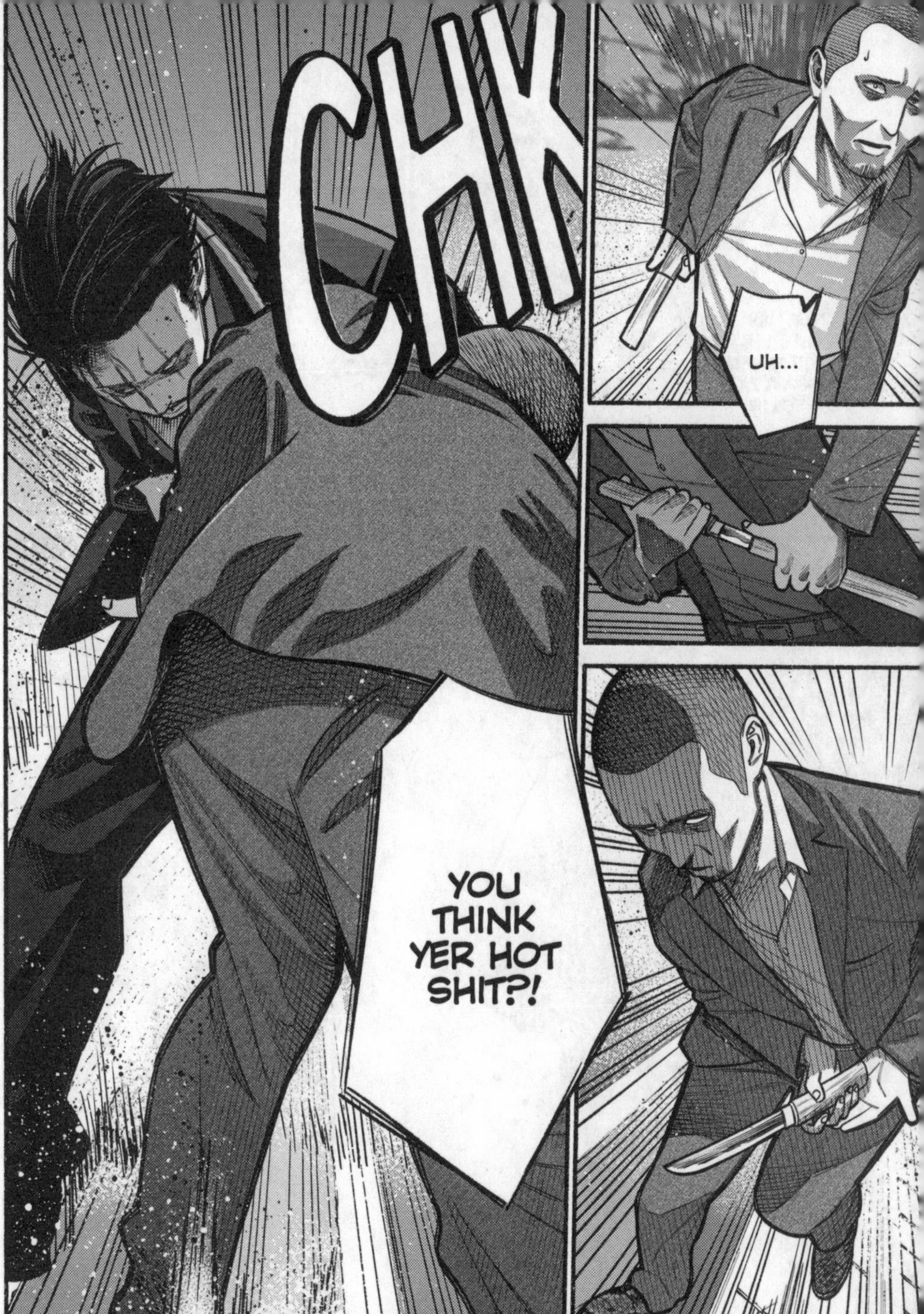
UH...
CHK
YOU THINK YER HOT SHIT?!

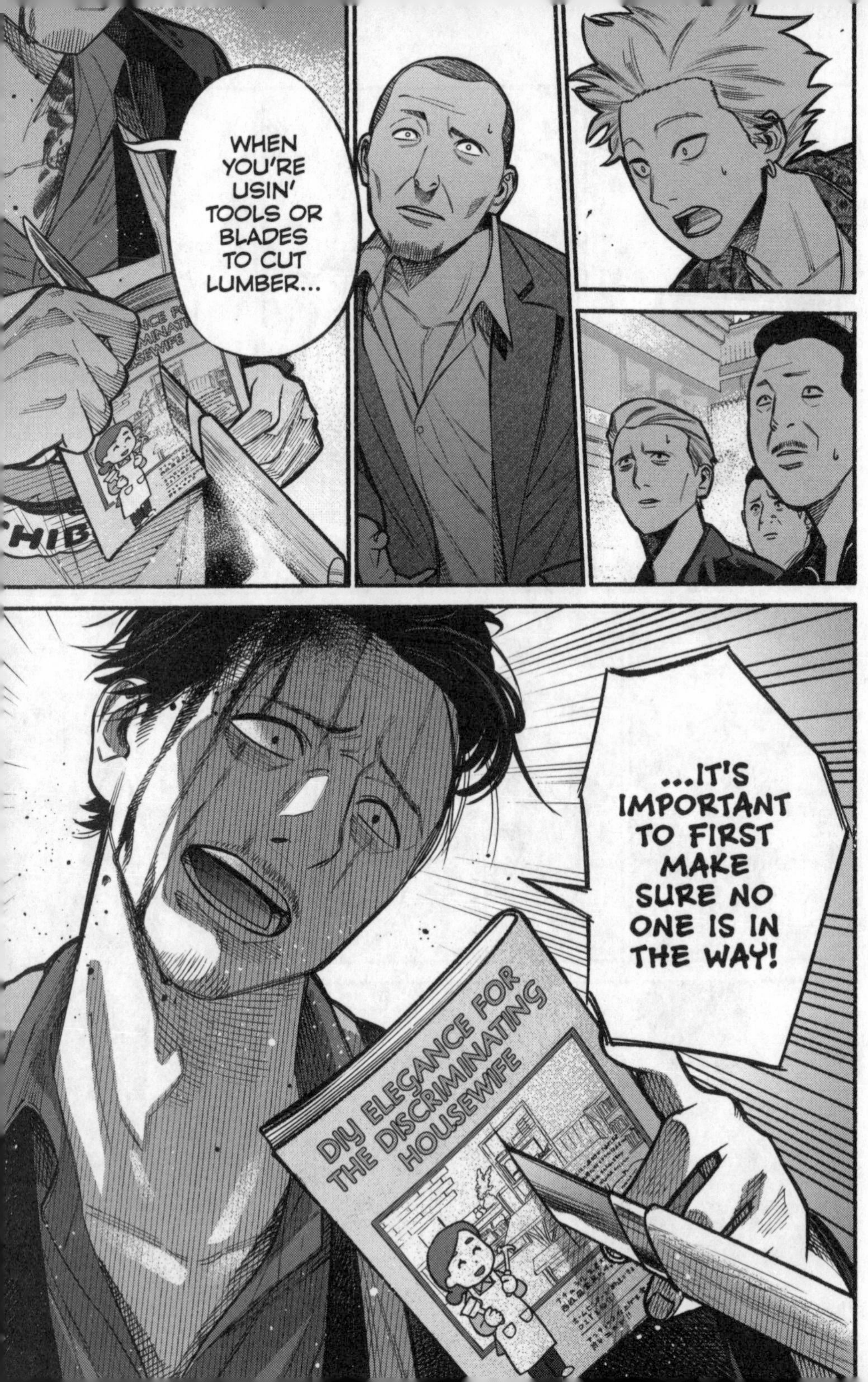
WHEN YOU'RE USIN' TOOLS OR BLADES TO CUT LUMBER...
...IT'S IMPORTANT TO FIRST MAKE SURE NO ONE IS IN THE WAY!
DIY ELEGANCE FOR THE DISCRIMINATING HOUSEWIFE

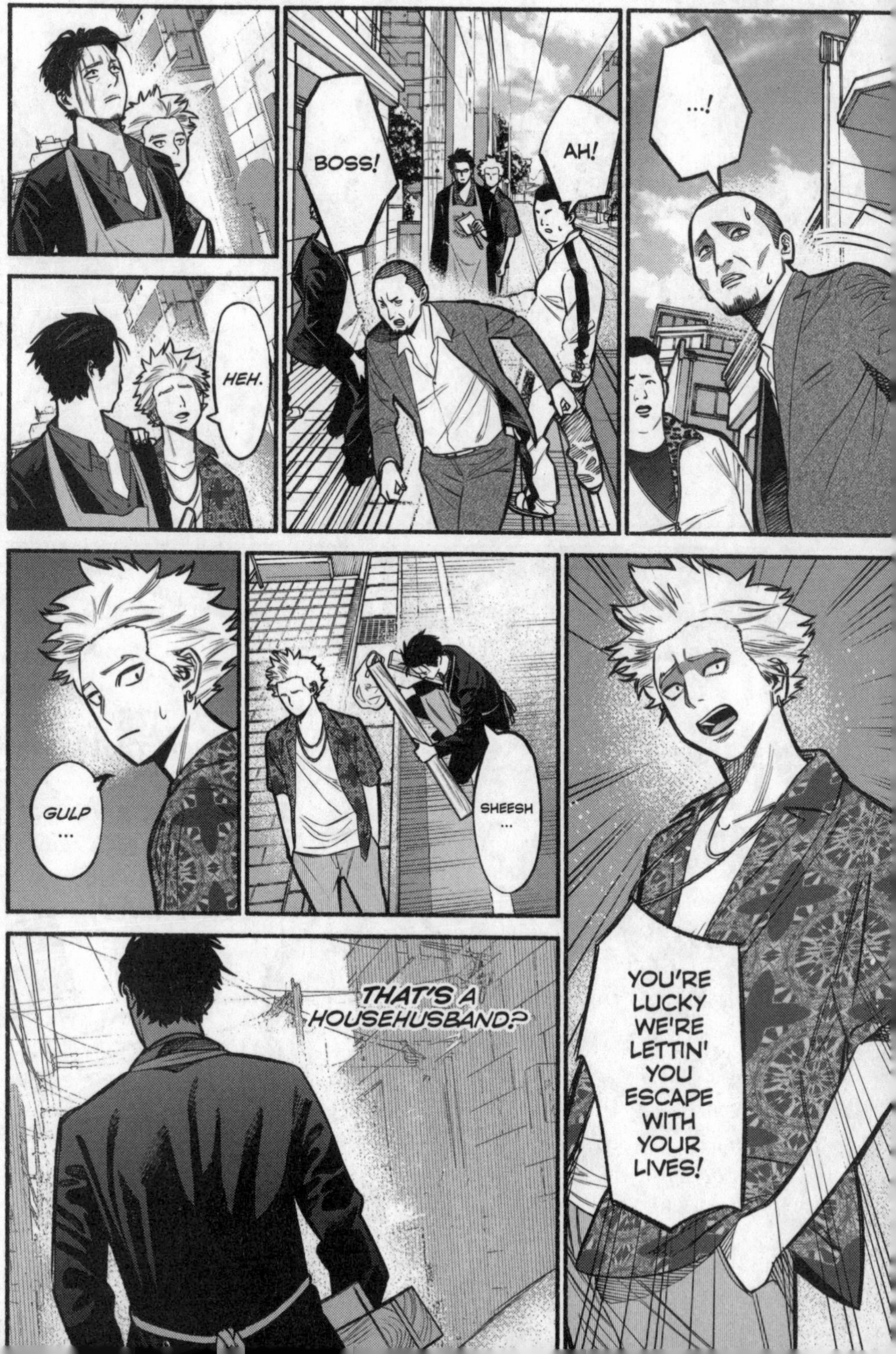
...!
AH!
BOSS!
HEH.
YOU'RE LUCKY WE'RE LETTIN' YOU ESCAPE WITH YOUR LIVES!
SHEESH ...
GULP ...
THAT'S A HOUSEHUSBAND?

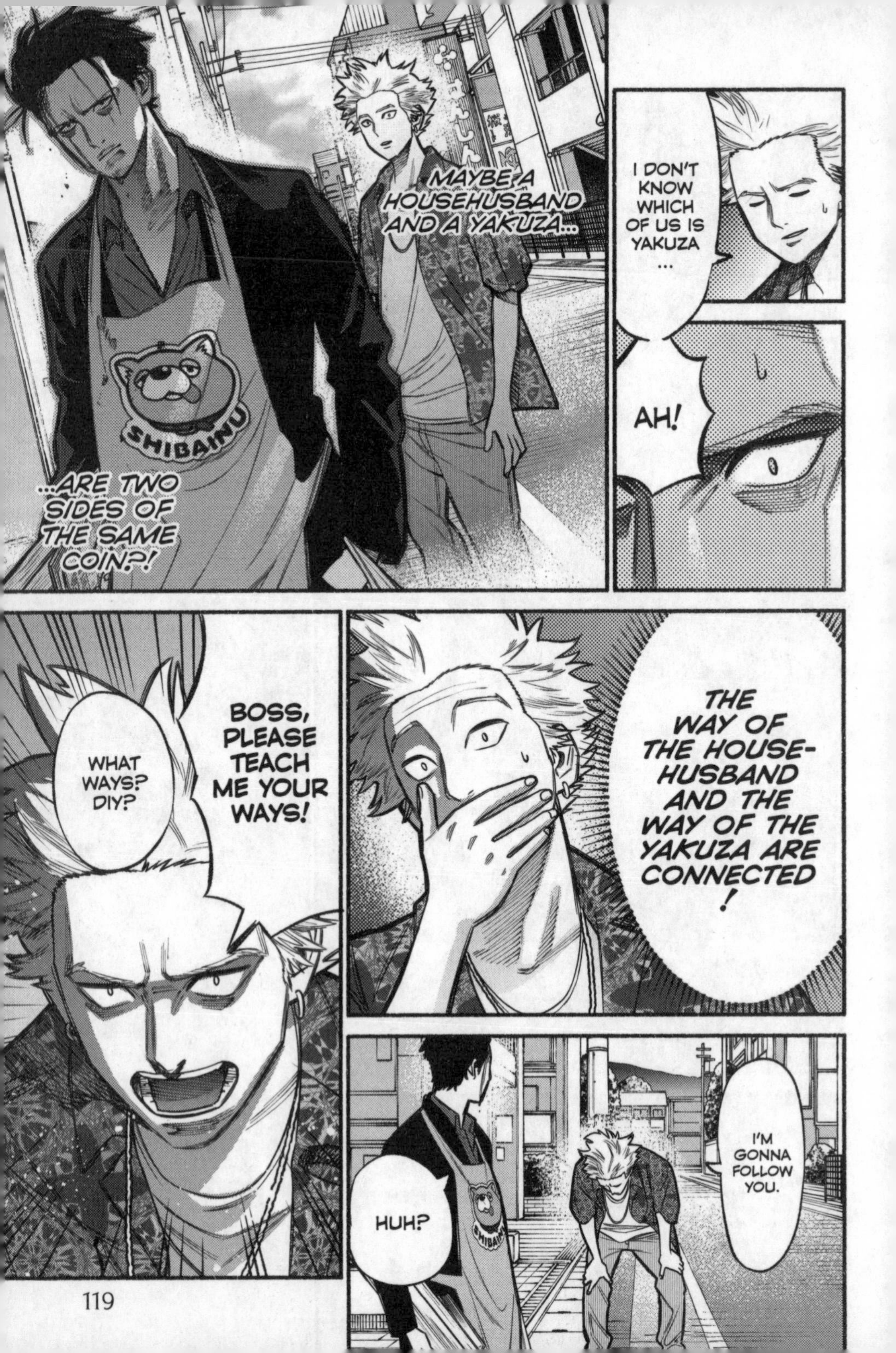

I DON'T KNOW WHICH OF US IS YAKUZA ...
AH!
MAYBE A HOUSEHUSBAND AND A YAKUZA...
...ARE TWO SIDES OF THE SAME COIN?!
THE WAY OF THE HOUSE-HUSBAND AND THE WAY OF THE YAKUZA ARE CONNECTED!
I'M GONNA FOLLOW YOU.
HUH?
BOSS, PLEASE TEACH ME YOUR WAYS!
WHAT WAYS? DIY?
SHIBAINU

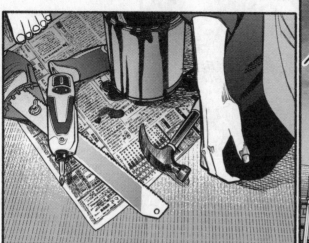

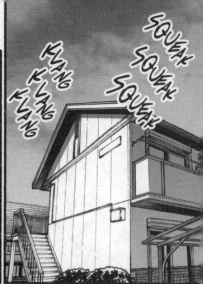

SQUEAK
SQUEAK
SQUEAK

KLANG
KLANG
KLANG

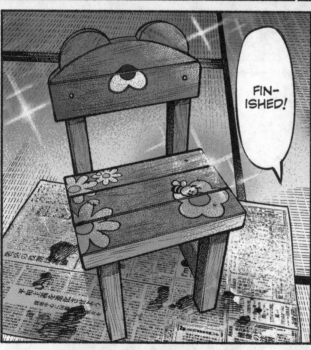

FIN-ISHED!

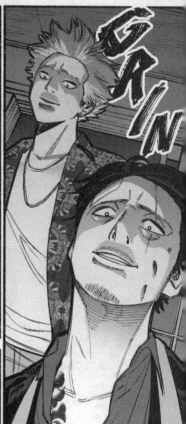

GRIN

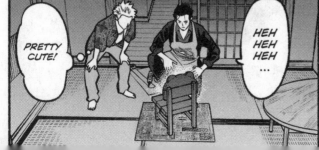

PRETTY CUTE!

HEH HEH HEH ...

120

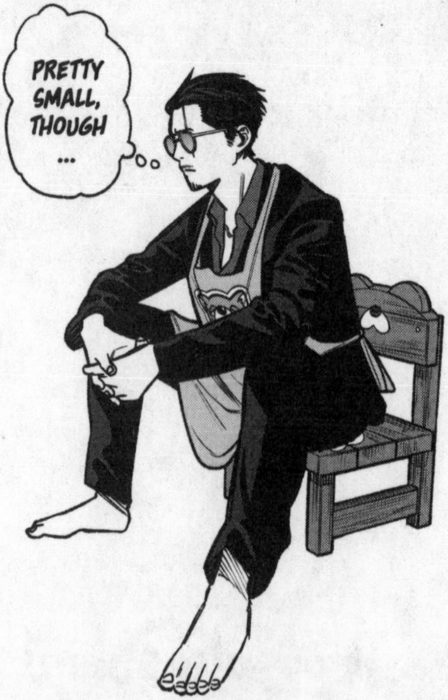
PRETTY SMALL, THOUGH ...

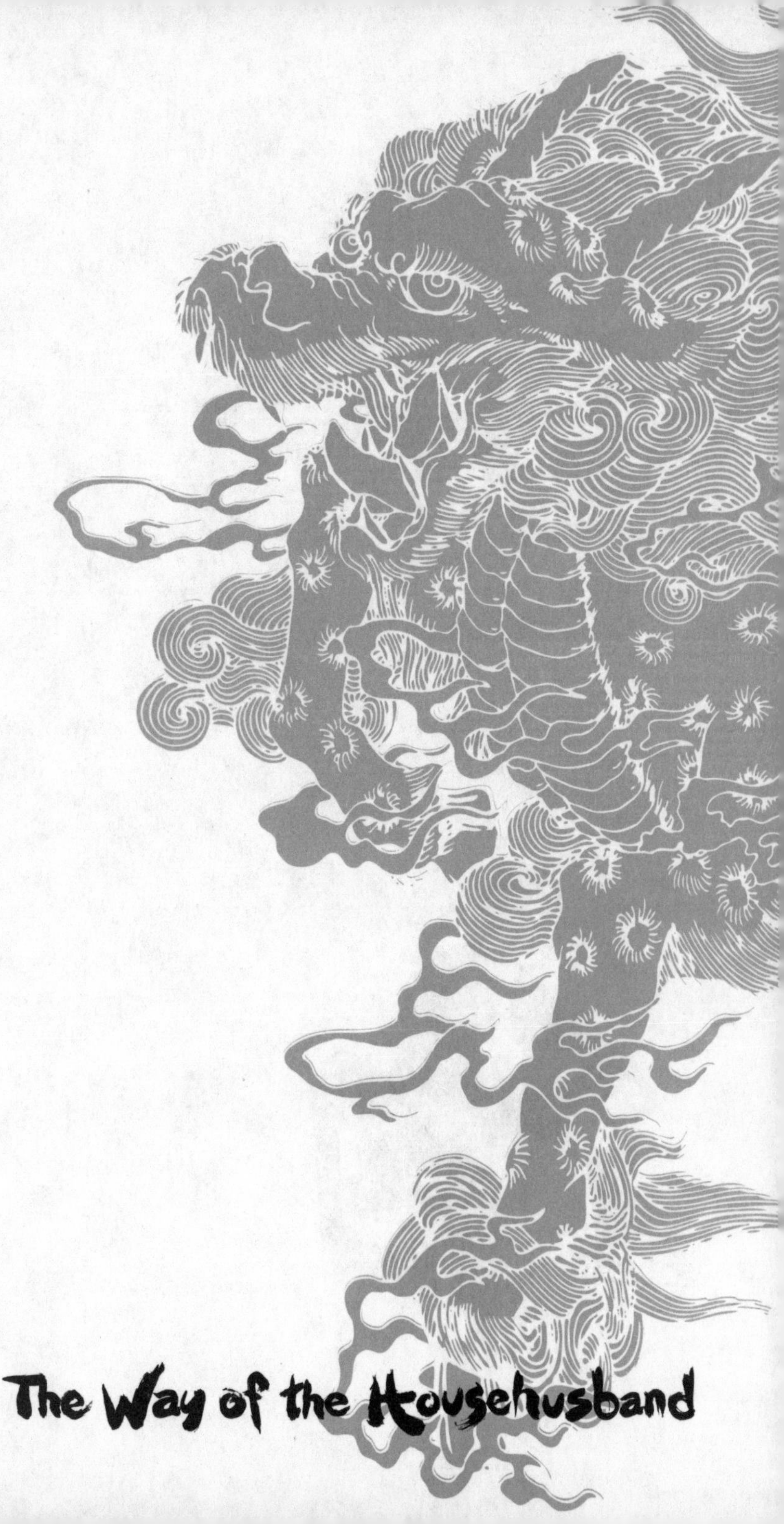
The Way of the Househusband

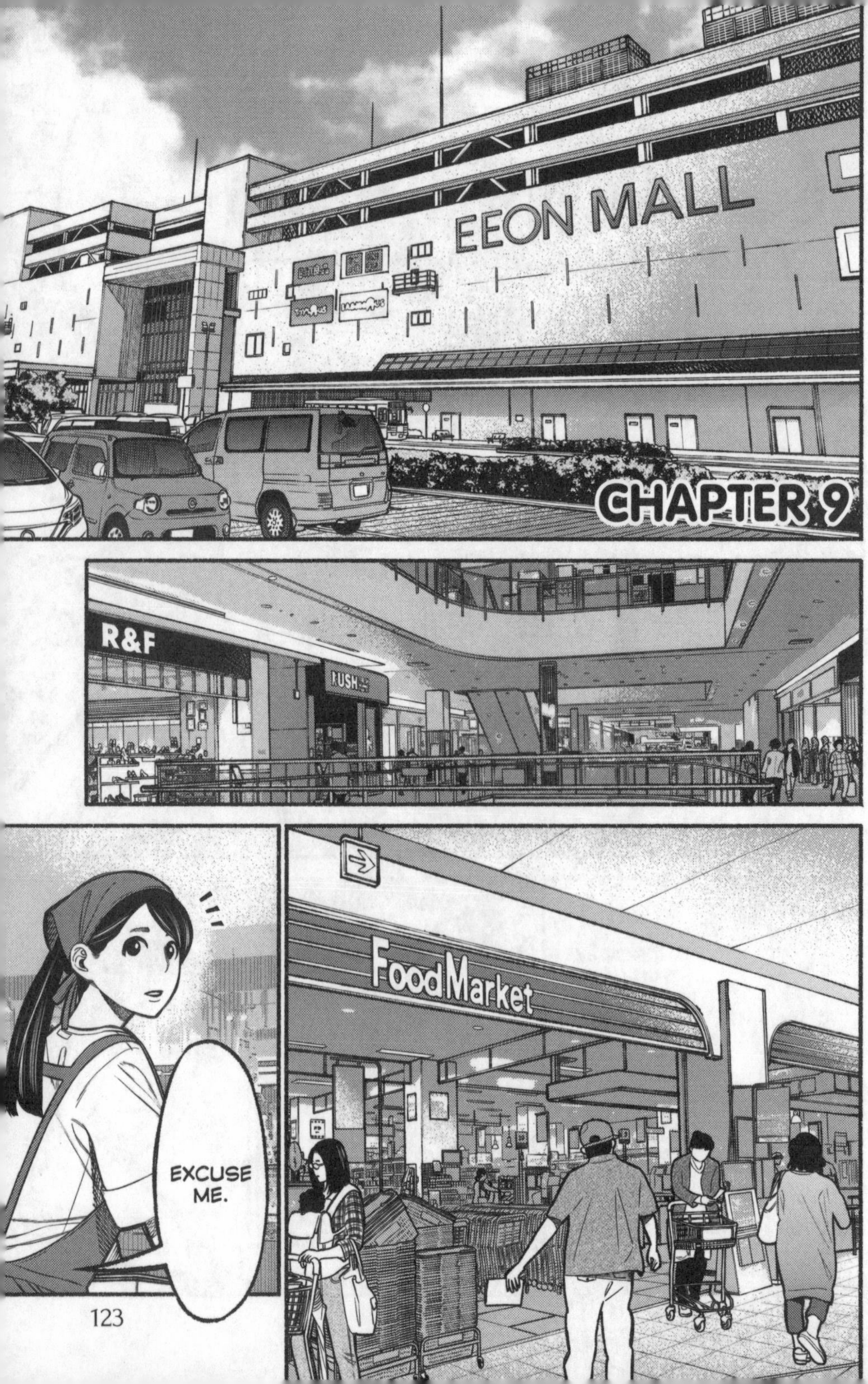
EEON MALL
CHAPTER 9
R&F
FoodMarket
EXCUSE ME.

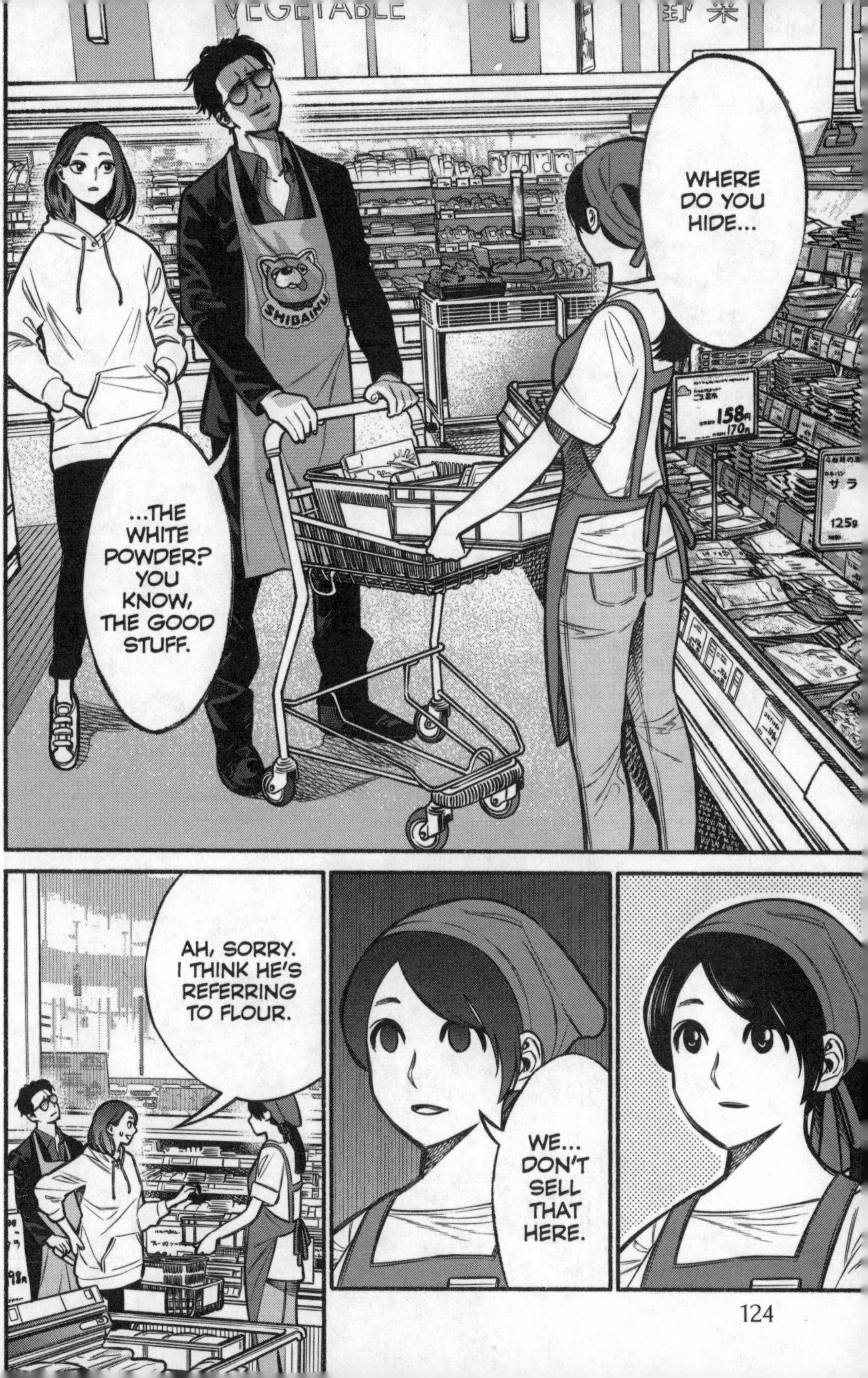
VEGETABLE
WHERE DO YOU HIDE...
...THE WHITE POWDER? YOU KNOW, THE GOOD STUFF.
SHIBAINU
158円
170円
125g
WE... DON'T SELL THAT HERE.
AH, SORRY. I THINK HE'S REFERRING TO FLOUR.

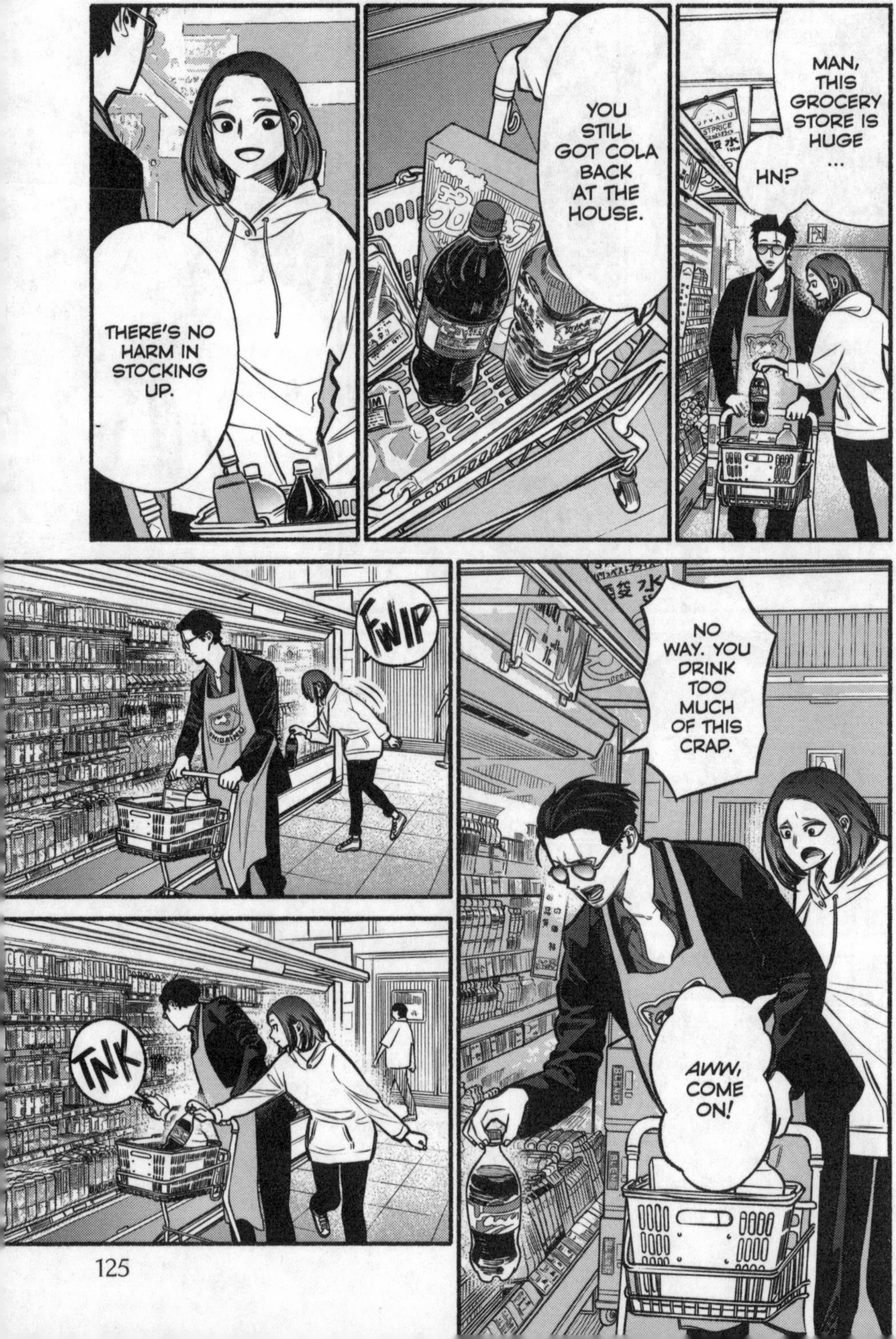
MAN, THIS GROCERY STORE IS HUGE ...
HN?
YOU STILL GOT COLA BACK AT THE HOUSE.
THERE'S NO HARM IN STOCKING UP.
NO WAY. YOU DRINK TOO MUCH OF THIS CRAP.
AWW, COME ON!
FWIP
TNK

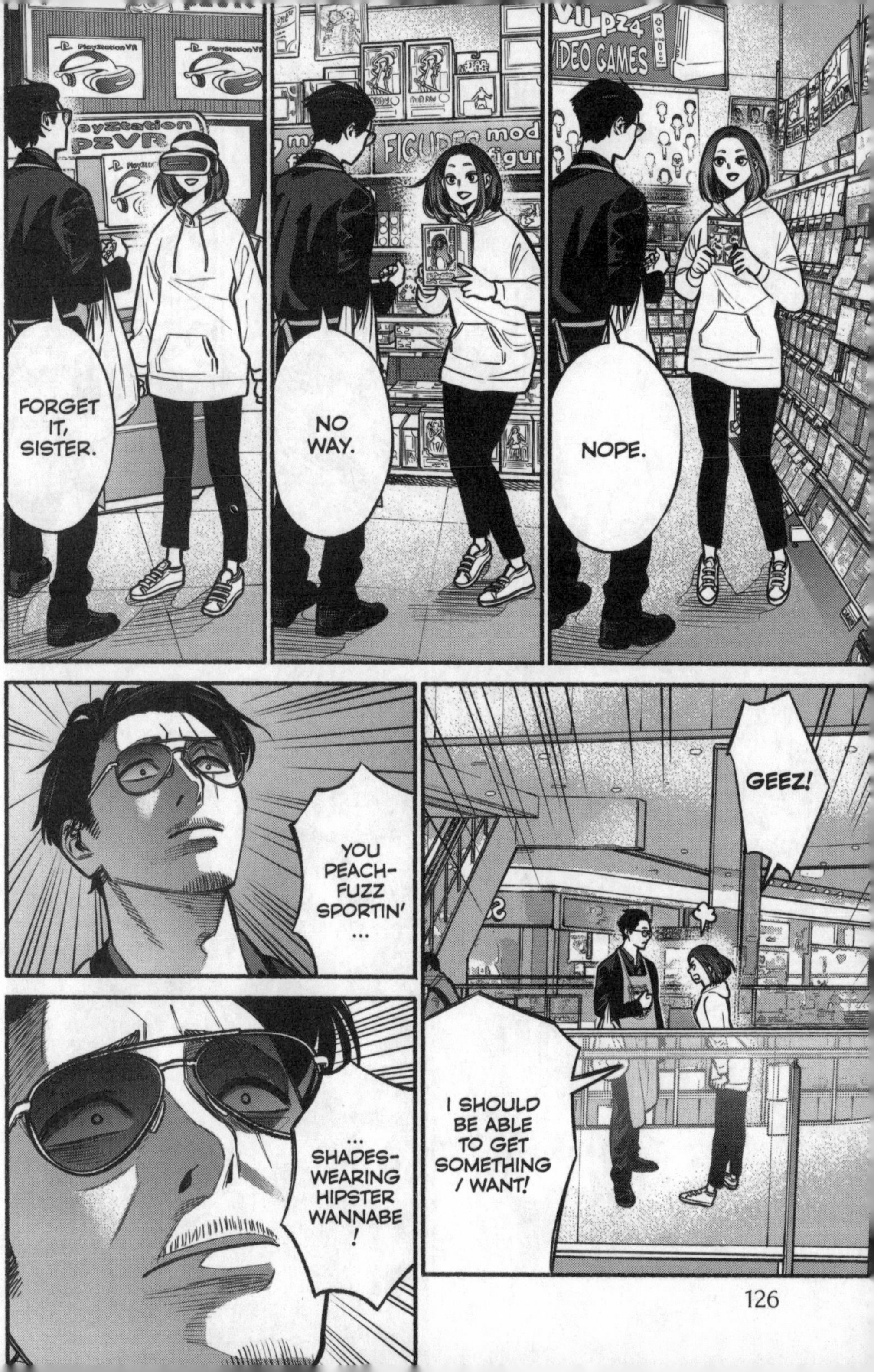
NOPE.
NO WAY.
FORGET IT, SISTER.
GEEZ!
I SHOULD BE ABLE TO GET SOMETHING I WANT!
YOU PEACH-FUZZ SPORTIN' ...
... SHADES-WEARING HIPSTER WANNABE!

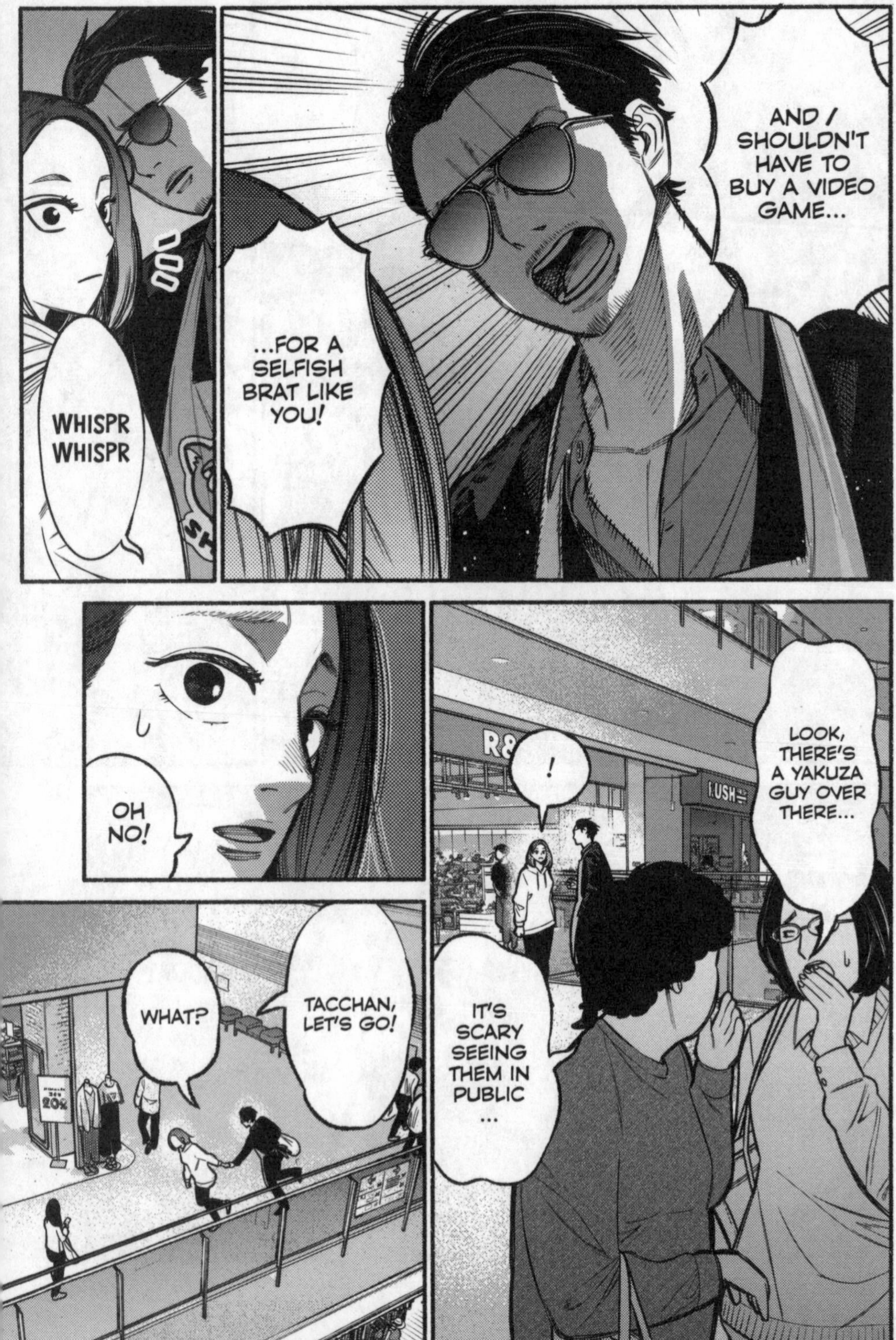
AND I SHOULDN'T HAVE TO BUY A VIDEO GAME...
...FOR A SELFISH BRAT LIKE YOU!
WHISPR WHISPR
LOOK, THERE'S A YAKUZA GUY OVER THERE...
!
IT'S SCARY SEEING THEM IN PUBLIC ...
OH NO!
TACCHAN, LET'S GO!
WHAT?

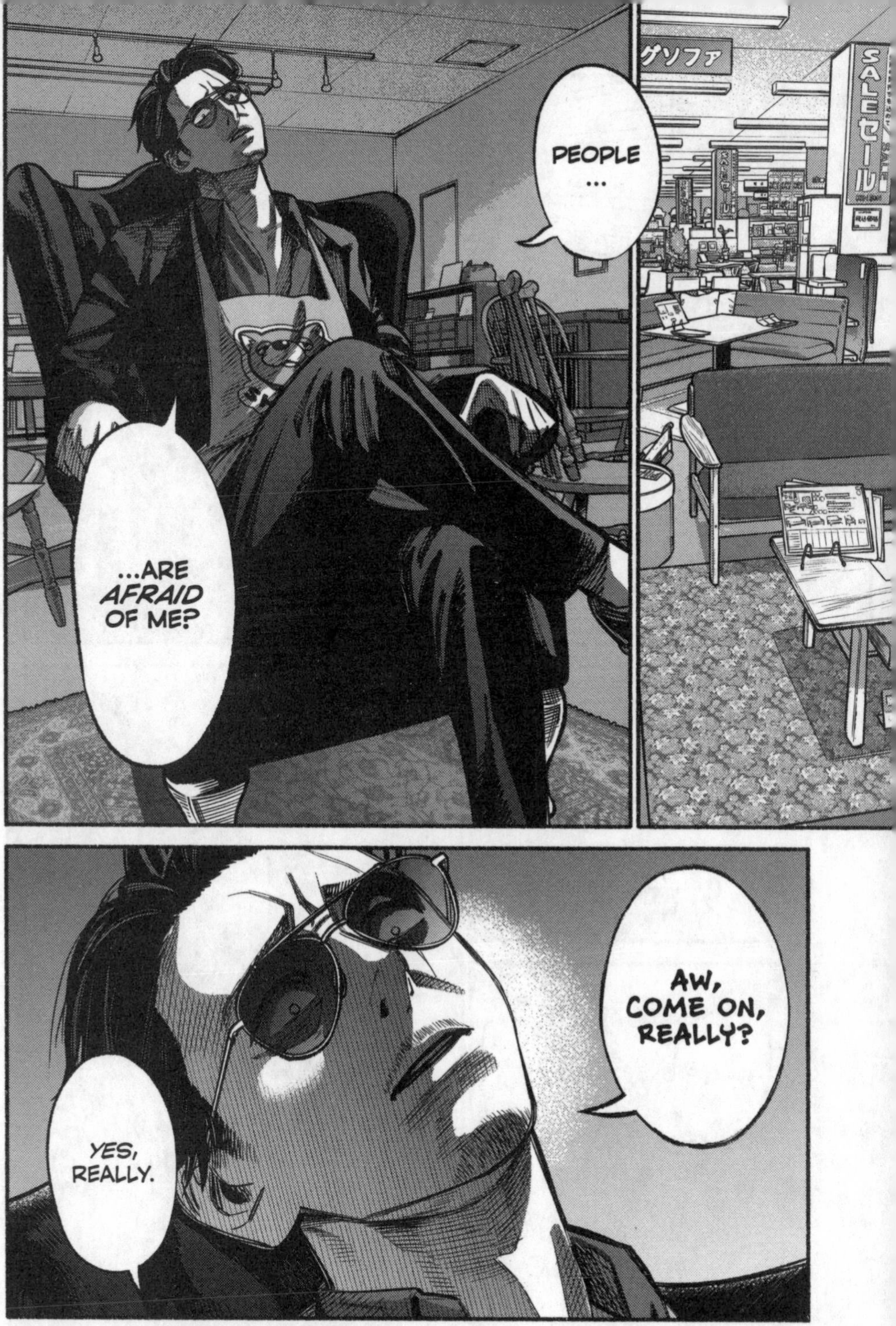
SALE セール
PEOPLE ...
...ARE AFRAID OF ME?
AW, COME ON, REALLY?
YES, REALLY.

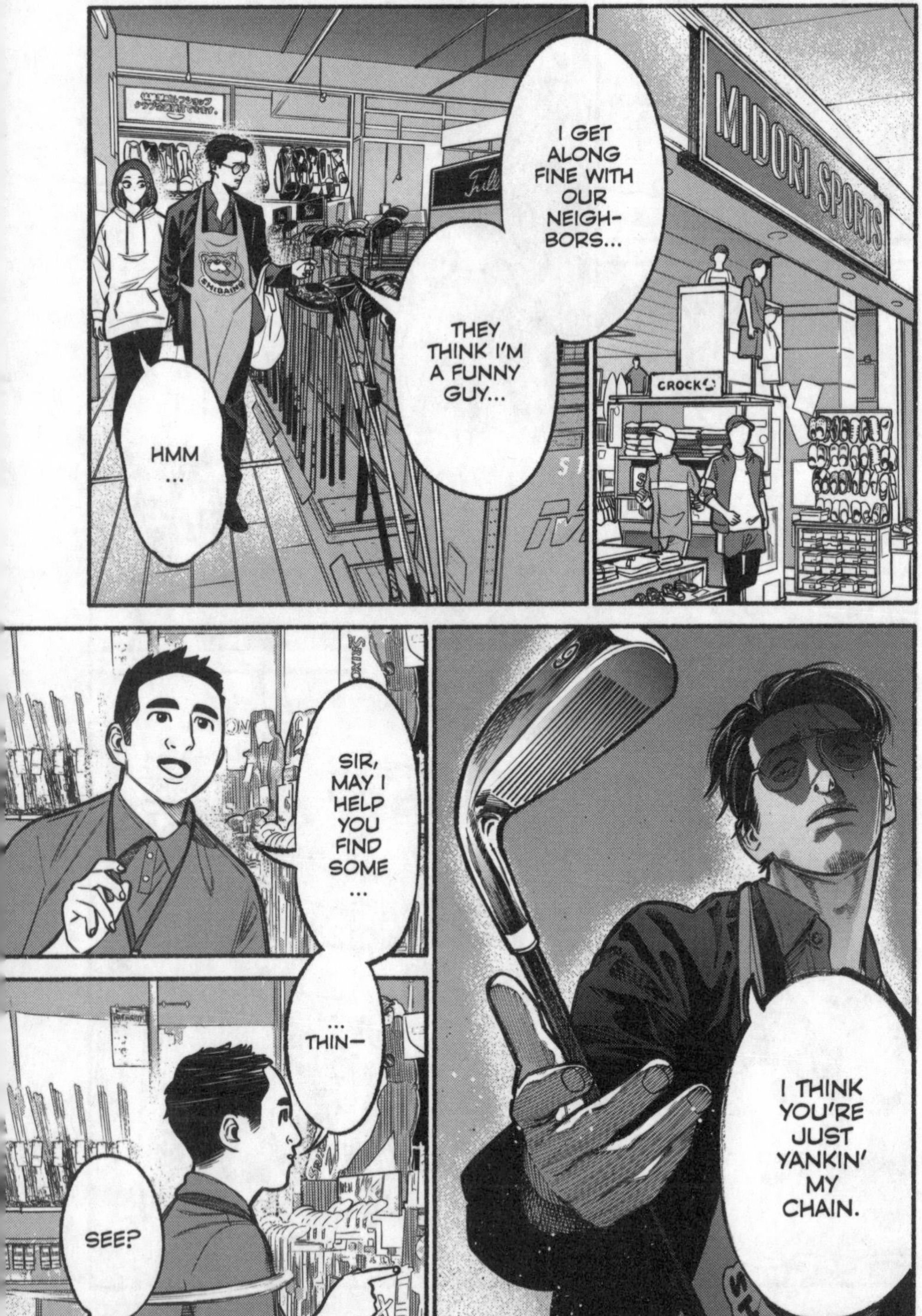
MIDORI SPORTS
CROCK
I GET ALONG FINE WITH OUR NEIGHBORS...
THEY THINK I'M A FUNNY GUY...
HMM ...
I THINK YOU'RE JUST YANKIN' MY CHAIN.
SHIBAINU
SIR, MAY I HELP YOU FIND SOME ...
... THIN—
SEE?

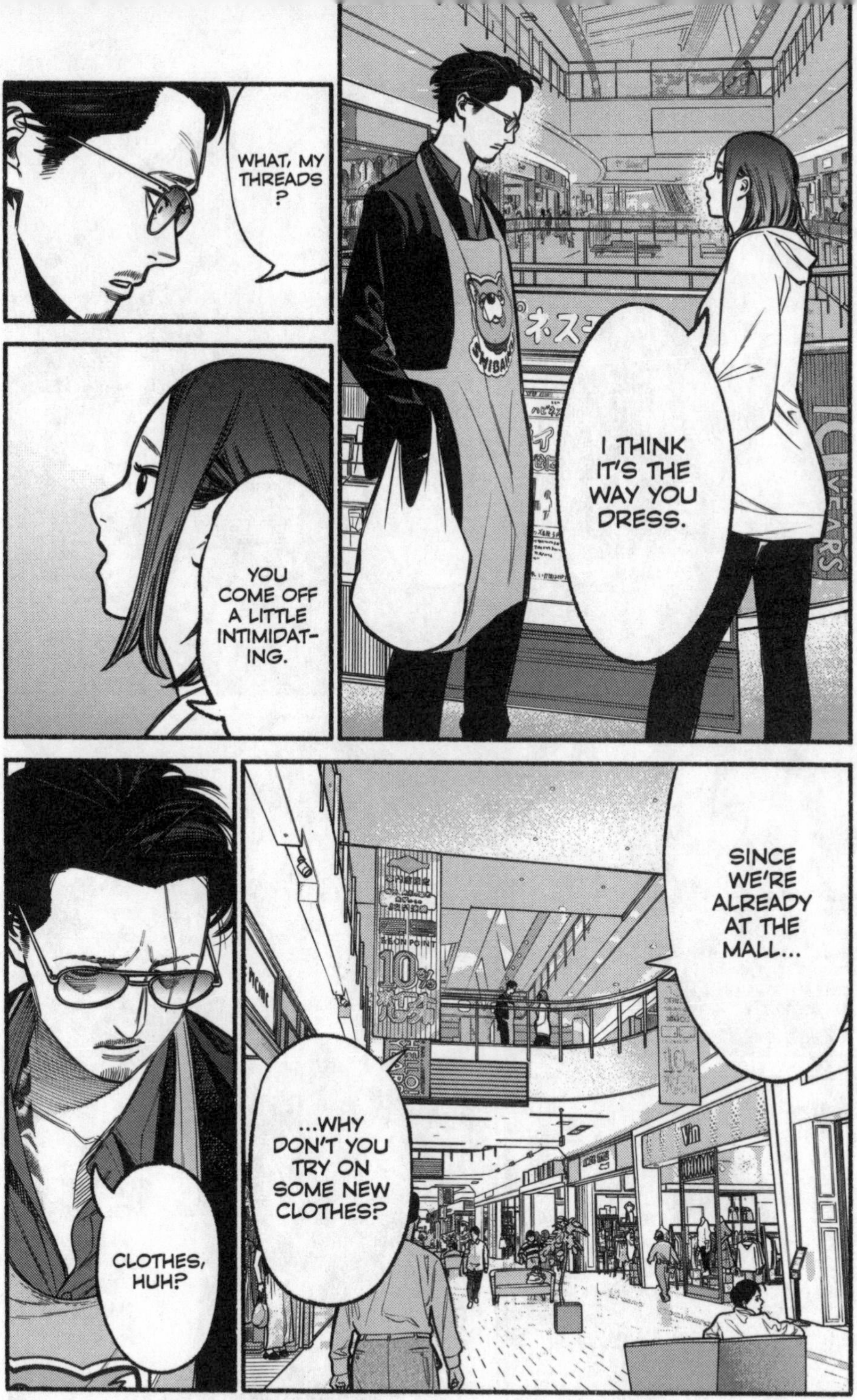
I THINK IT'S THE WAY YOU DRESS.
WHAT, MY THREADS?
YOU COME OFF A LITTLE INTIMIDATING.
SINCE WE'RE ALREADY AT THE MALL...
...WHY DON'T YOU TRY ON SOME NEW CLOTHES?
CLOTHES, HUH?

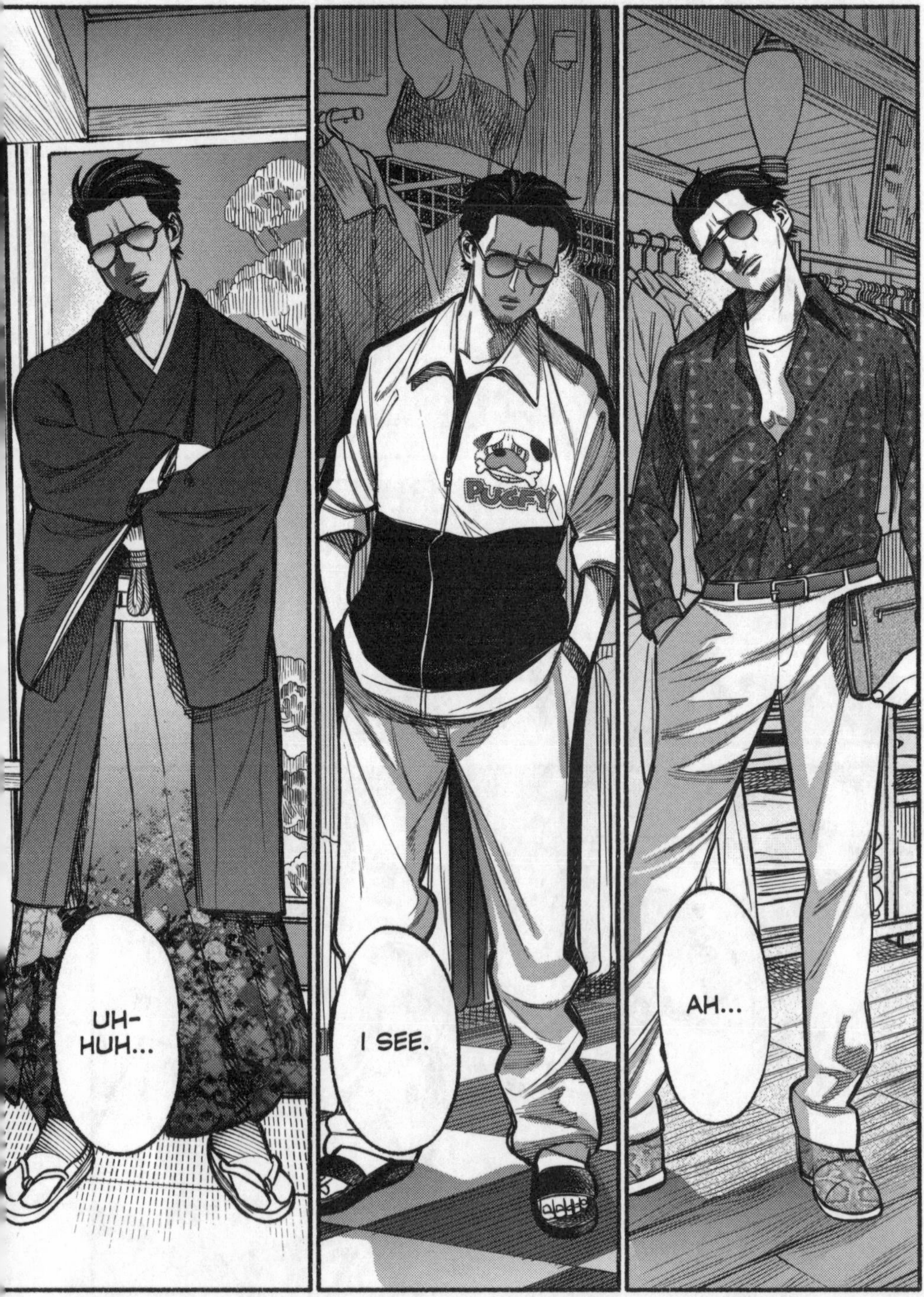
AH...
PUGFY
I SEE.
UH-HUH...

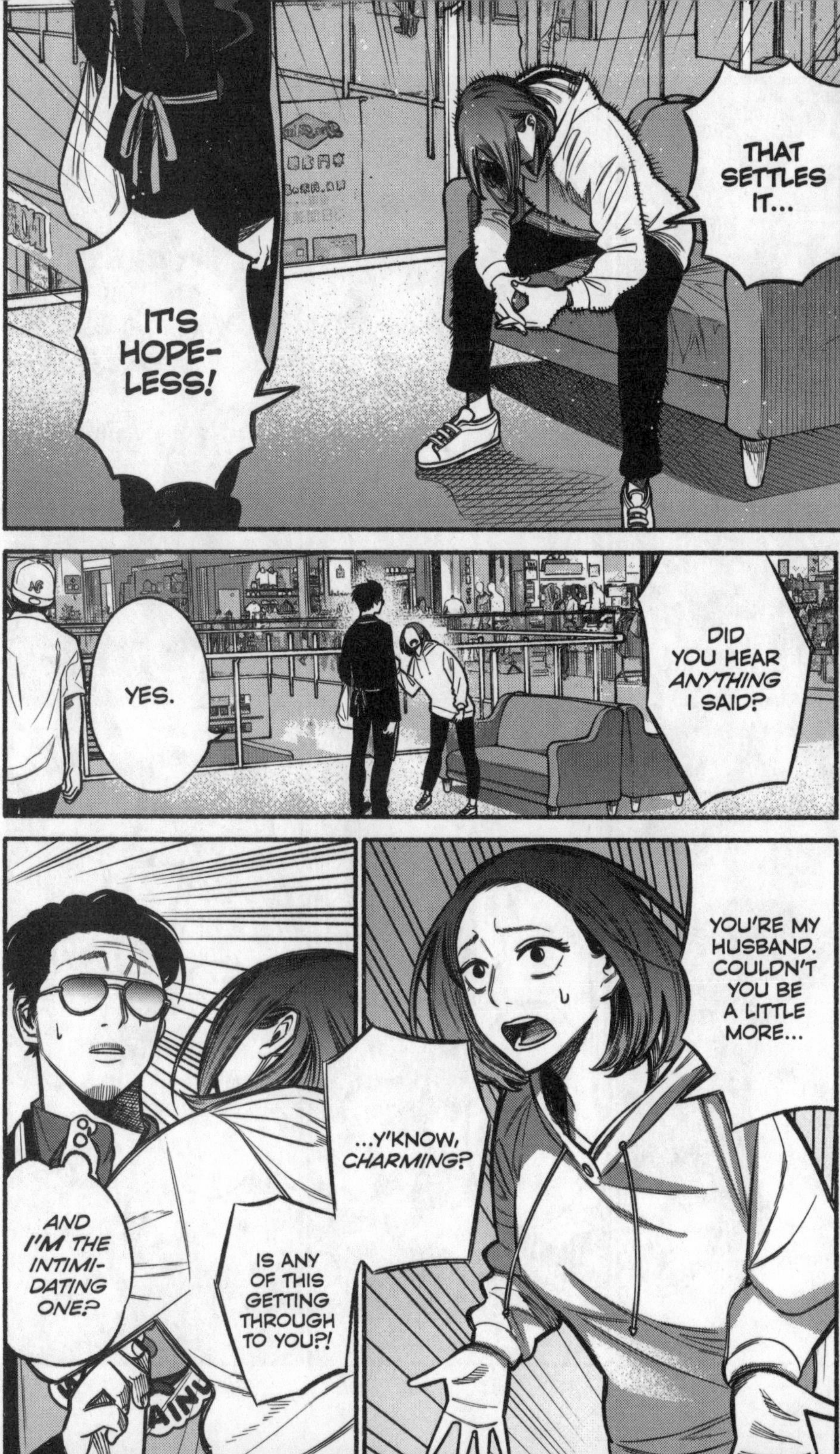
THAT SETTLES IT...
IT'S HOPE-LESS!
DID YOU HEAR *ANYTHING* I SAID?
YES.
YOU'RE MY HUSBAND. COULDN'T YOU BE A LITTLE MORE...
...Y'KNOW, *CHARMING*?
IS ANY OF THIS GETTING THROUGH TO YOU?!
AND *I'M* THE INTIMI-DATING ONE?

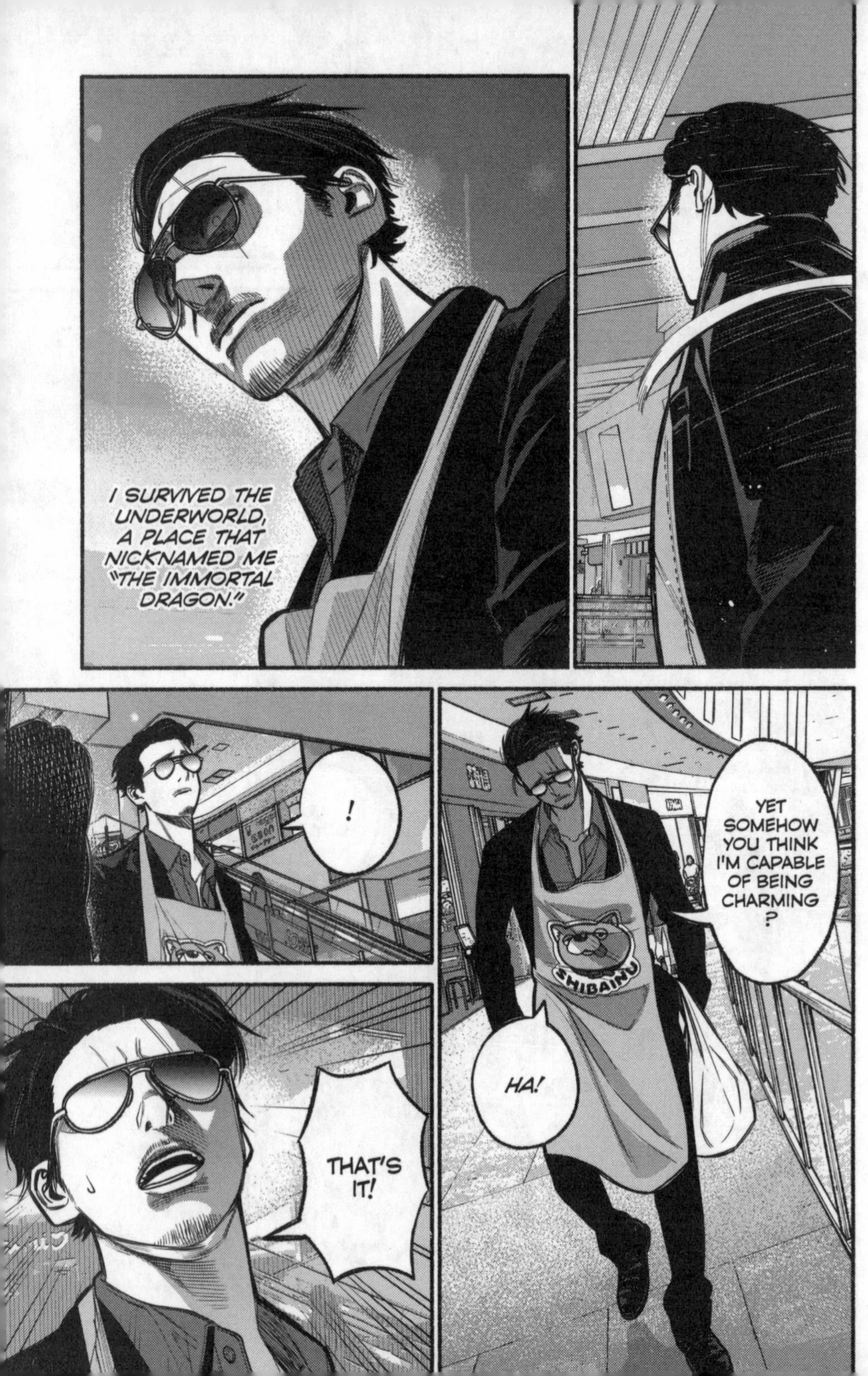
I SURVIVED THE UNDERWORLD, A PLACE THAT NICKNAMED ME "THE IMMORTAL DRAGON."
YET SOMEHOW YOU THINK I'M CAPABLE OF BEING CHARMING?
SHIBAINU
HA!
!
THAT'S IT!

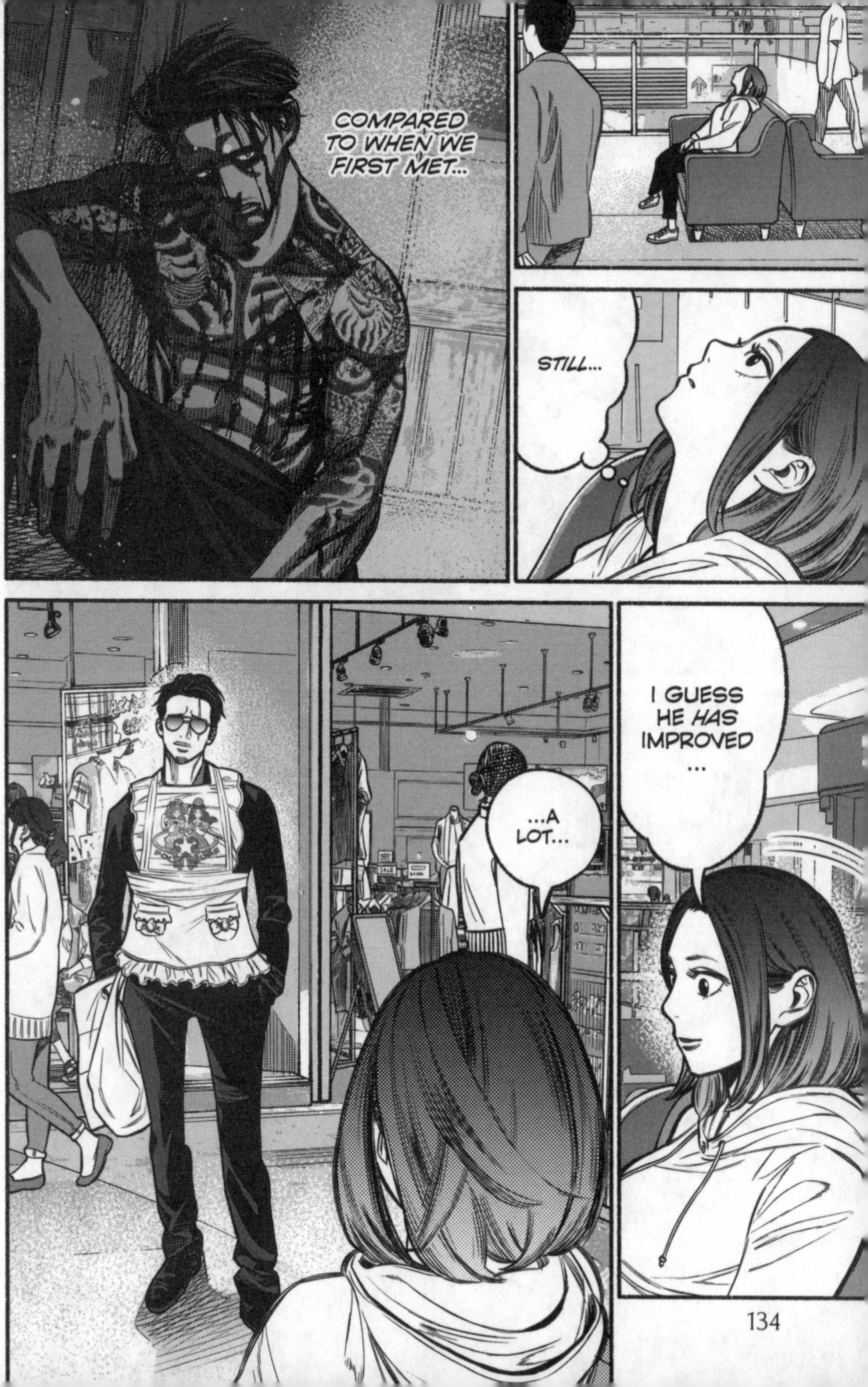
STILL...
COMPARED TO WHEN WE FIRST MET...
I GUESS HE *HAS* IMPROVED ...
...A LOT...

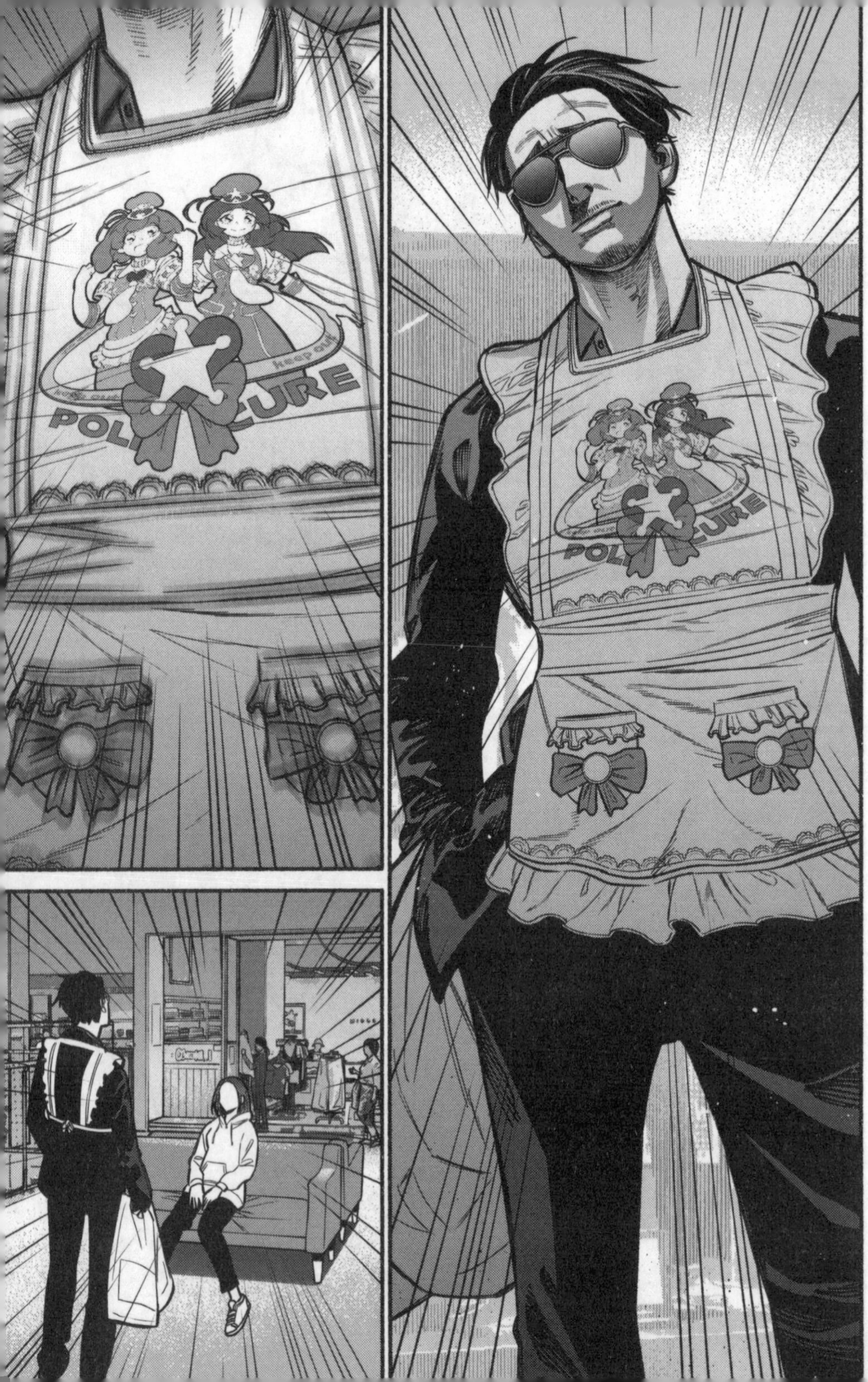
keep out
POLI
CURE
keep out
POLI
CURE

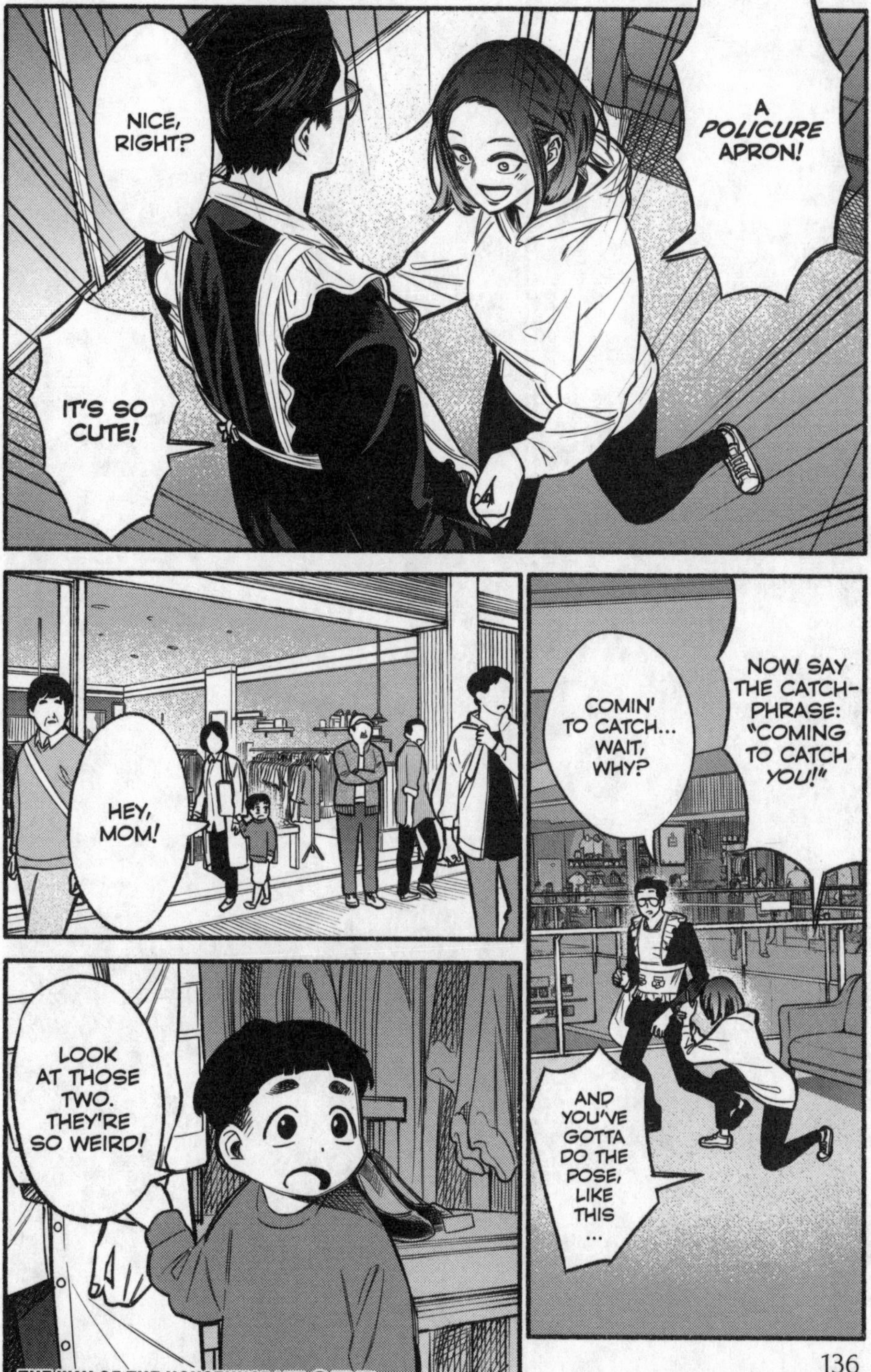
A *POLICURE* APRON!
NICE, RIGHT?
IT'S SO CUTE!
NOW SAY THE CATCH-PHRASE: "COMING TO CATCH *YOU!*"
COMIN' TO CATCH... WAIT, WHY?
AND YOU'VE GOTTA DO THE POSE, LIKE THIS ...
HEY, MOM!
LOOK AT THOSE TWO. THEY'RE SO WEIRD!
THE WAY OF THE HOUSEHUSBAND ① END

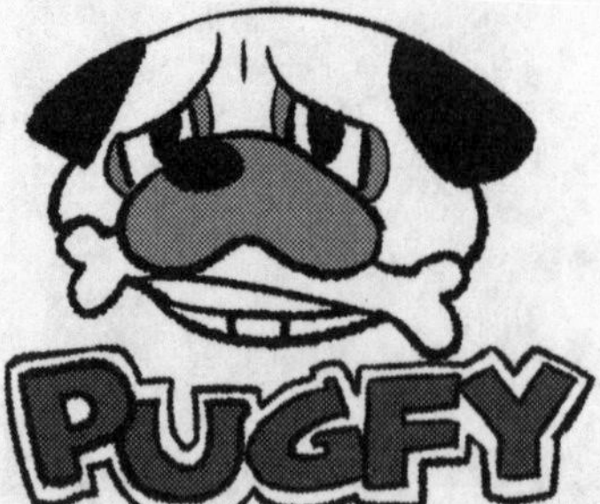
PUGFY

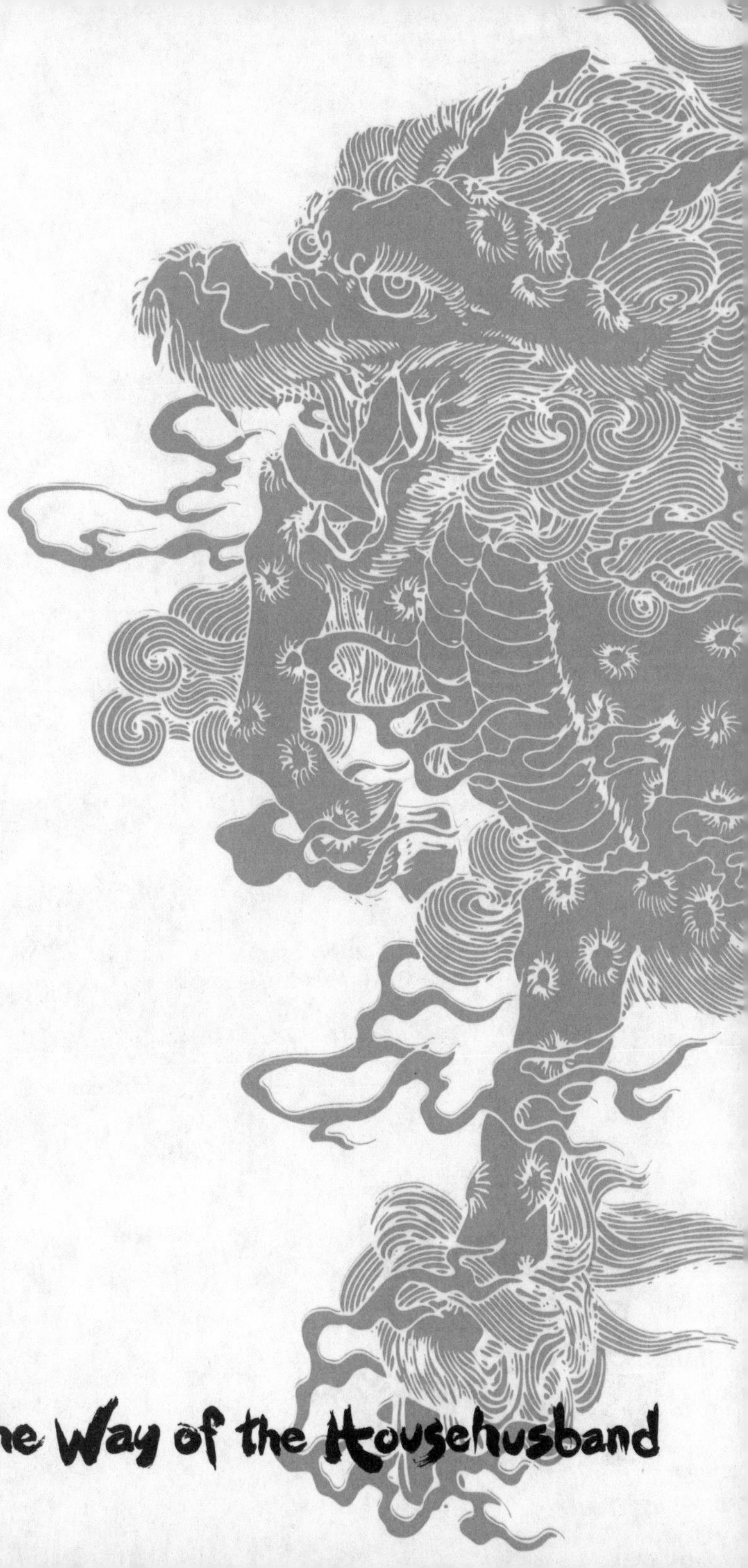

# The Way of the Househusband

# BONUS MANGA ① GIN'S WALK

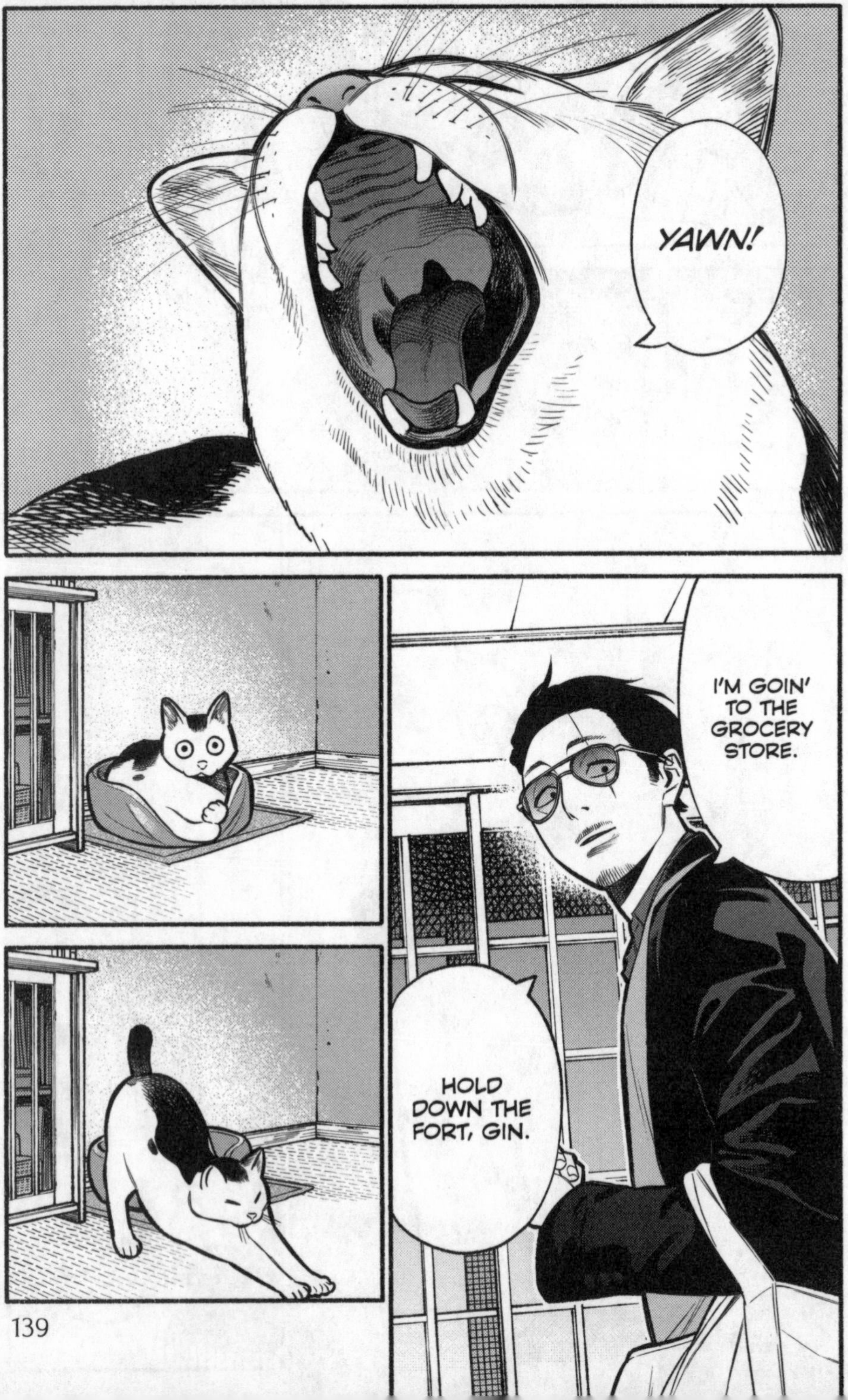
YAWN!
I'M GOIN' TO THE GROCERY STORE.
HOLD DOWN THE FORT, GIN.

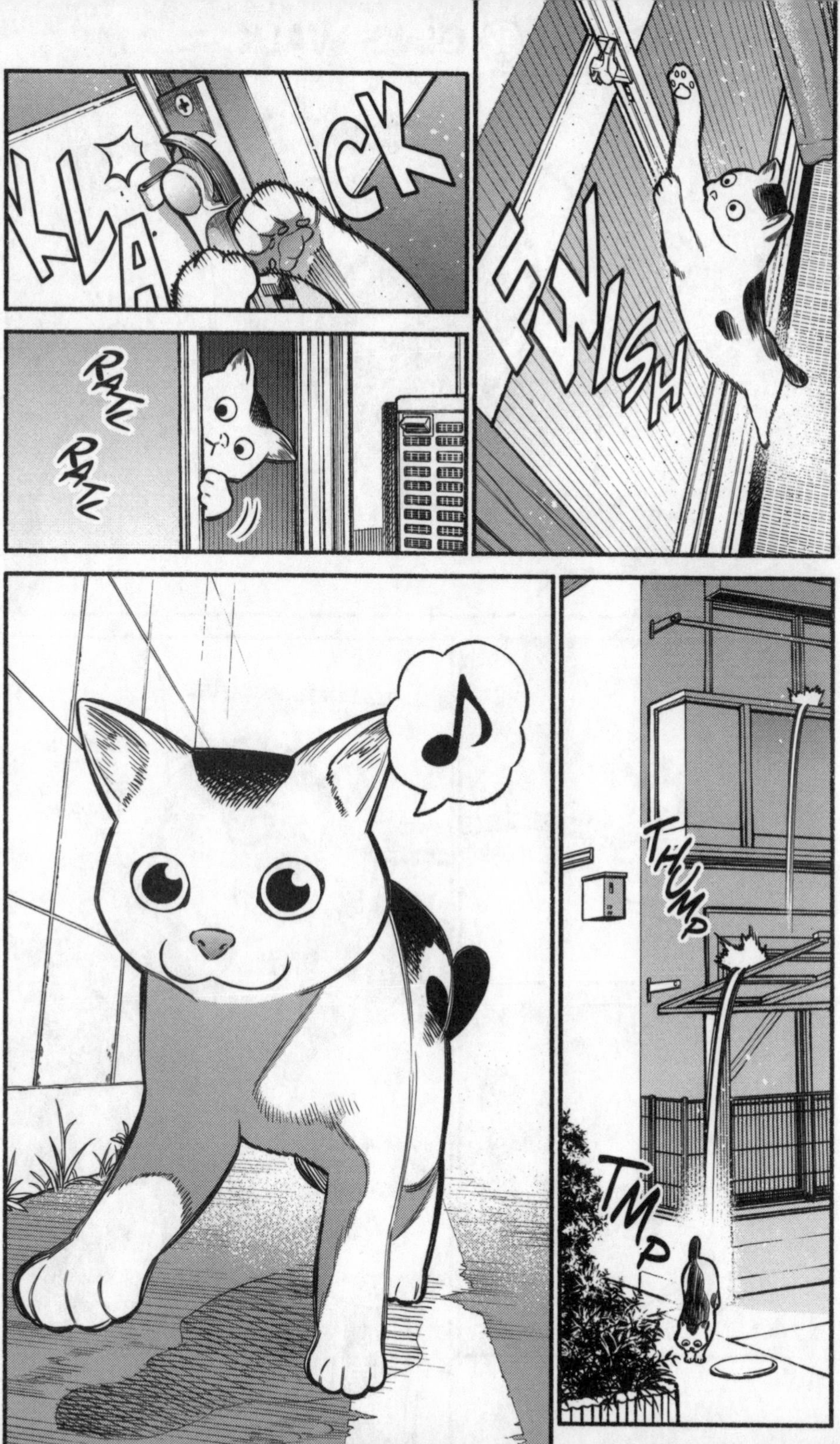
SWISH
KLACK
RATL RATL
THUMP
TMP
♪

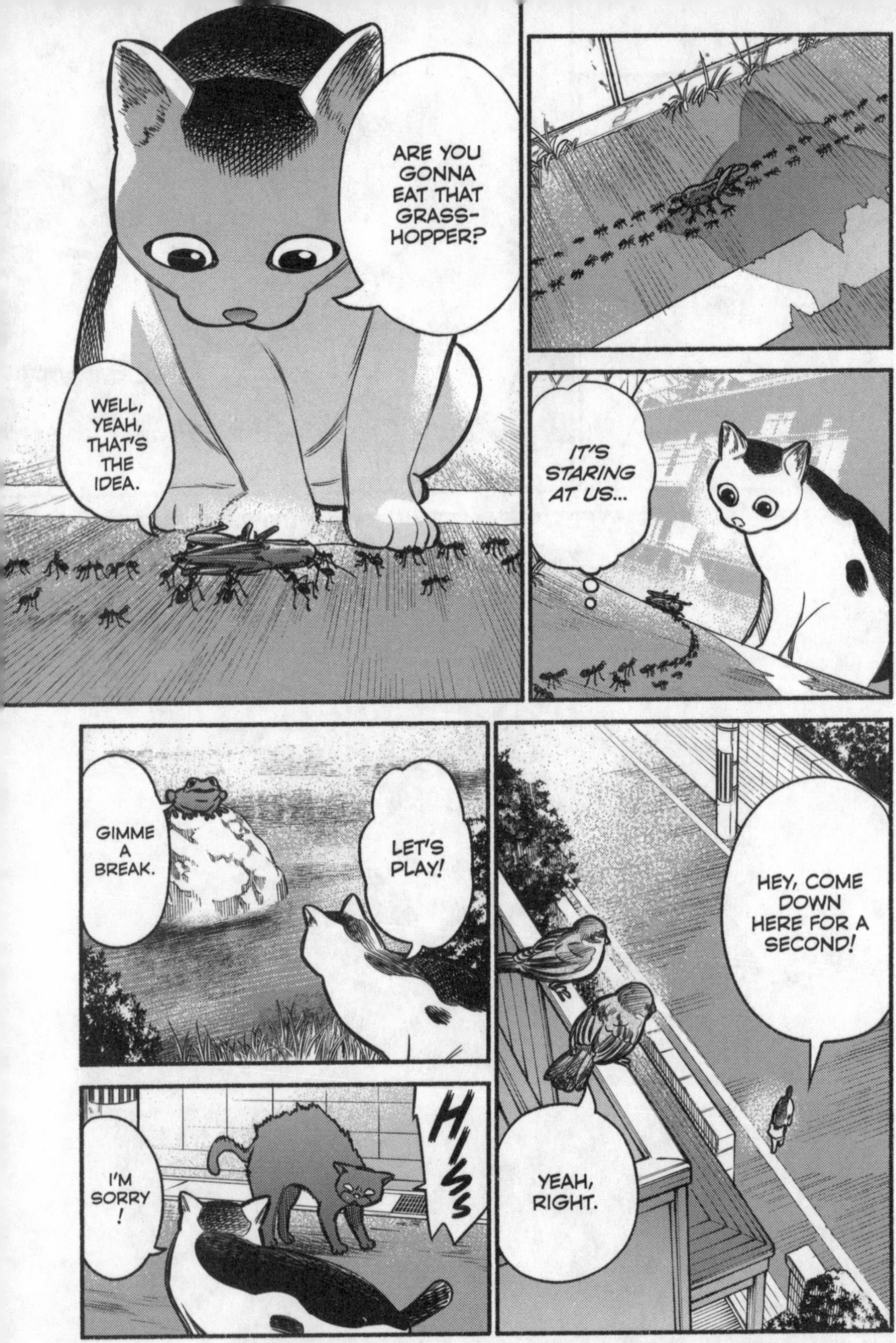
IT'S STARING AT US...
ARE YOU GONNA EAT THAT GRASS-HOPPER?
WELL, YEAH, THAT'S THE IDEA.
HEY, COME DOWN HERE FOR A SECOND!
YEAH, RIGHT.
LET'S PLAY!
GIMME A BREAK.
HISS
I'M SORRY!

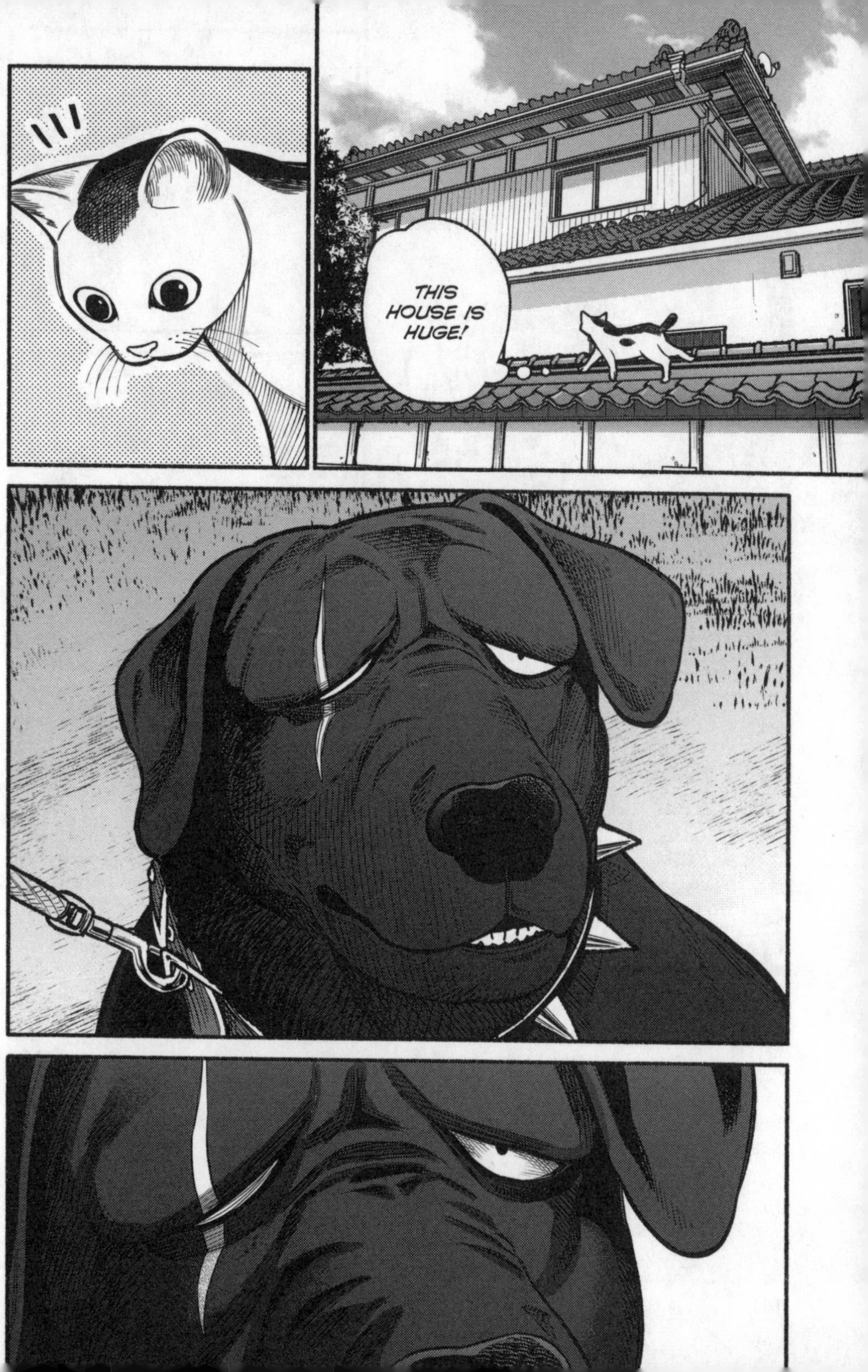
THIS HOUSE IS HUGE!

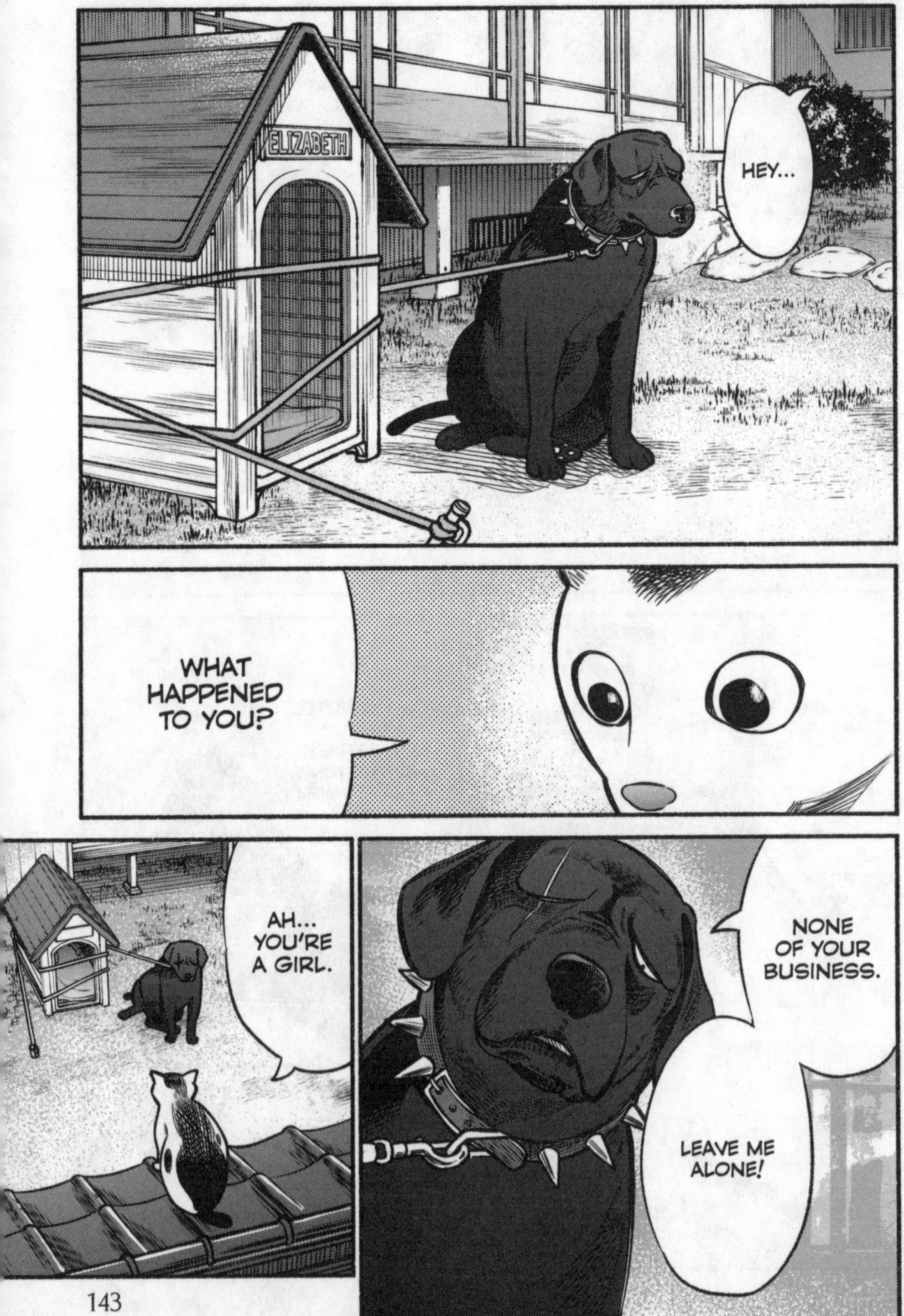
ELIZABETH
HEY...
WHAT HAPPENED TO YOU?
NONE OF YOUR BUSINESS.
LEAVE ME ALONE!
AH... YOU'RE A GIRL.

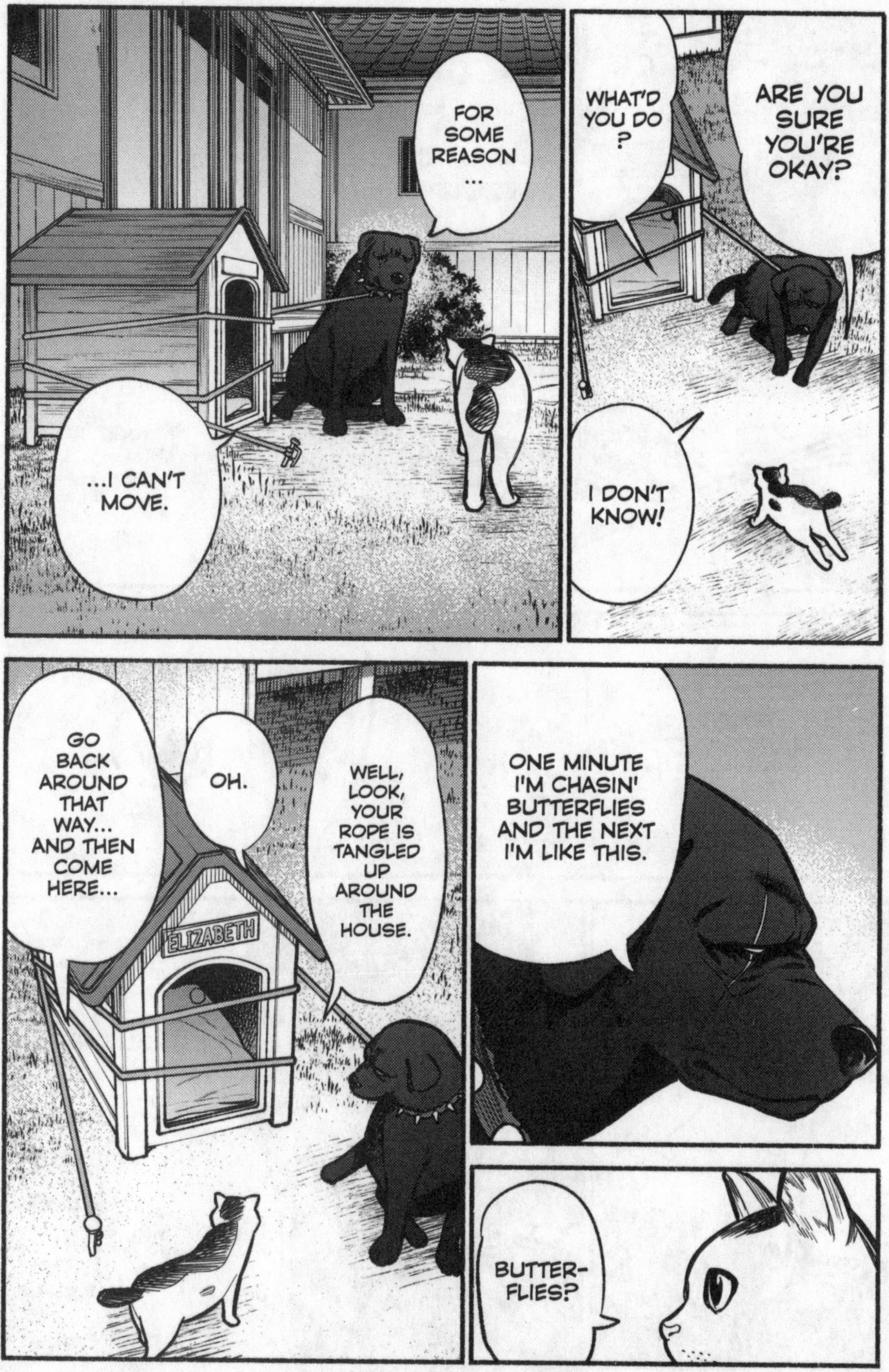
ARE YOU SURE YOU'RE OKAY?
WHAT'D YOU DO?
I DON'T KNOW!
FOR SOME REASON...
...I CAN'T MOVE.
ONE MINUTE I'M CHASIN' BUTTERFLIES AND THE NEXT I'M LIKE THIS.
BUTTER-FLIES?
WELL, LOOK, YOUR ROPE IS TANGLED UP AROUND THE HOUSE.
OH.
ELIZABETH
GO BACK AROUND THAT WAY... AND THEN COME HERE...

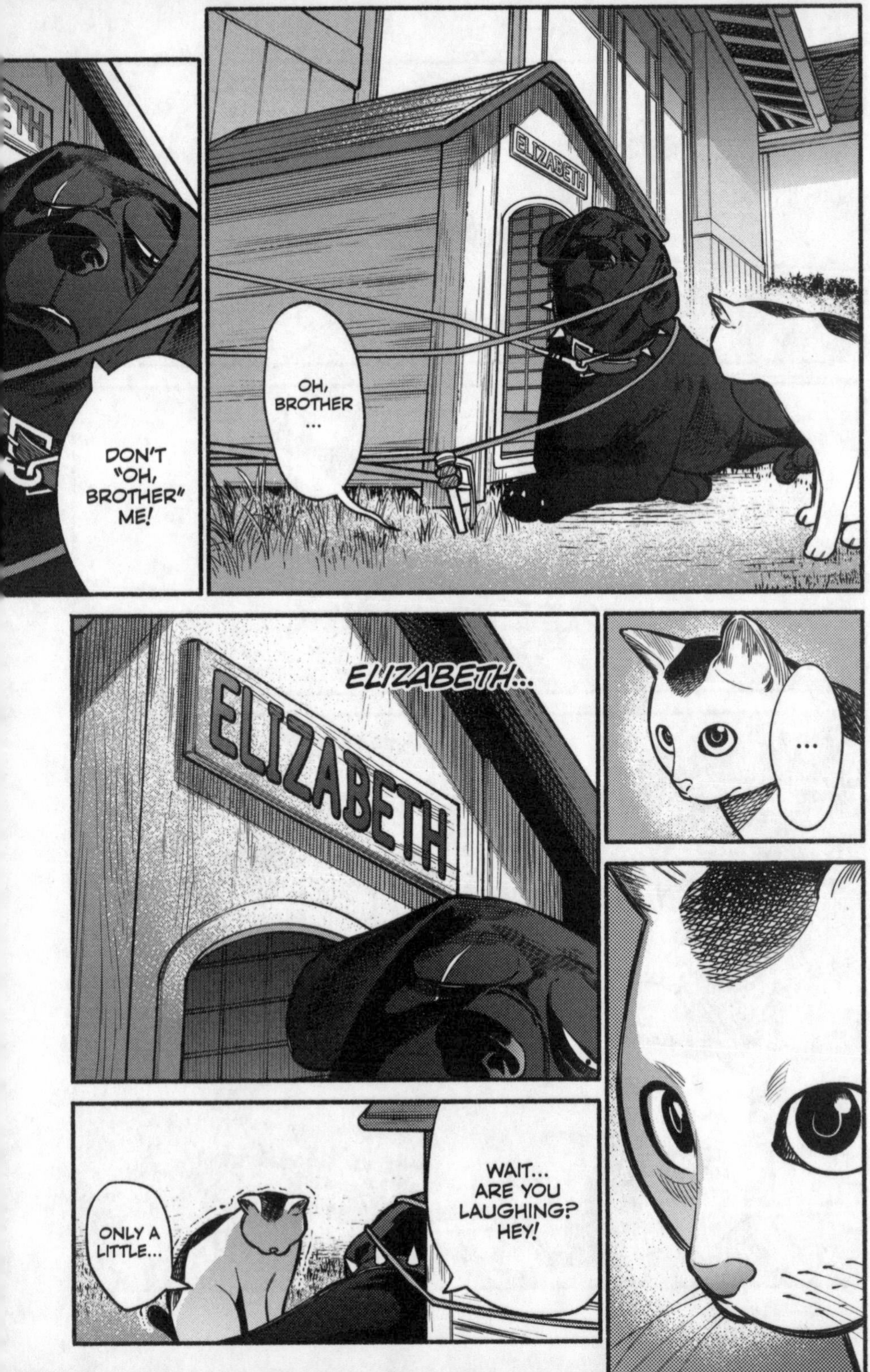
ELIZABETH
OH, BROTHER ...
DON'T "OH, BROTHER" ME!
...
ELIZABETH...
ELIZABETH
WAIT... ARE YOU LAUGHING? HEY!
ONLY A LITTLE...

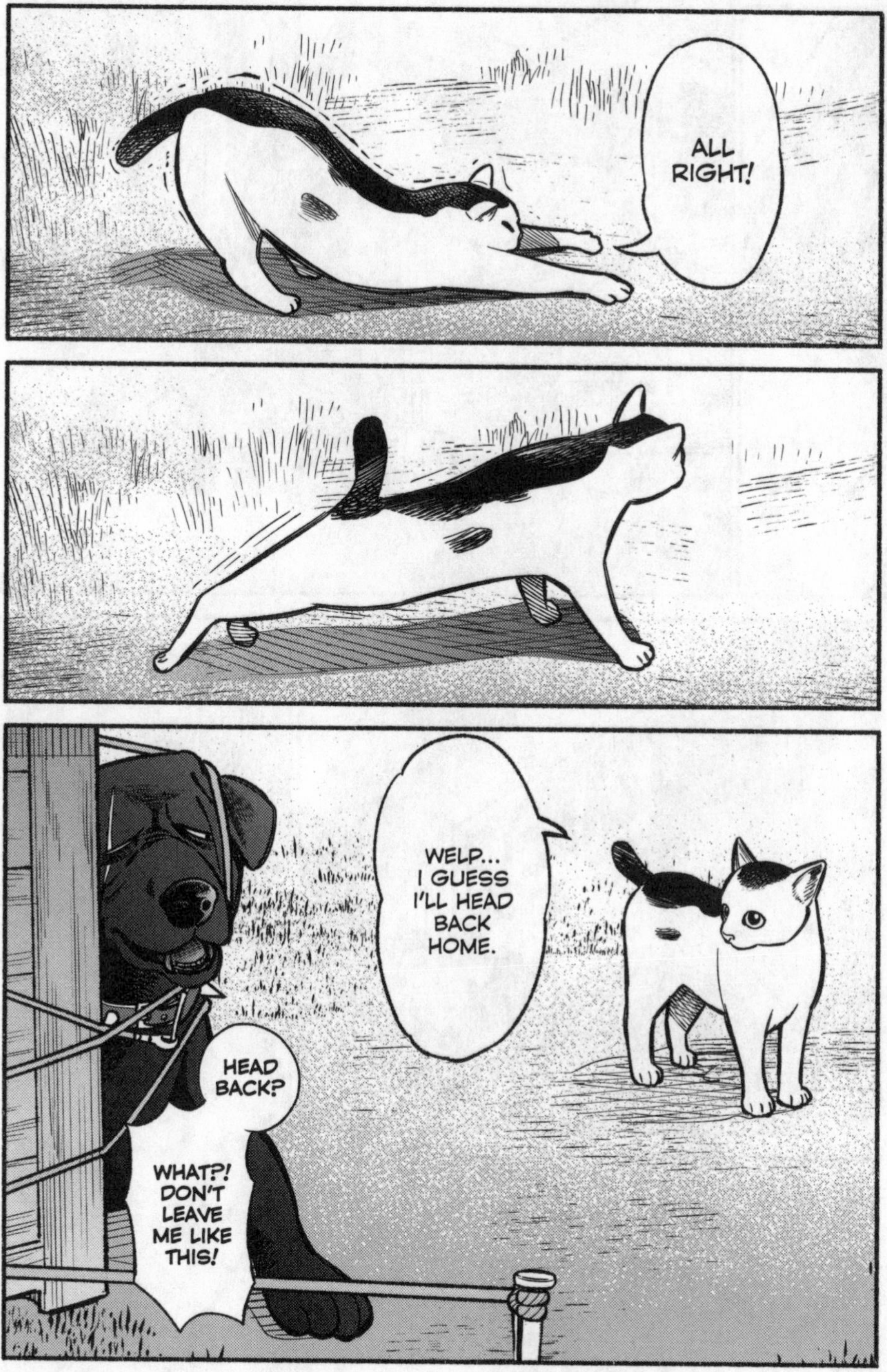
ALL RIGHT!
WELP... I GUESS I'LL HEAD BACK HOME.
HEAD BACK?
WHAT?! DON'T LEAVE ME LIKE THIS!

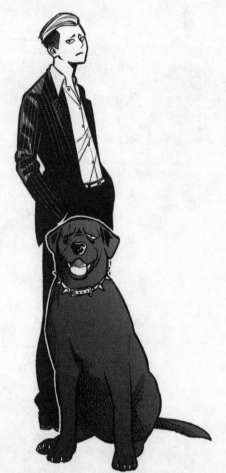

ELIZABETH KUNIMI (5)

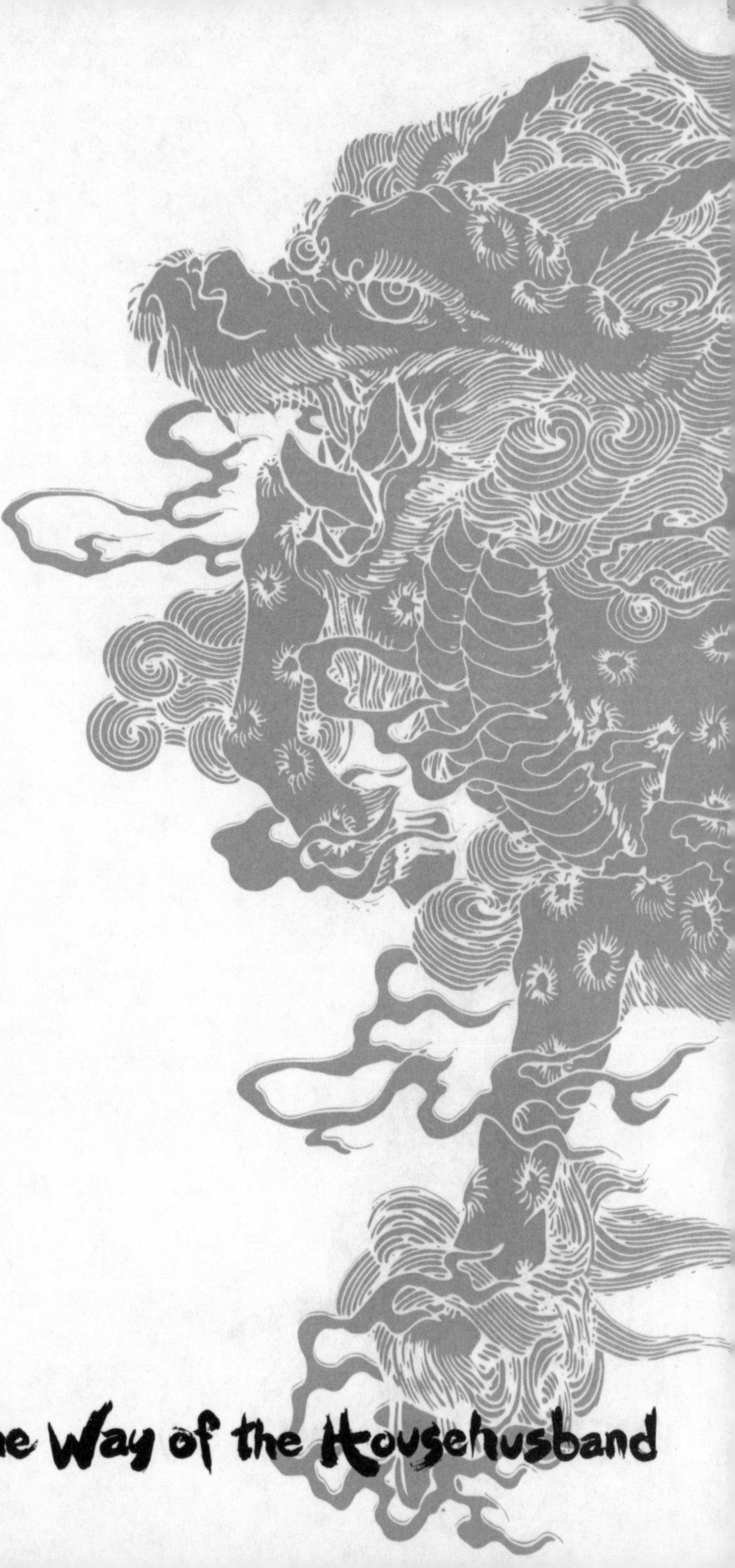

# The Way of the Househusband

## BONUS MANGA ② THIS IS MASA STYLE

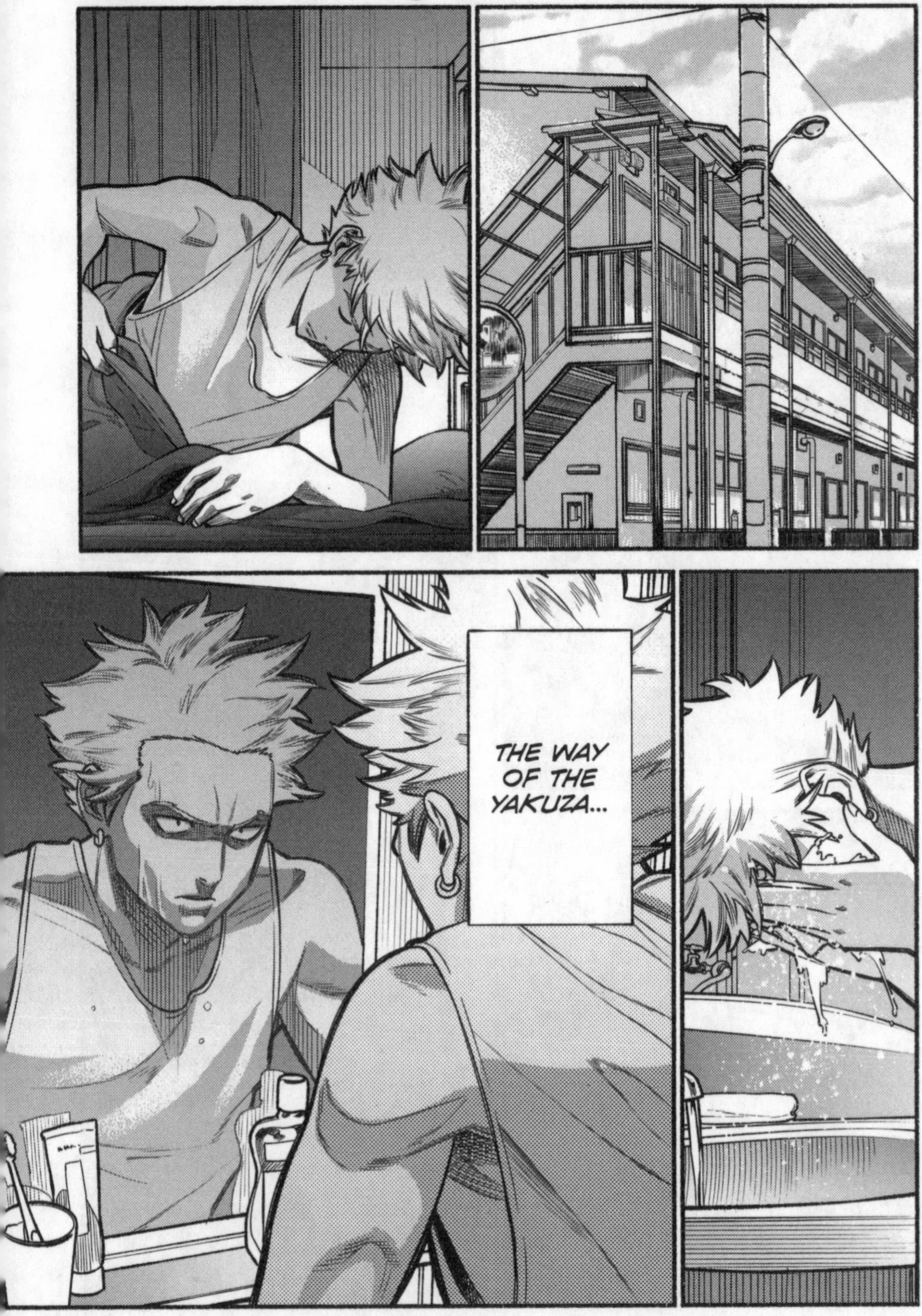
THE WAY OF THE YAKUZA...

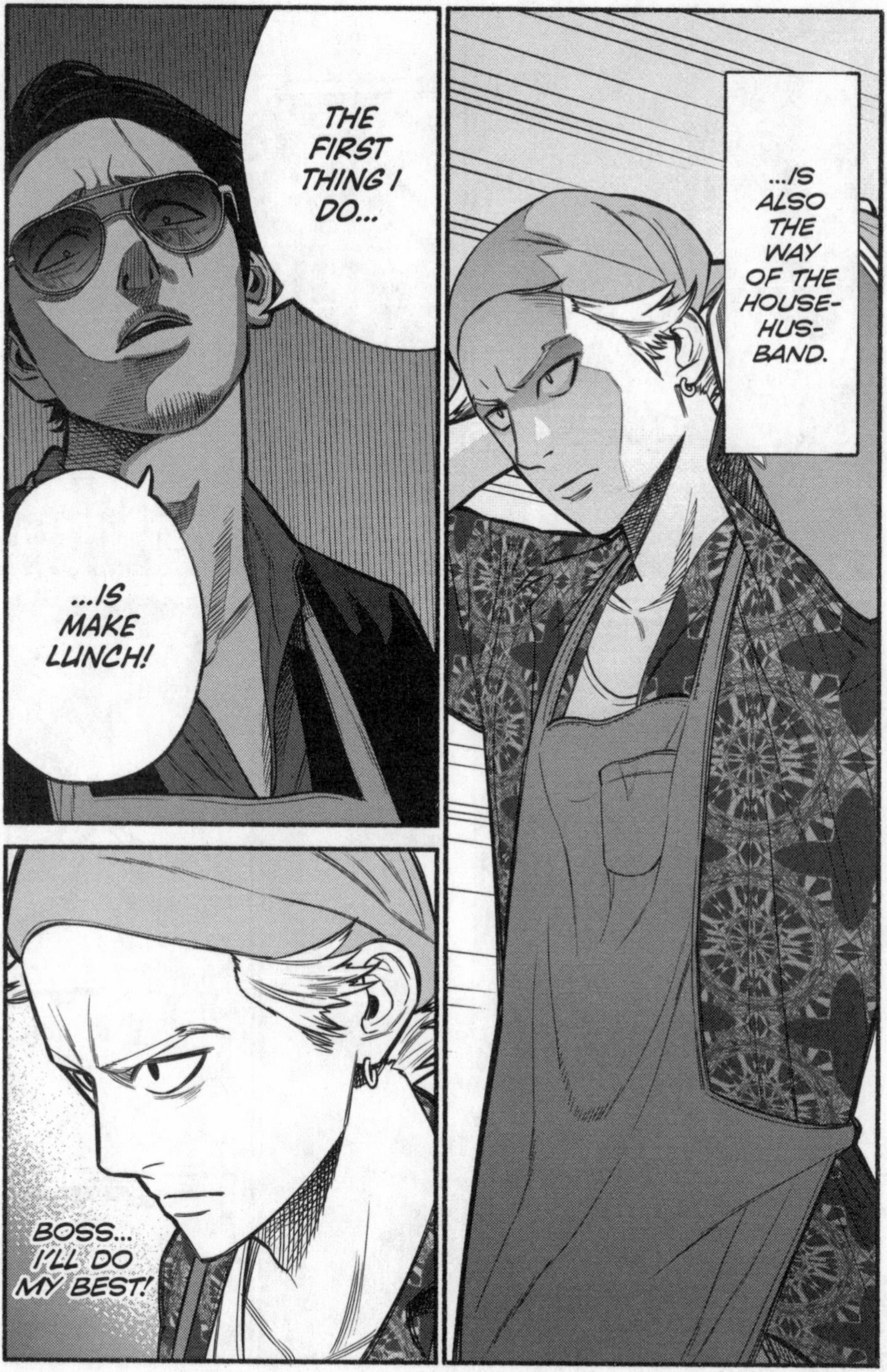
...IS ALSO THE WAY OF THE HOUSE-HUSBAND.
THE FIRST THING I DO...
...IS MAKE LUNCH!
BOSS... I'LL DO MY BEST!

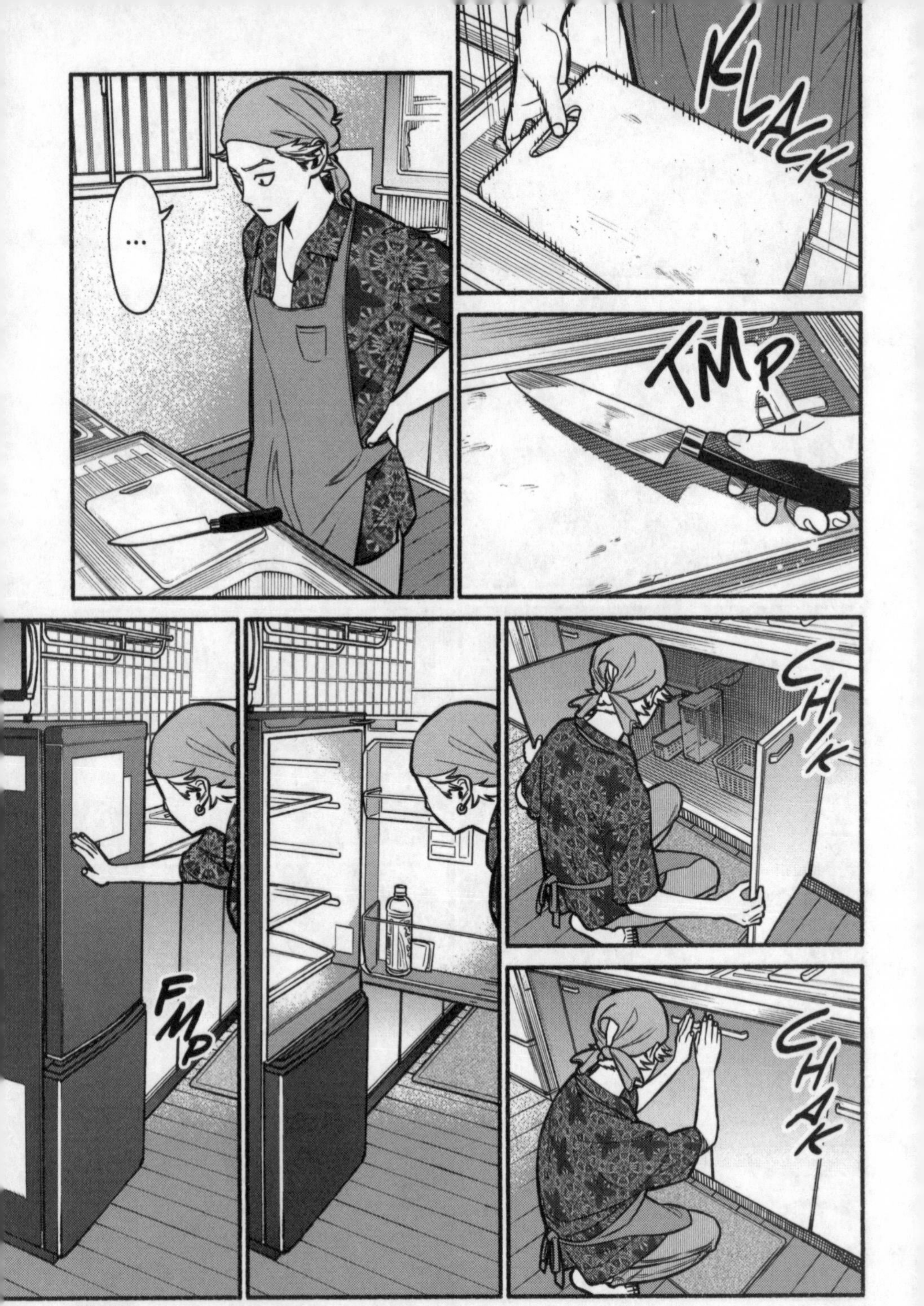
KLACK
TMP
...
CHIK
CHAK
FMP

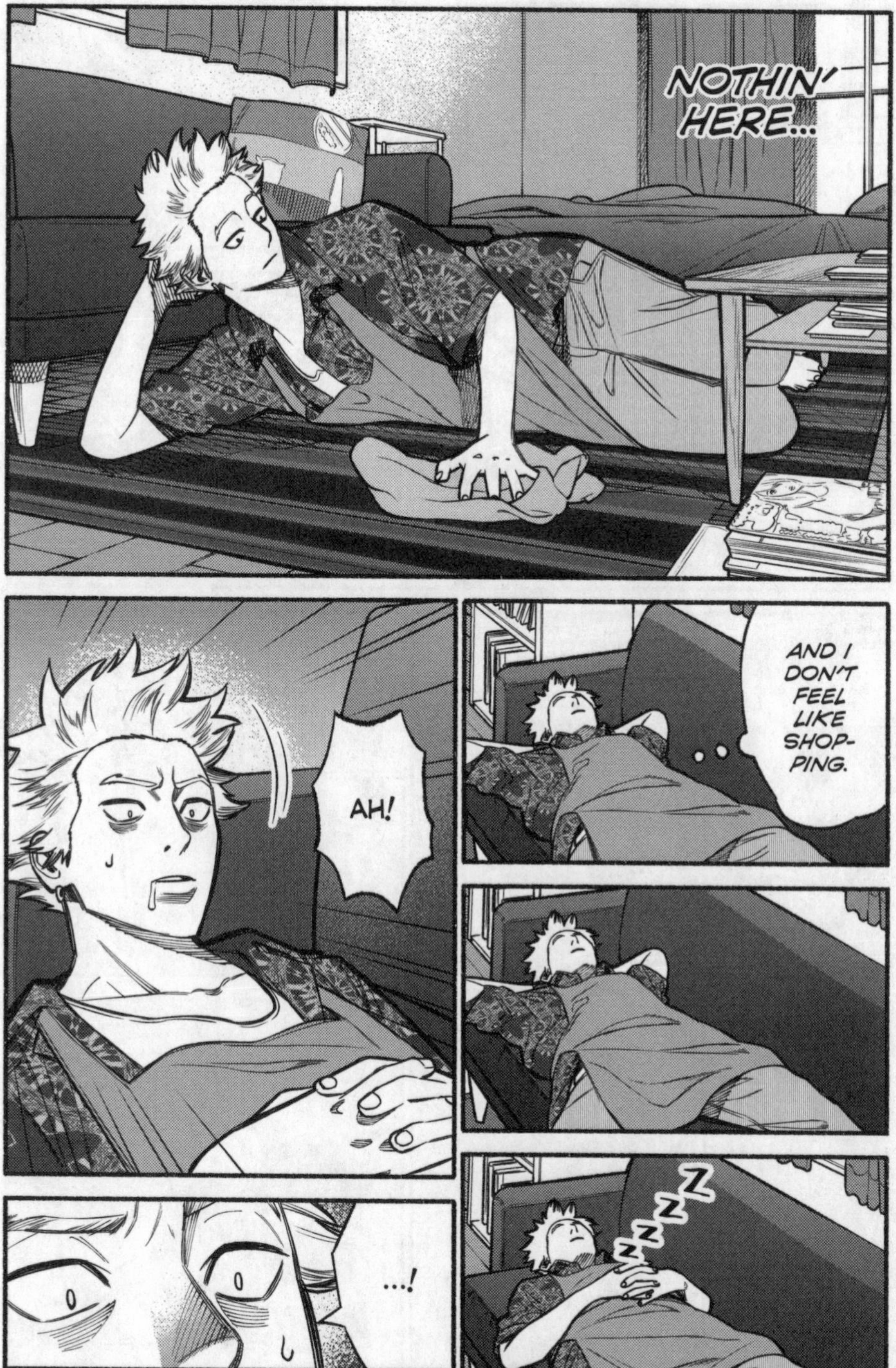
NOTHIN' HERE...
AND I DON'T FEEL LIKE SHOPPING.
ZZZZ
AH!
...!

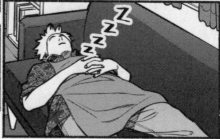

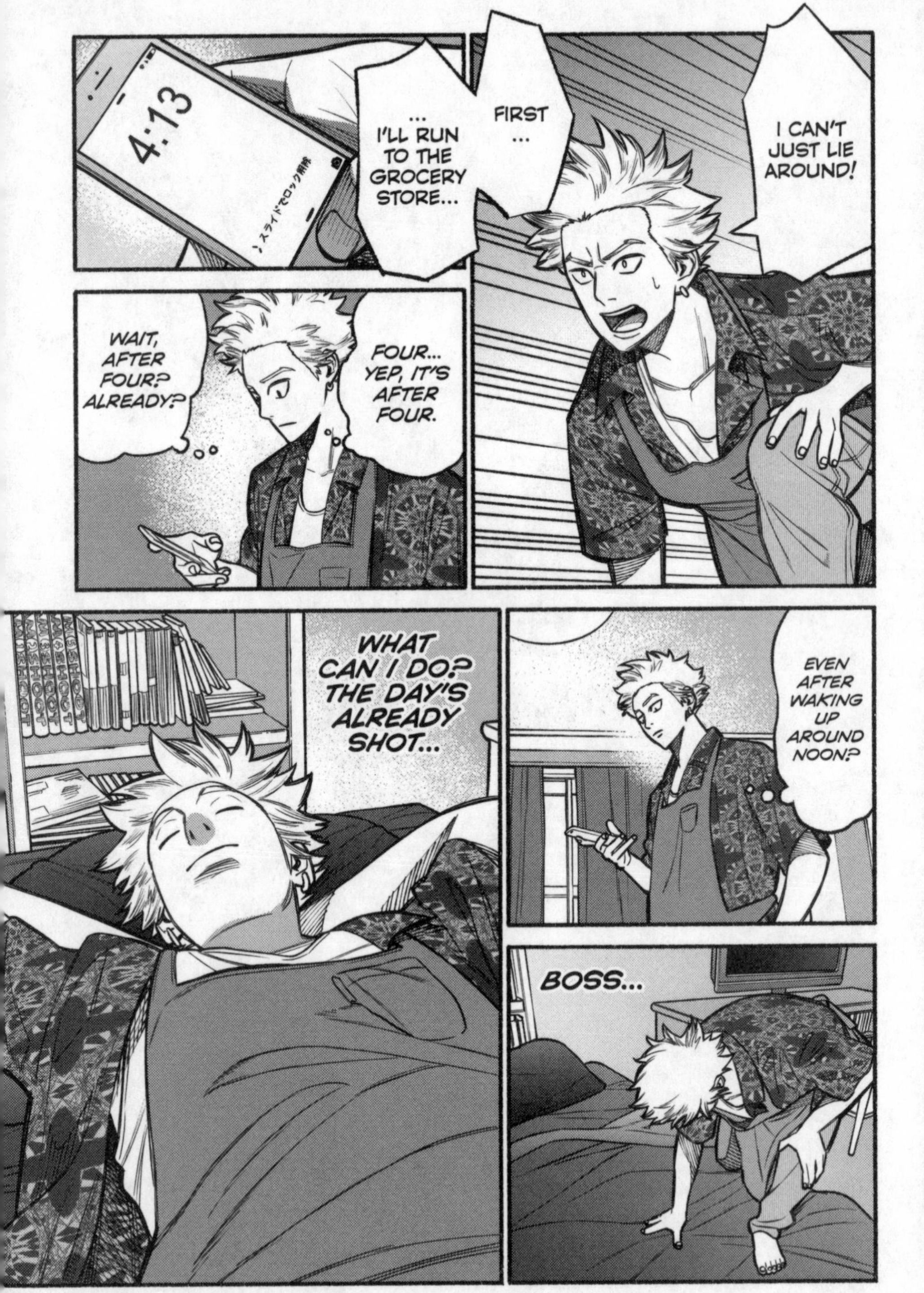
I CAN'T JUST LIE AROUND!
FIRST ...
... I'LL RUN TO THE GROCERY STORE...
4:13
スライドでロック解除
FOUR... YEP, IT'S AFTER FOUR.
WAIT, AFTER FOUR? ALREADY?
EVEN AFTER WAKING UP AROUND NOON?
BOSS...
WHAT CAN I DO? THE DAY'S ALREADY SHOT...

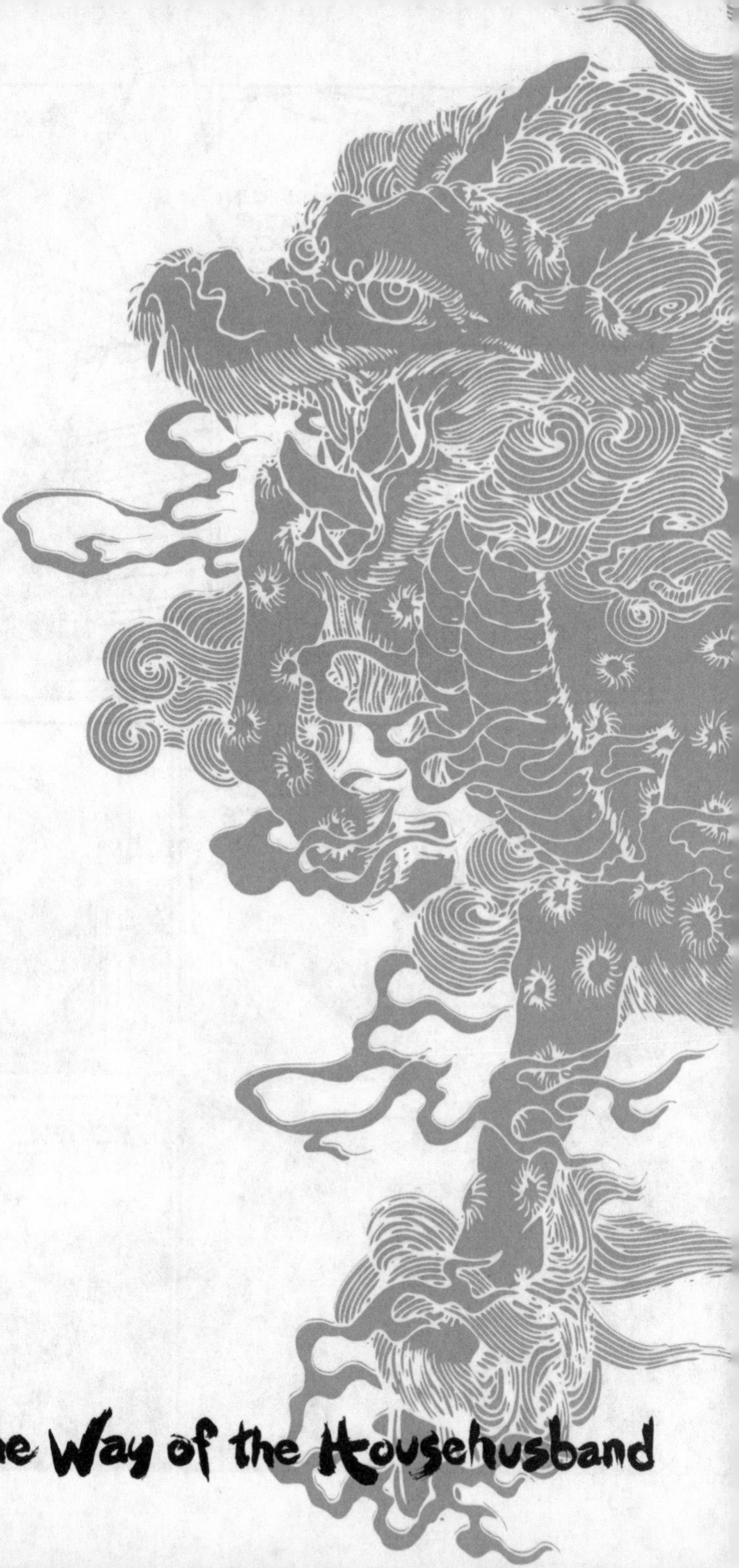

# The Way of the Househusband

# BONUS MANGA ③ LET'S HAVE A FAIR FIGHT

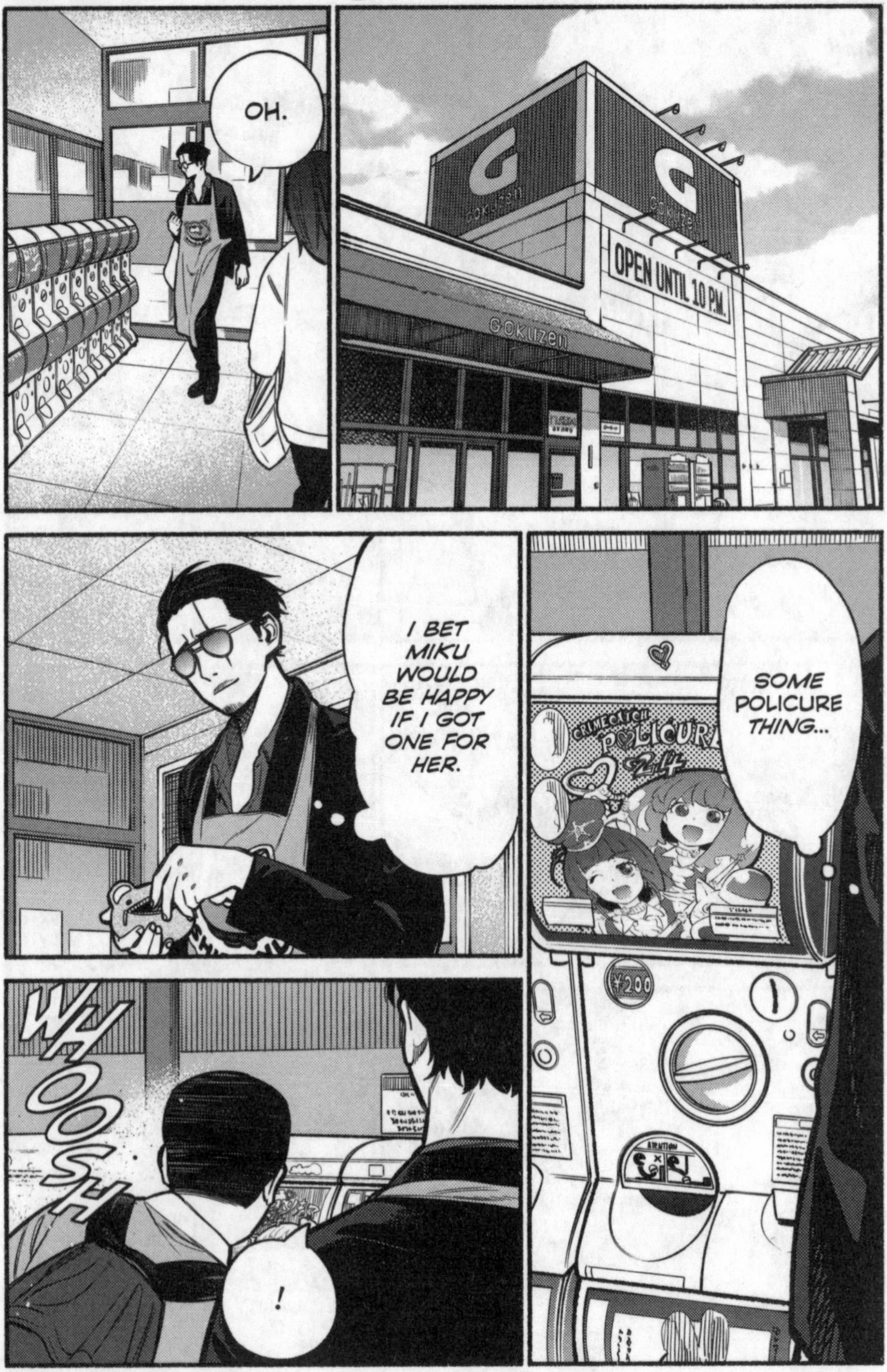

OPEN UNTIL 10 P.M.
GOKUZEN
OH.
SOME POLICURE THING...
¥200
I BET MIKU WOULD BE HAPPY IF I GOT ONE FOR HER.
WHOOSH
!

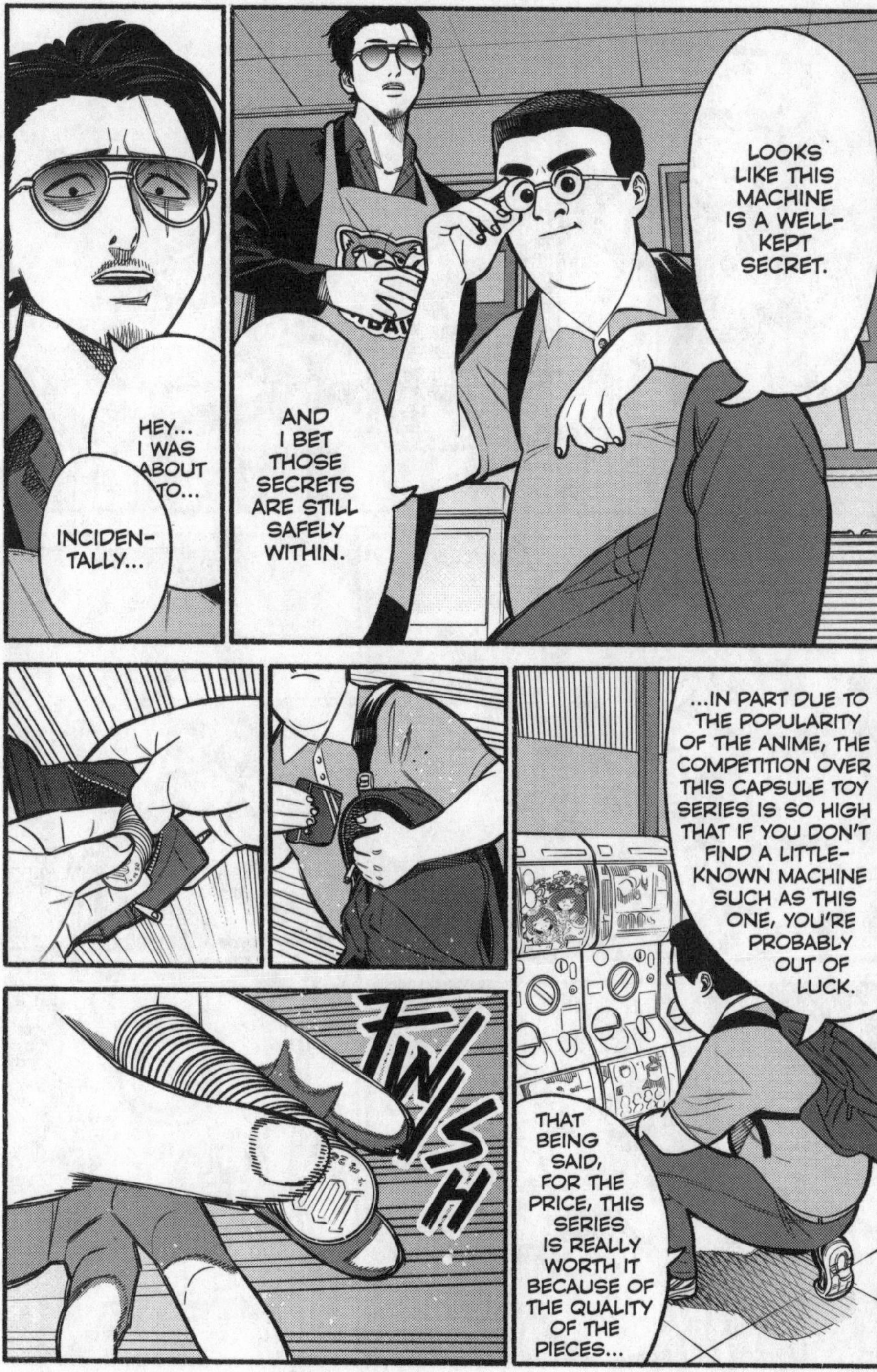
LOOKS LIKE THIS MACHINE IS A WELL-KEPT SECRET.
AND I BET THOSE SECRETS ARE STILL SAFELY WITHIN.
HEY... I WAS ABOUT TO...
INCIDEN-TALLY...
...IN PART DUE TO THE POPULARITY OF THE ANIME, THE COMPETITION OVER THIS CAPSULE TOY SERIES IS SO HIGH THAT IF YOU DON'T FIND A LITTLE-KNOWN MACHINE SUCH AS THIS ONE, YOU'RE PROBABLY OUT OF LUCK.
THAT BEING SAID, FOR THE PRICE, THIS SERIES IS REALLY WORTH IT BECAUSE OF THE QUALITY OF THE PIECES...
FWISH

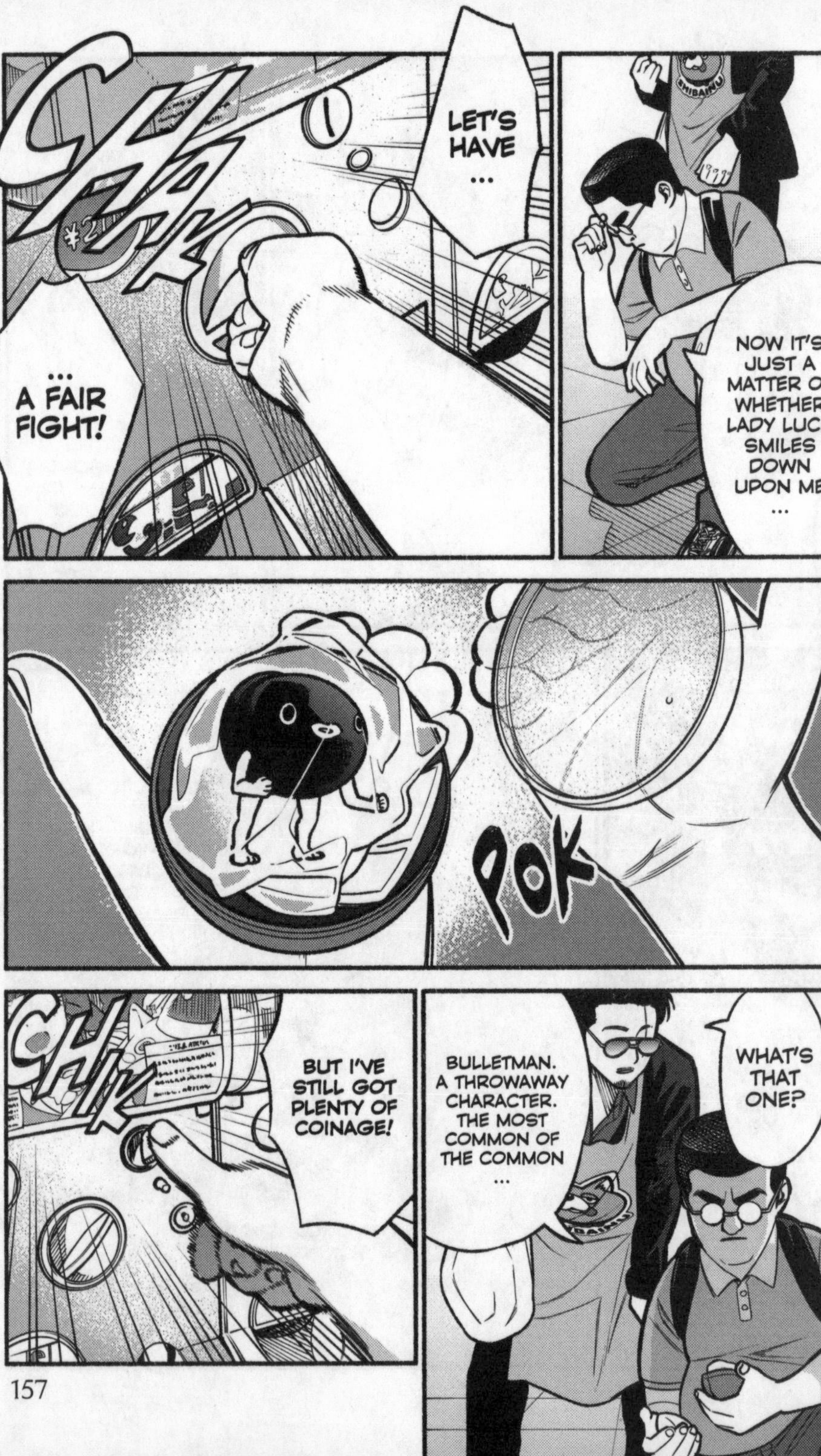
NOW IT'S JUST A MATTER OF WHETHER LADY LUCK SMILES DOWN UPON ME ...
LET'S HAVE ...
CHAK
... A FAIR FIGHT!
POK
WHAT'S THAT ONE?
BULLETMAN. A THROWAWAY CHARACTER. THE MOST COMMON OF THE COMMON ...
BUT I'VE STILL GOT PLENTY OF COINAGE!
CHK

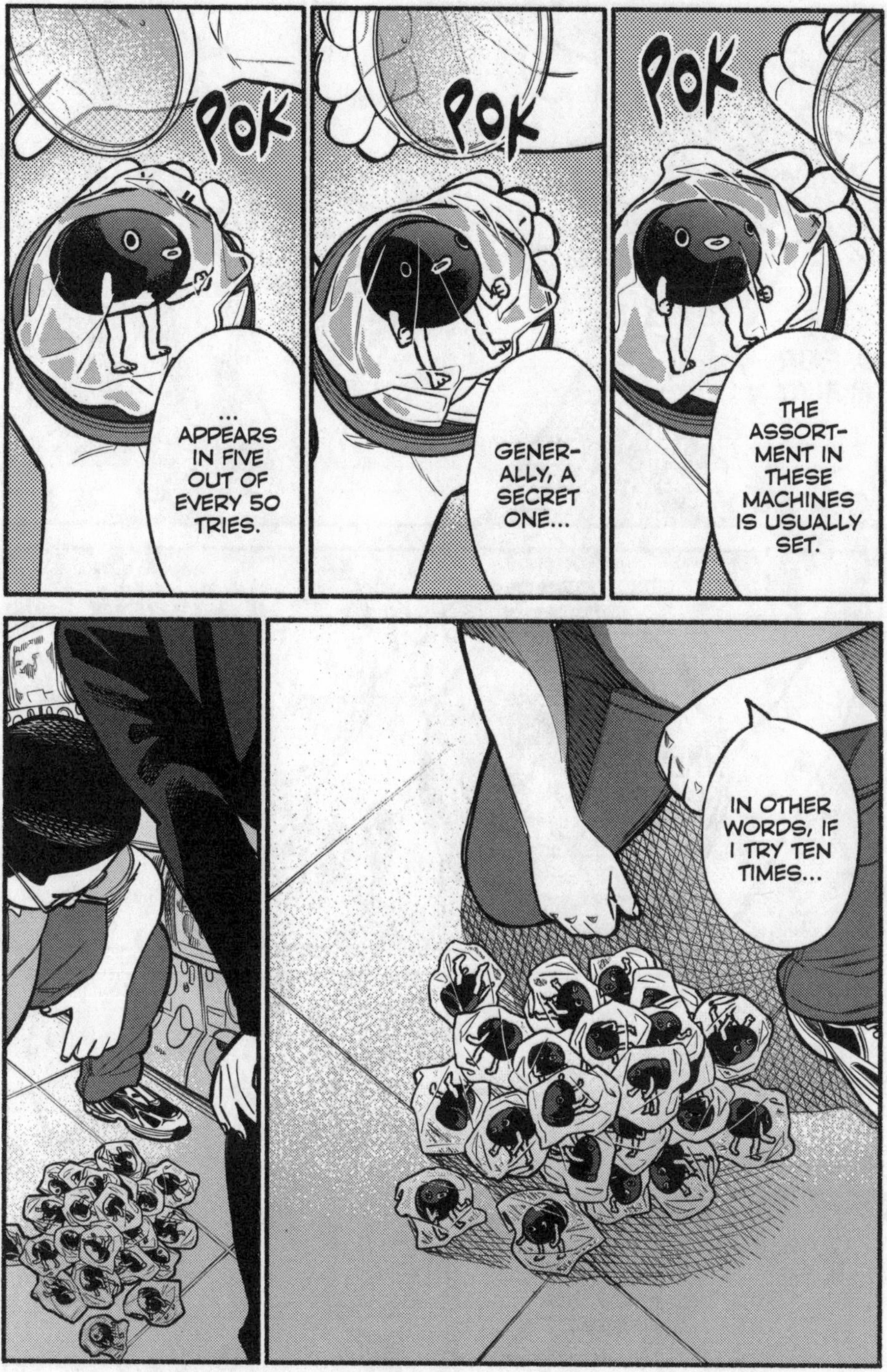
POK
THE ASSORTMENT IN THESE MACHINES IS USUALLY SET.
POK
GENERALLY, A SECRET ONE...
POK
... APPEARS IN FIVE OUT OF EVERY 50 TRIES.
IN OTHER WORDS, IF I TRY TEN TIMES...

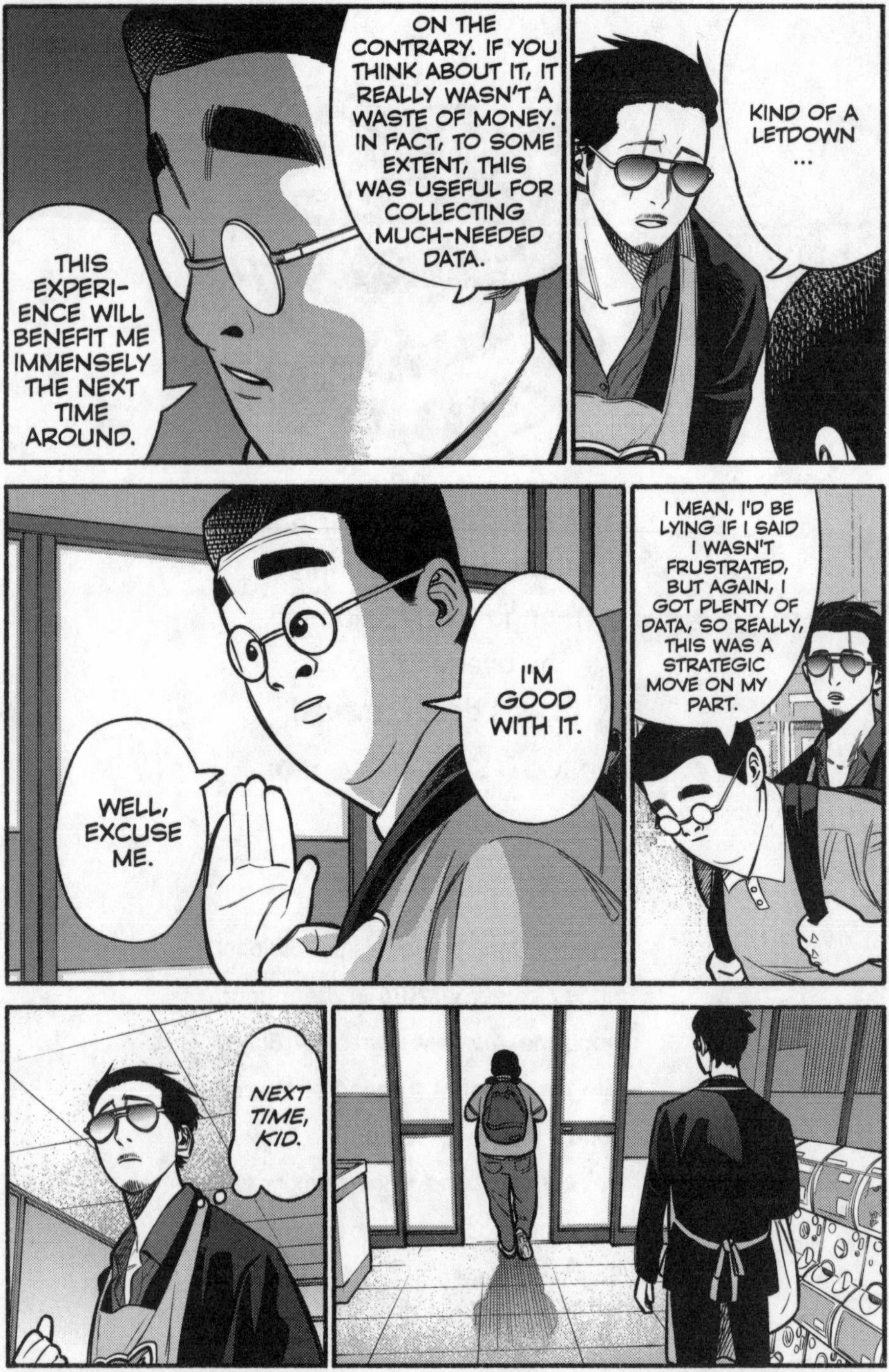
KIND OF A LETDOWN ...
ON THE CONTRARY. IF YOU THINK ABOUT IT, IT REALLY WASN'T A WASTE OF MONEY. IN FACT, TO SOME EXTENT, THIS WAS USEFUL FOR COLLECTING MUCH-NEEDED DATA.
THIS EXPERI-ENCE WILL BENEFIT ME IMMENSELY THE NEXT TIME AROUND.
I MEAN, I'D BE LYING IF I SAID I WASN'T FRUSTRATED, BUT AGAIN, I GOT PLENTY OF DATA, SO REALLY, THIS WAS A STRATEGIC MOVE ON MY PART.
I'M GOOD WITH IT.
WELL, EXCUSE ME.
*NEXT TIME, KID.*

THANK YOU FOR READING TO THE VERY END. I'M HOPING TO GET VOLUME 2 OUT AROUND DECEMBER... THAT'S THE IDEA, ANYWAY.

SPECIAL THANKS - KIMURA . HIROE . SOEN

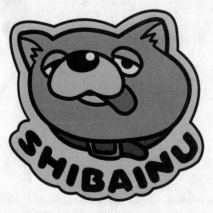

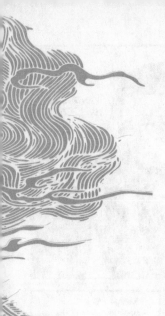

This is my first graphic novel.
When I showed this
manga to my Shiba Inu,
he averted his eyes.
I was deeply moved.

**KOUSUKE OONO**

---

Kousuke Oono began his professional
manga career in 2016 in the manga
magazine *Monthly Comics @ Bunch*
with the one-shot "Legend of Music."
Oono's follow-up series, *The Way of
the Househusband*, is the creator's first
serialization as well as his first English-
language release.

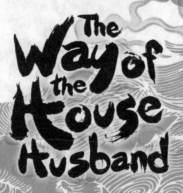

# The Way of the House Husband

**VOLUME 1**

**VIZ SIGNATURE EDITION**

**STORY AND ART BY**
**KOUSUKE OONO**

TRANSLATION: Sheldon Drzka
ENGLISH ADAPTATION: Jennifer LeBlanc
TOUCH-UP ART & LETTERING: Bianca Pistillo
DESIGN: Alice Lewis
EDITOR: Jennifer LeBlanc

GOKUSHUFUDO volume 1
© Kousuke Oono 2018
All Rights Reserved
English translation rights arranged
with SHINCHOSHA PUBLISHING CO.
through Tuttle-Mori Agency, Inc., Tokyo

Printed in Canada

Published by VIZ Media, LLC
P.O. Box 77010
San Francisco, CA 94107

10 9 8 7 6 5 4 3
First printing, September 2019
Third printing, November 2020

**VIZ** MEDIA    *VIZ SIGNATURE*
viz.com            vizsignature.com

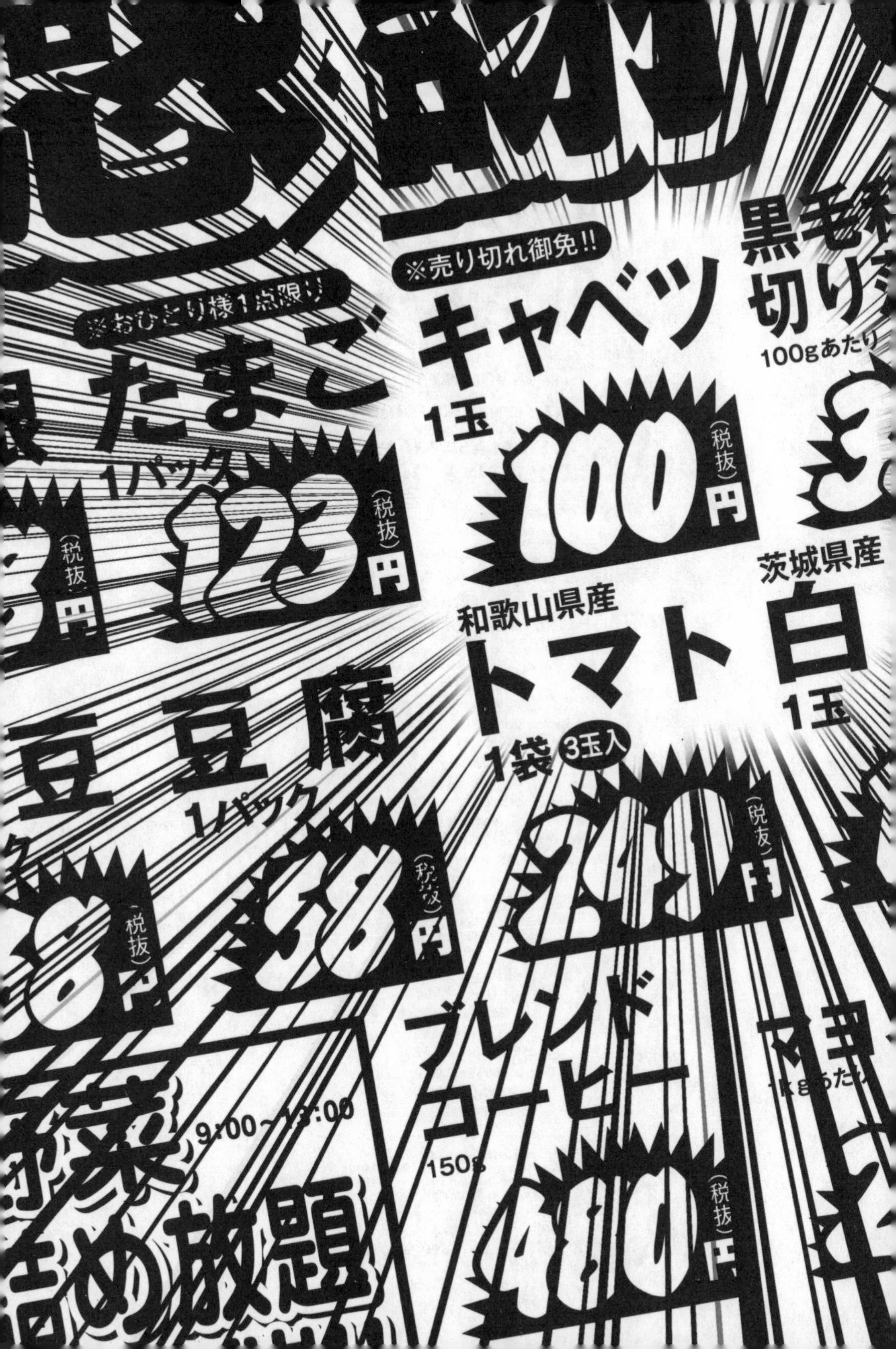

※売り切れ御免!!
黒毛
切り
100gあたり
キャベツ
1玉
100(税抜)円
※おひとり様1点限り
たまご
1パック
123(税抜)円
(税抜)円
茨城県産
白
1玉
和歌山県産
トマト
1袋 3玉入
(税抜)円
豆腐
1パック
(税抜)円
(税抜)円
ブレンド
コーヒー
150g
(税抜)円
9:00~13:00
放題

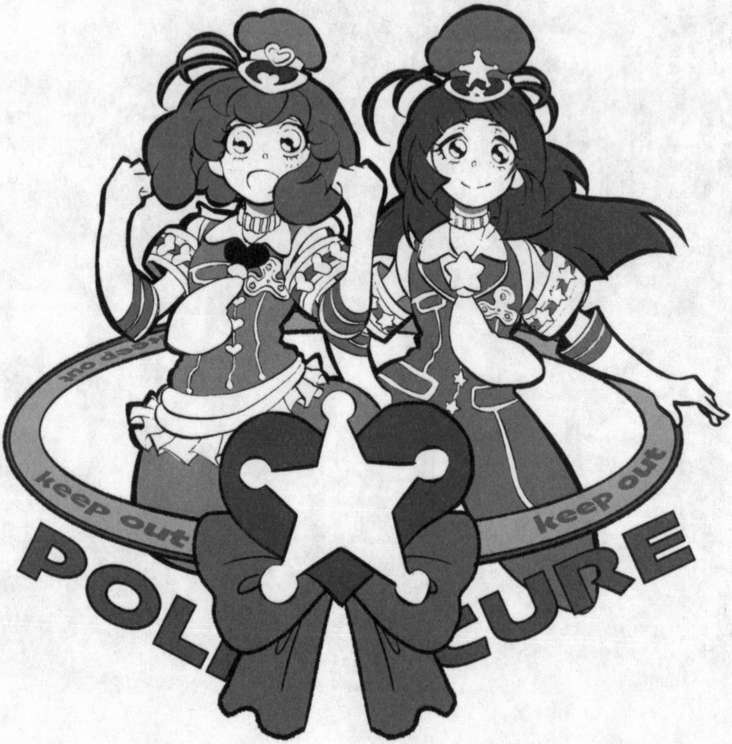
keep out
keep out
keep out
POL
CURE

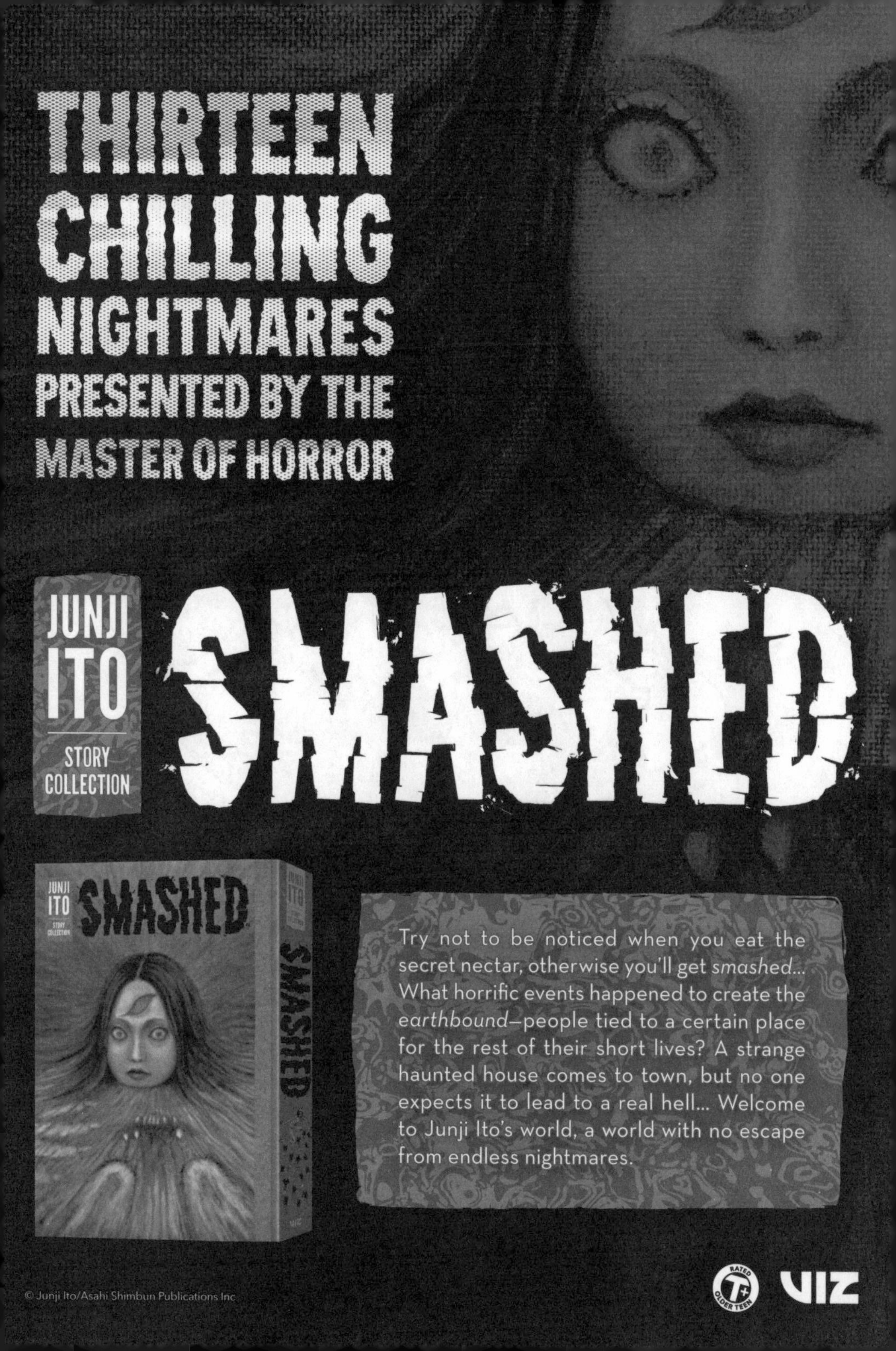

THIRTEEN CHILLING NIGHTMARES PRESENTED BY THE MASTER OF HORROR
JUNJI ITO STORY COLLECTION
SMASHED
JUNJI ITO SMASHED STORY COLLECTION
Try not to be noticed when you eat the secret nectar, otherwise you'll get *smashed*... What horrific events happened to create the *earthbound*—people tied to a certain place for the rest of their short lives? A strange haunted house comes to town, but no one expects it to lead to a real hell... Welcome to Junji Ito's world, a world with no escape from endless nightmares.
© Junji Ito/Asahi Shimbun Publications Inc.
RATED T+ OLDER TEEN
VIZ

# CHILDREN OF THE WHALES

In this postapocalyptic fantasy, a sea of sand
swallows everything but the past.

In an endless sea of sand drifts the
Mud Whale, a floating island city
of clay and magic. In its chambers a
small community clings to survival,
cut off from its own history by the
shadows of the past.

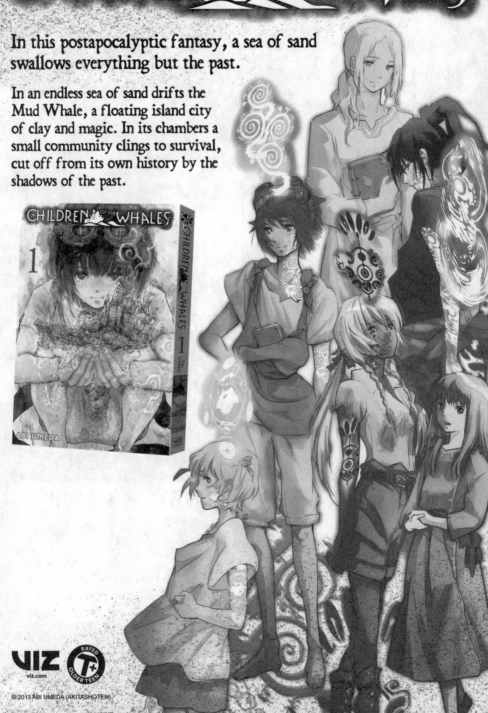

CHILDREN OF THE WHALES

1

ABI UMEDA

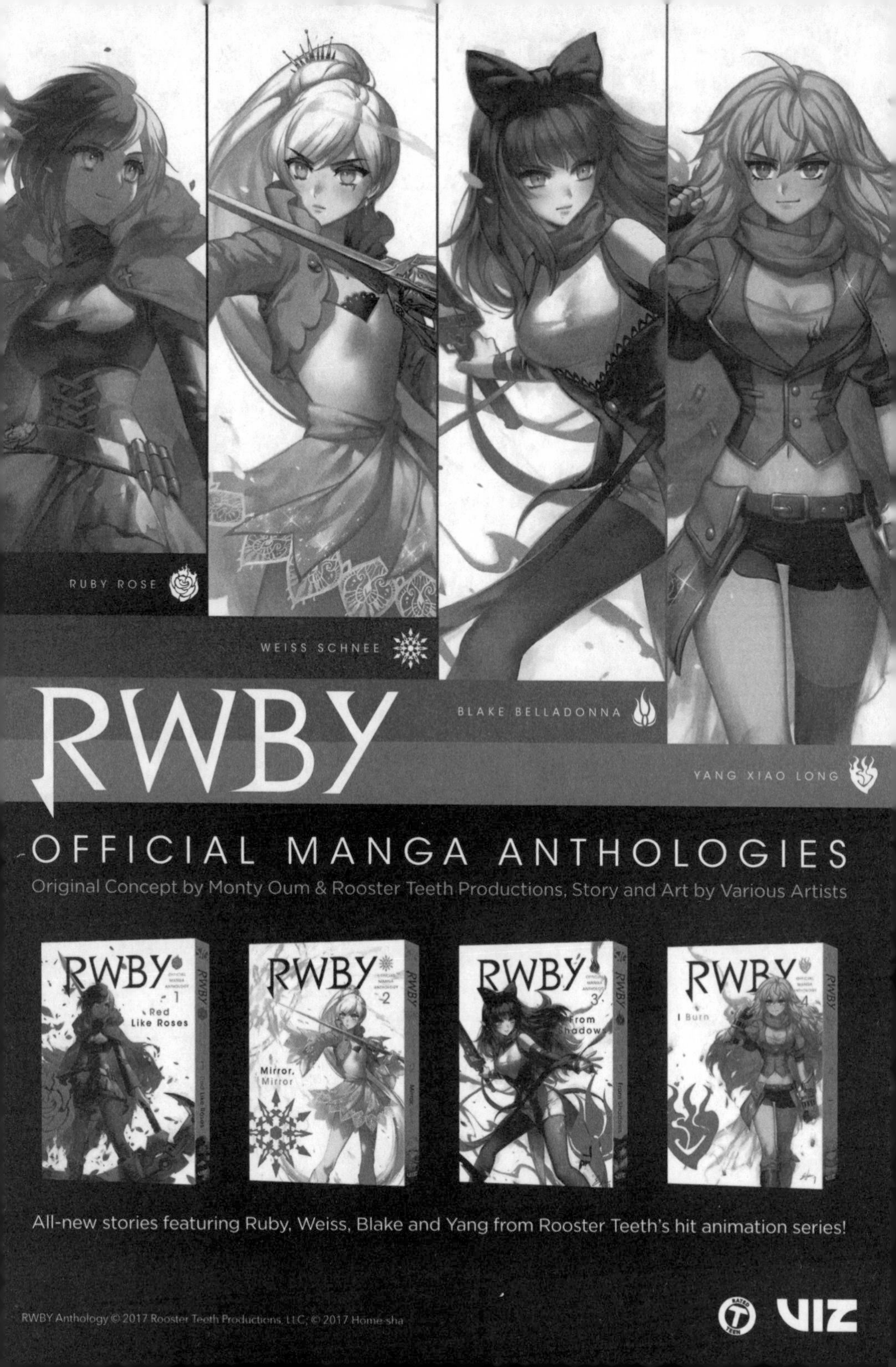
RUBY ROSE
WEISS SCHNEE
BLAKE BELLADONNA
YANG XIAO LONG
RWBY
OFFICIAL MANGA ANTHOLOGIES
Original Concept by Monty Oum & Rooster Teeth Productions, Story and Art by Various Artists
RWBY 1 Red Like Roses
RWBY 2 Mirror, Mirror
RWBY 3 From Shadows
RWBY 4 I Burn
All-new stories featuring Ruby, Weiss, Blake and Yang from Rooster Teeth's hit animation series!
RWBY Anthology © 2017 Rooster Teeth Productions, LLC; © 2017 Home-sha
VIZ

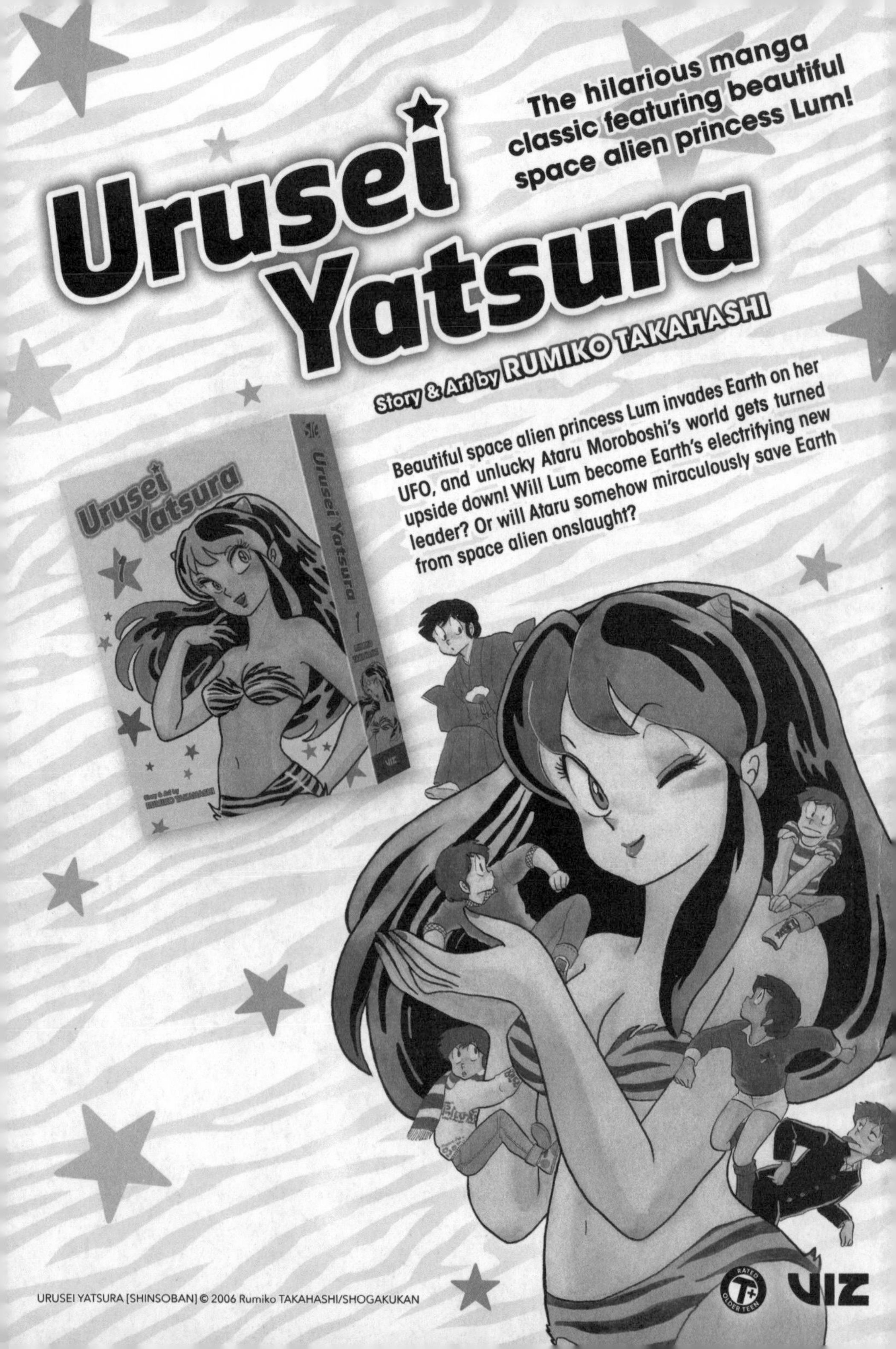
The hilarious manga classic featuring beautiful space alien princess Lum!
Urusei Yatsura
Story & Art by RUMIKO TAKAHASHI
Beautiful space alien princess Lum invades Earth on her UFO, and unlucky Ataru Moroboshi's world gets turned upside down! Will Lum become Earth's electrifying new leader? Or will Ataru somehow miraculously save Earth from space alien onslaught?
Urusei Yatsura
1
Urusei Yatsura
1
URUSEI YATSURA [SHINSOBAN] © 2006 Rumiko TAKAHASHI/SHOGAKUKAN
RATED T+ OLDER TEEN
VIZ

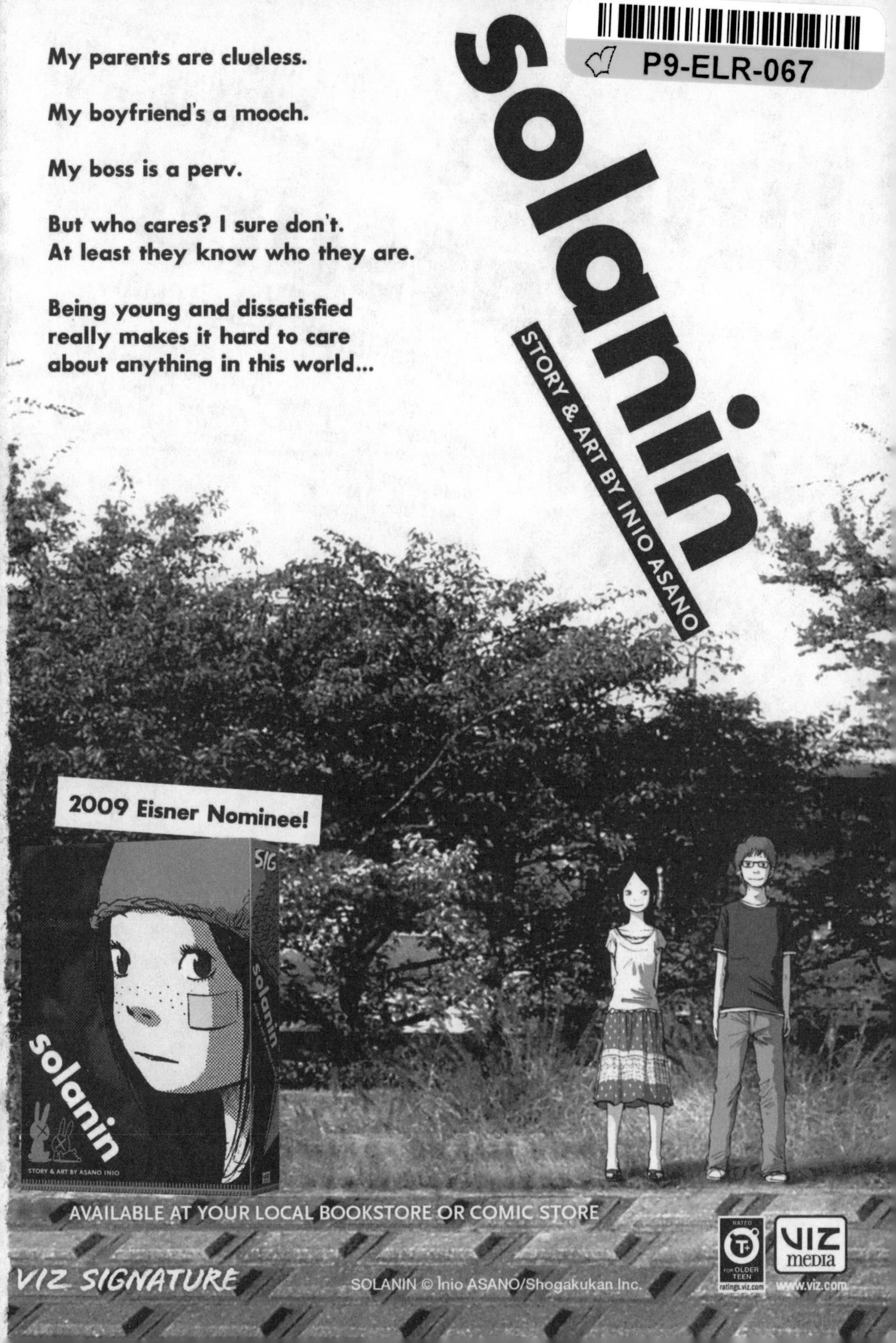
My parents are clueless.
My boyfriend's a mooch.
My boss is a perv.
But who cares? I sure don't.
At least they know who they are.
Being young and dissatisfied
really makes it hard to care
about anything in this world...
solanin
STORY & ART BY INIO ASANO
2009 Eisner Nominee!
SIG
solanin
solanin
STORY & ART BY ASANO INIO
AVAILABLE AT YOUR LOCAL BOOKSTORE OR COMIC STORE
RATED
T+
FOR OLDER TEEN
ratings.viz.com
VIZ media
www.viz.com
VIZ SIGNATURE
SOLANIN © Inio ASANO/Shogakukan Inc.